THE CRC
THE Y

Gardening with God
in Eastertide and Summer

By the same author and published by Burns & Oates

GARDENING WITH GOD: Light in Darkness
THORN, FIRE AND LILY:
Gardening with God through Lent to Easter

THE CROWN
OF THE YEAR

*Gardening with God
in Eastertide and Summer*

JANE MOSSENDEW

BURNS & OATES
A Continuum imprint
LONDON • NEW YORK

Burns & Oates
A Continuum imprint
The Tower Building
11 York Road
London SE1 7NX

15 East 26th Street
New York
NY 10010

www.continuumbooks.com

© Jane Mossendew 2005

Line drawings by Penelope Harter

First published 2005

British Library Cataloguing-in-Publication Data
A catalogue record for this book is available from the British Library

ISBN 0–8601–2385–5

Typeset by Bookens Ltd, Royston, Herts
Printed and bound in Great Britain by MPG Books Ltd, Bodmin, Cornwall

Dedicated to Our Lady of Consolation
in memory of
Dame Felicitas Corrigan OSB,
and Rumer Godden, novelist and poet

CONTENTS

Part 3: SOLEMNITIES AND SAINTS' DAYS

CONTENTS

ACKNOWLEDGEMENTS

Copyright material is quoted by permission of the following: Paul Burns, for extensive reference to and a quotation from *Butler's Lives of the Saints, New Concise Edition*, Burns & Oates, 2003; The Continuum International Publishing Group for Caryl Houselander's prayer poem, 'Breath of Heaven', Sutton's Consumer Products Ltd, for quotations on the runner bean and wallflower from *The Culture of Flowers and Vegetables*, Sutton and Sons, 1904. Hymns from *The New English Hymnal* and are quoted by kind permission of SCM-Canterbury Press. Scripture quotations are from the Revised Standard Version of the Bible, © 1946, 1952 and 1971 by the Division of Christian Education of the National Council of the Churches of Christ in the USA. Lines from 'The Lake Isle of Innisfree' are quoted by permission of A. P. Watt Ltd. on behalf of Michael B. Yeats.

Every effort has been made to contact copyright holders and any inadvertent omissions will be made good in future editions.

Much-appreciated spiritual and/or temporal support has continued without stint from friends and colleagues mentioned in *Gardening with God: Light in Darkness* and *Thorn, Fire and Lily*. My wholehearted gratitude goes to them again with the addition of Timothy Burnham, Pen Campbell, Mark Clifford, Revd Dr Alasdair Coles, Dee Dean, Dame Julian Falkus OSB (Stanbrook), Rosemary and Patrick Findlater, the Revd and Mrs Andrew Francis, Moyra Goodban (Buckingham Nurseries), Julian Kent, Jane Murray-Flutter; Barty Phillips (The Herb Society), Robert Proctor, David Richards, Jayne Sambrook-Smith (King Alfred's, Winchester), Elizabeth Sawday (Apuldram Roses), Yvonne Guerin and Elizabeth Stafford of Wells Cathedral and Maggie Tarbox (Royal National Rose Society).

Profound thanks also to Miriam Cooper of Tasmania, whose visit to France in the sunny sowing and planting days of late spring this year brought great happiness, peace and healing; in England to Jonathan Childs and Kenneth Stanion, without whose patient and generous technical help, my books would never reach the publisher; to Margaret Woods and Laura Brombjerb for their moral and practical support; and to Jack Edwards (Opera Restor'd) and Canon Russell Bowman-Eadie (Wells Cathedral) for their recent hospitality, and for the love and encouragement each has given me over the past forty years. In France, *merci mille fois* to Brigittte and Serge Bonneau, Rosemonde Noga, and Annick and Jean-Philippe Quanté for looking after house, cats and garden during my absences; and to Franck Petit, for continued use of his fax machine, and through which during recent months when I have been in London and my husband in France, he has ensured that 'les vieux amants séparés' are kept in touch with each other.

I continue to be richly blessed in the friendship of Sue and John Gregson; the patience and experience of my editor Paul Burns; the delightful illustrations of Penelope Harter; the sound professional advice of Martin Dillon; the spiritual guidance, particularly in times of stress and doubt, of the Revd Dr Stephen Young; and finally in the understanding and love of my husband Colin Fulthorpe who in the daily trials of being married to me, comes closer to fulfilling 1 Corinthians 13:4–8a than any wife has a right to expect!

J. M.
London, 7 November 2004

Warning
Always consult a qualified medical practitioner before taking herbal
remedies.

You crown the year with your goodness.
Abundance flows in your steps,
in the pasture of the wilderness it flows.
(Psalm 65:11)

This blood, which flowed from its source in the secret recesses of his heart,
gave the sacraments of the Church power to confer the life of grace, and
for those who already live in Christ was a draught of living water welling
up to eternal life.
(from St Bonaventure, *Opus 3*)

The loving kindness of the heart of our God
who visits us like the dawn from on high:
(from the *Canticle of Zachariah;* Luke 1: 68–79)

INTRODUCTION

O muckle is the powerful grace that lies
In plants, herbs, stones, and their true qualities:
For nought so vile that on the earth doth live,
But to the earth some special good doth give.
(Friar Lawrence in Shakespeare's
Romeo and Juliet Act II, scene ii, 15–18)

The present volume is the third in a series of four, and an explanation of
how and why I first came to envisage the project appears in the
Introduction to the first volume, *Gardening with God: Light in Darkness*.
Since then I have written the Introductions as each book is finished. This
is because I have not necessarily selected all the plants that will eventually
be included.

People often ask me how I choose individual plants to match the
liturgical themes or the different characters and experiences of the saints.
The answer is, 'In several ways'. In many cases, plants 'self-seed' so to
speak, and are chosen for their names, structure, characteristics or
meaning in folklore or the nineteenth-century language of flowers. And so
we have, for instance, Spanish Bayonet for St Ignatius of Loyola, Trillium
for the Holy Trinity, Star of Bethlehem for Epiphany-tide, Chamomile for
humility, Snakeshead Lily for persecution and so on. It is astonishing how
frequently even these obvious choices provide springboards to quite
lengthy meditation; and often the humbler the plant, the deeper the
reflection it stimulates. Sometimes I do not know until I study and
meditate on the life of a saint, or on the themes of a liturgical day (or
week, as in the present volume), which plant will match them, and
sometimes the choice will be made while I am actually gardening. Myrtle
for the seventeenth week of Ordinary Time came in the former way, and
Eglantine for St John of the Cross in the latter. Other plants suggest
themselves at church or at work, or again I may discover appropriate
named varieties when leafing through plant catalogues. At yet other times
through observation and thought, or engagement with a familiar plant, I
notice something about it that can be turned to spiritual account.
Occasionally, that engagement is of a spiritual nature in itself, as when I
touched a Snapdragon, during the preparation of the entry for St Thomas

the Apostle (see page 188). Nor do I disdain weeds, or even poisonous plants, as a stimulus to meditation. In the past Shepherd's Needle has led to a reflection on neighbourliness, Speedwell to one on faithfulness and Blessed Thistle to the holiness attained by the young St Aloysius Gonzaga. Dock, with its deep root and terrible self-seeding propensities, led to a consideration of the nature of sin, while Corncockle, detested by farmers, is offered to St James the Greater as a 'lily of the field'. And yet Dock has the famous property of soothing nettle stings, and Corncockle is beautiful if kept well away from fields of grain. Most weeds do in fact have redeeming features: it is just that they insist on growing where they are not wanted, much as sin does. Shakespeare, in the guise of Friar Lawrence, further reflects:

> Within the infant rind of this weak flower
> Poison hath residence, and medicine power ...
> Two such opposed kings encamp them still,
> In man as well as herbs – grace and rude will:
> And where the worser is predominant,
> Full soon the canker death eats up the plant.
> (*Romeo and Juliet*, II, ii, 23–4, 27–30)

And so, whether the plant leads me to meditation and prayer or whether I have to look for a plant to suit a particular liturgical theme or saint's day, the amazing fact is that so far the right one has always suggested itself in one way or another. And yet, I should not really be surprised, because an instinct to faith told me beforehand that it would be so.

Another major reason why I prefer to write the Introduction when the book itself is complete is that, during the course of writing, I may be given an insight into the book's underlying cohesion, which I had not perceived at the outset. For instance, the title of the present volume was originally chosen to evoke a green, golden and abundant time of year and to reflect our thanksgiving to God for the burgeoning of nature in spring and summer. But then in late June came the Solemnity of The Most Sacred Heart of Jesus, and I saw it as another kind of crowning, in which God, out of his love for us, sent his Son to redeem us. Christ then, is not only the crown of the year but the crown of life itself, that eternal life which, because of his love for us, he fought for and won through his passion, death and resurrection. It is *this* crown of love that is at the core of the book.

Everything else springs from it and leads back to it, not only in a return of human love for God in the lives of the saints, but through our own also.

The yearly round of gardening tasks is comparable with the liturgical cycles in which we annually revisit the same truths, problems, joys and victories. And, in spite of inevitable failures, if all is going well in garden and soul we are deepening our knowledge of plants, improving our plots, and entering more profoundly into the mysteries of faith. And yet at the same time, although we long for permanence, and to achieve perfection in our gardens, the pilgrimage of the soul continues, and we face the fact that for most of us there will be no permanence, no perfection, until and unless heaven is gained. Nowadays, because of humankind's generally appalling stewardship of the planet God gave us, gardeners welcome the seasons as they turn, with a tinge of relief, and are dismayed at signs of the climactic change we believe is being brought about by pollution.

This only serves to increase our joy as praying gardeners, in the one true certainty, namely our security in the promises of Christ, even if, against the yearly backdrop of work and prayer, we can at any time be depressed and discouraged by loss of plants or by aridity of soul, or be oppressed by doubt in our faith. But then, beyond all hope, a plant will crop which has always failed before, our souls will suddenly be illuminated with the sunlight of grace, or we will receive an unasked-for and unmerited spiritual gift. Such a one came for me this year in the shape of a friend I had not seen for nearly forty years. She brought a breath of air into my spiritual house and helped me to spring-clean it. And as we gardened together, I experienced, for the first time, the joy and exhilaration of working with someone of a different Christian tradition who shares my approach to gardening. I was deeply moved when, with great delight, she found an oak sapling growing behind my hazel tree of reconciliation and then weeded, watered and mulched it, firmly instructing me to care for it until she came again. As if I would not! It will be 'Miriam's Oak' from now on and outlive us both. But these things are not just a matter of parallels, symbolism or metaphor. From experience I know that after a time they become integral to prayer, so that my delight in the discovery of the oak, and indeed in Miriam herself, was not merely a cause of prayer, but was in itself the prayer of joyful praise and thanksgiving. Similarly, to watch the sapling grow will be to pray for Miriam, just as to look at any plant becomes a prayer of intercession. Thus, being with a Chaste Tree is to pray for all Benedictines; with an *Aloe vera*, to pray for the victims of burns; to tread upon chamomile, to seek humility. Reaction to the loss of plants can be a prayer of resignation to God's will, and dealing with Eglantine and Teasel a prayer in aridity or suffering. Pruning a rose can be a meditation on martyrdom, the touching of a Snapdragon an apprehending of the reality of the resurrection, and a close study of the Heartsease an overwhelming appreciation of Christ's love for us, and be the beginning of an increase in a previously lamentably weak desire for union with him.

Throughout the writing of these books, my life has unavoidably been arranged so that I have had periods of intense practical labour 'in the world', interspersed with equally intense periods 'on retreat' in my French garden. Indeed, these latter times are almost eremitic. (My husband is another hermit in another cell all day, until in the evening we turn into far from silent and fasting cenobites!). The garden is my daytime cell, and during ten years it has been a place of solace, where I have very rarely felt lonely in solitude. However, I have always been conscious that gardening can encourage a navel-gazing insularity, which is why there is always a list of intercessions at the end of each entry in my books. As a writer, however, I lived in a vacuum until, in Lent 2004, I had the tremendous privilege, pleasure and encouragement of meeting many of my readers. I concluded the introduction of the previous two books with a prayer for them, and do so again, but this time I pray for them as known companions on the earthly pilgrimage of the people of God. And my prayer is this: 'As the Easter lily blooms, may you meet the Risen Lord and hasten into the world with the Good News; when the swallow is on the wing, may you rejoice in the Spirit and receive his gifts; at the season of sowing and planting, may you grow in the Word; and at the time of harvest, may you reap in joy and bear a rich harvest home to God.'

J.M.
London, Feast of SS Michael, Gabriel and Raphael; 29 September 2004

Part 1

Eastertide to Pentecost

EASTERTIDE
TO PENTECOST

EASTER SUNDAY

SHEEPSBIT SCABIOUS *Jasione montana*; Sheep's Rampion; Blue Bonnets
SCABIOUS *Scabiosa caucasica*; mourning bride

Cultivation notes
This attractive blue-flowered
perennial grows wild in
western England and in my
own region of south-west
France. It has hairy and
spreading stems, each one
bearing a single bloom
between May and August,
and can reach a height of
20 inches. Avoid bruising the
leaves and stems as they emit
an unpleasant smell. In spite of
its resemblance to a true
scabious, sheepsbit belongs
to the bellflower family. It
has leaves arranged spirally
round the stem, whereas
scabious has leaves paired in
opposite positions. Sheepsbit seed is
available from purveyors of wild flower mixtures, but in a traditionally
cultivated garden true scabious may be preferred. *S. caucasica* grows to 2
feet with a spread of 18 inches, and its blue or white flowers are excellent
for cutting. The seed heads can be dried for arrangements. Both these
plants like limy soil and a sunny position. Plant in groups from October to
April. *S. Columbaria var. ochroleuca* has pretty, pale yellow petals
surrounding a domed centre, and grows to 3 feet in height and spread.

History and lore

'Sheepsbit' denotes the way the plant is cropped or bitten by sheep in rough pasture, and the Latin name may indicate a connection with Jason and the golden fleece. The word *scabious* comes from the Latin *scabies* or 'the itch', which the roughness of the plant's leaves was supposed to cure. Native to the Caucasus, Northern Turkey and Iran, true scabious is thought to have arrived in Britain early in the nineteenth century. The flower heads of both sheepsbit and scabious consist of small florets and appear to pollinating wasps as one large flower. Pollination causes each flower to produce a seed capsule.

Towards meditation

Many pagan belief systems feature a figure who is killed and who rises from the dead, usually a characterization of the re-burgeoning of nature in spring. Elsewhere (holy water and Baptism in *Gardening with God*, p. 90) I express the feeling that those who claim that the Christian Church merely exploited these systems to promote its own tenets are looking through the wrong end of the telescope. For me, the fact that the Church transmuted these rites of spring is not a reason for disbelief. Far from that, I believe that, in the cycle of the life, death, passion, resurrection and ascension of Christ, God fulfils our pagan dream (which God had put into our natures in the first place) and makes it an astonishing reality.

Towards the end of *Thorn, Fire and Lily* I described coming home from church after the Easter Vigil and expressed a wish to stay in the Garden of Resurrection with Mary Magdalene during the remaining hours of darkness. This year in a small sense that wish was granted because I was in France and therefore unable to attend the Vigil. There in my own garden, until I recognized the Risen Lord, I was, like Mary, a 'mourning bride'. But the main reason why sheepsbit scabious is chosen today is because of the reference to sheep in the Easter Sequence that we hear first during the Mass of Easter Day: 'Christian, to the Paschal Victim offer sacrifice and praise. The sheep are ransomed by the Lamb.' (*Victimae Paschali laudes* is attributed to a priest named Wipso, chaplain to Conrad II [d. *c*.1048], and was possibly initially part of a mystery play.) And indeed, 'Tell us, Mary: say what thou didst see upon the way', has the feel of a questioning chorus, which is then answered by the Magdalene, as in the last six lines. The style of the Sequence, whether it is said, read or sung, lends a homely intimacy, and makes me feel closely connected to the events of Easter morning. But there are other reasons for the choice of sheepsbit. Christ ransomed us but he continues to cherish us, and to feed us. He is our food and cures the restlessness of our spirits, and, if we will heed and follow him, prevents us from becoming lost sheep. The many florets making one flower are symbolic of the Church being the Body of Christ with us as its members who are individually pollinated by the Word and Sacraments.

We can also say of the unpleasant smell emitted when the plant is bruised that it is a reminder of the stench of earthly decay and corruption, or symbolic of what will happen to our souls if they are bruised by sin. And so we are brought to the contrast between ourselves and Christ, who was not subject to corruption of the flesh and who did not sin. Like all human beings he was born and he died, but in the way these two events happened, God altered the natural order of creation, so that Christ, born of a virgin and risen from the dead, ensured that we too may achieve incorruptibility and forgiveness of our sins.

My own favourite Easter carol enables expression of a deeply personal jubilation in these aspects of the resurrection of our Lord:

> This joyful Eastertide,
> Away with sin and sorrow.
> My love the Crucified,
> Hath sprung to life this morrow:
> Had Christ that once was slain
> Ne'er burst his three day prison,
> Our faith had been in vain:
> But now is Christ arisen, arisen, arisen, arisen!
>
> My flesh in hope shall rest,
> And for a season slumber
> Till trump from east to west
> Shall wake the dead in number:
> Had Christ that once was slain
> Ne'er burst his three day prison,
> Our faith had been in vain:
> But now is Christ arisen, arisen, arisen, arisen!
>
> Death's flood hath lost his chill,
> Since Jesus crossed the river:
> Lover of souls, from ill

My passing soul deliver:
Had Christ that once was slain
Ne'er burst his three day prison
Our faith had been in vain:
But now is Christ arisen, arisen, arisen, arisen!

(G. R. Woodward, 1848–1934)

Readings and other suggested plants
John 20:1-9: Summoned by Mary Magdalene, Peter and John hasten to the empty tomb (Roses: 'Pascali', 'Easter Morning, 'St John', 'St Pier', 'Mary Magdalene'; Narcissus 'Easter Moon', 'Easter Bonnet'; Royal Fern; Water forget-me-not; Water lily 'Sunrise').

Intercessions
For shepherds and their flocks, for sheep farmers and those who work in the wool industry; for sufferers from skin disease; for the bereaved; for unbelievers;

For the Church, that she may spread the seed of the gospel, and for ourselves as members of Christ's Body;

Thanksgiving and joy in the resurrection of our Lord.

Place of spiritual retreat
With Peter and John, and then with Mary Magdalene, as in John 20.

EASTERTIDE WEEK ONE

BAPTISIA *Baptisia tinctoria;* Wild Indigo; Rattleweed

Cultivation notes
This perennial is native to eastern North America. Of some seventeen species two are grown in borders for their yellow, white or blue lupin-like flowers, which appear in June and July. They are upright and clump-forming and have attractive clover-like leaves. Baptisia will grow to a height of 4 feet and spread for 2 feet. It likes rich moisture-retentive soil in sun. Sow seed in spring or plant in groups from October to March. Propagate by division when dormant, but remember that larger roots do not respond well to disturbance. Support in windy areas.

History and lore

The botanical name comes from *bapto*, Greek for 'to wash' or 'to dye', and indeed it does produce an indigo dye as its common English name suggests. Charles Millspaugh in his *Medicinal Plants* (1892), wrote that the shoots resembled asparagus and in New England were used instead of this in soup, and it is mentioned in the US *Pharmocopoeia* of 1831. The Mohicans made a decoction of roots as an antiseptic wash for wounds, and it is effective against bacterial infections, lowers fever and has laxative, emetic effects. It is used in modern herbalism to treat boils, ulcers and gum disease. Lift the roots in autumn and dry for decoctions and tinctures.

Towards meditation

There is much in the liturgy this week about how we should behave as Christians, and, as is often the case, the characteristics of good Christians are also to be found in good gardeners: patience, vigilance and good stewardship for instance. On Monday, St Peter tells us in the responsory to the first Office reading that we must be mentally stripped for action, and this spiritual truth in our active lives as Christians certainly has a practical application as we embark on the busiest time of the gardening year. As Lent prepared us for Easter and our continuing Christian pilgrimage, so all our winter planning for the new season in the garden can now be put into practice. And as we sow and plant for food crops, we may reflect on Wednesday's first reading. This is from a paschal homily by an ancient writer and dwells on Christ as the author of life and of spiritual nourishment. There are also several occasions when the liturgy chimes with our joy in the rebirth of nature around us. At Prayer during the Day on Tuesday, Psalm 23 reminds us of the symbolism of the fresh green pastures where the Lord gives us repose; on Wednesday the Office begins with Psalm 104, which is a hymn of wonder and gratitude for God's provision in nature. When reading it my gardener's heart leaps, and farming blood is stirred: 'You make the grass grow for the cattle/and the plants to serve man's needs ...'

This psalm emphasizes God's provision of water. Beasts of the field, wild asses, trees of the Lord, the earth itself, all drink their fill of God's gift. And this reminds me that I chose *Baptisia* because Baptism is a particular theme this week. Tuesday's midday scripture reading (1 Pet. 3:21–22a) recalls the fact that our baptism saves us through the resurrection of Jesus Christ, and the second Office reading on Thursday is from the *Instruction to the Newly Baptized at Jerusalem*. Here Baptism is explored as a symbol of Christ's passion. The newly baptized are buried with Christ into death and yet come from the font filled with radiance. For, as the midday reading (Titus 3:5b–7) tells us, through the Holy Spirit they and we are given new birth and new life by Baptism. The continuation of *The Instruction* on Friday explains that through Baptism we have put on Christ and share in him. For that reason it is correct to call ourselves 'anointed ones'. At midday on Friday the reading stresses the unifying power of baptism (Gal. 3:27–8): 'No more Jew or Gentile, no more slave and freeman, no more male and female: you are all one person in Jesus Christ.'

Readings and other suggested plants with their meanings

Ps 1: He is like a tree whose leaf does not wither (Berberis, evergreen).
1 Pet. 1:22–2:10: Spiritual honesty, no spite, deceit or envy (*Lunaria*, honesty; Fern, sincerity; Orange Tree, generosity).
1 Pet. 3:1–17: Influence of women on men; husbands to be considerate (Linden, conjugal love); against over-adornment (Stock, lasting beauty).
Acts 4:1–12: The name by which we are saved (Clematis, safety).
1 Pet. 3:18–4:12: Good stewardship (Flax, Sage and Mint, industry and domestic virtue); *Physotegia Virginiana*, 'Obedience Plant'.
1 Pet. 4:11–5:14: Crown of glory (Bay, victory); Humility, obedience, servanthood (Service Tree); unload your worries on the Lord (Milk vetch, 'Your presence softens my pains'); Calm vigilance against the devil (Dame's Violet, watchfulness).

Intercessions

For victims of drought and famine; for an increase in the virtues mentioned in the week's liturgy; for good stewardship of the earth and of our individual charges; for God's blessing on our gardens.

Thanksgiving for our Baptism, and for the wonders of nature.

Places of spiritual retreat

Monday: with the women receiving Christ's instructions to tell the disciples they will see him in Galilee, as in Matthew 26:8–15.

Tuesday: with Mary Magdalene in the garden of Christ's burial, as in John 20:11–18.

Wednesday: with Luke and Cleopas on the road to Emmaus, as in Luke 24:13–35.

Thursday: with Luke and Cleopas when Jesus appears, eats with them and then teaches them, as in Luke 24:35–48.

Friday: with the disciples when Jesus appears to them by the Sea of Tiberias, as in John 21:1–14.

Saturday: with the Eleven being told by the Risen Christ to go out and proclaim the good news, as in Mark 16:9–15.

LOW SUNDAY
(*Quasimodo* or White Sunday)

PRIMROSE *Primula vulgaris*

Cultivation notes

This familiar and much-loved perennial is native to temperate and mountainous areas of the northern hemisphere. It thrives in borders and naturalizes well in the garden. The primrose produces two types of flower and seeds only appear when pollen from one sort is transferred to the other. Since they bloom when there are few insects about, the flowers frequently die un-pollinated. Ants like the sticky seeds and carry them off, thus aiding dispersal. Sow seed in a semi-shaded site in late summer or divide established clumps in late spring or early autumn. Regular division encourages the plant's strength. Plant close together to see whether they will hybridize and produce yellow polyanthus.

History and lore

Shakespeare knew about the plant's pollination system, since he writes in *The Winter's Tale* (Act IV, sc. iii, l. 122), 'pale primroses,/that die unmarried ere they can behold/bright Phoebus in his strength ...'

In the language of flowers primroses signify early youth, and it was an old custom to plant them on the graves of children. From these churchyard plants have come the many primroses that now grow wild, although not so plentifully as in the past because of over-picking. The early flowering of primroses led to their being used to decorate churches at Easter, and indeed the name means 'first rose'. In parts of England they were also known as the 'butter rose', in an attempt to make an accurate description of its colour. But perhaps Lesley Gordon is more charmingly correct when she says that the shade of its yellow 'may be compared only to the wings of the Brimstone butterfly, itself a wavering primrose on wings' (*Green Magic*, Webb & Bower, 1977). The primrose was fashionable in Victorian times, perhaps because it was supposed to be Disraeli's favourite flower, and Queen Victoria sent him many from her gardens. On his death she sent a large wreath of them to mark her affection and respect for him. Pliny recommended primrose to treat paralysis, gout and rheumatism, and in modern herbalism an infusion of the roots is taken as a remedy for these complaints and for nervous headaches. A tincture of the whole plant is sedative and reduces tension. In the kitchen flowers and young leaves may be added to salads and the flowers used to decorate puddings and desserts. Soak them in distilled water to make a wash for spots and wrinkles. Pick the flowers in spring to use fresh or dried. Cut the whole plant when flowering and do not lift the roots for drying until the second spring or autumn.

Note: Primrose remedies are not given during pregnancy or to anyone with whom aspirin disagrees. Avoid giving to patients who are taking anti-coagulant drugs such as warfarin. Leaves can irritate sensitive skins.

Towards meditation

Today I want to reflect on the names given to this Sunday:

First, *Quasimodo* is taken from the first word of today's Mass introit, in which Peter tells us, 'Like newborn children you should thirst for milk, on which your spirit can grow in strength' (1 Pet. 2:2). As the primrose is associated with extreme youth, it is appropriate here, and my meditation may be on this text of Peter, bearing in mind that in the first Office reading St Paul exhorts us to cut away earthly desires and hateful feelings and, in compassion, kindness, humility, gentleness and patience, to do just as the Introit (Col. 3:1–17) has told us. (And that cutting away, also reminds me that my pruning programme in the garden should be well completed by now, particularly if Easter has been late.)

Second, in the old Missal and Breviary this day was called *Dominica in Albis*, hence the English 'White Sunday'. The name alludes to the white robes of the newly baptized, worn for the last time on the Sunday after Easter. There is reference to them in the early Ambrosian Vespers hymn of the pre-conciliar Breviary, '*Ad regias Agni dapes*': 'The Lamb's high banquet we await/In snow-white robes of royal state ...' (trans. J. M. Neale, 1818–66).

In the Collect of the old Low Sunday Mass, the Church called on the newly baptized to prolong the feast of Easter in themselves by remaining faithful to the graces they had drawn from it. And she speaks to us, as well as to those who have just entered the Christian body: 'May we ... who have celebrated the paschal solemnity ... remain faithful to it in the conduct of our lives.'

Third, the name 'Low Sunday' possibly originated in the contrast between the high solemnity and joy of Easter Day and the quieter atmosphere of the Sunday following. That it came to mark the end of Easter is witnessed in another Latin name, *Pascha Clausum*. Nowadays Eastertide officially lasts until Pentecost, and in this the post-conciliar liturgy is perhaps truer to the spirit of the old hymn and Collect than one might first think. With our spiritual lives renewed and rejuvenated by the Easter celebration, we are the stronger to continue in the life we have embraced. Through being fed by the pure milk of the Word and with the bread of the Eucharist, we are helped to be witnesses of Christ's resurrection and victory over death and evil. And if we are tempted at times to excessive frivolity and to a neglect of these keys to salvation, there is an old Flemish legend about the primrose that is worth pondering: When God created the flowers in all their variety of colour he kept them all in heaven. Then he began to think about the time of year when each would blossom and noticed some yellow ones with five, six or seven umbels on a stalk. They were cheerful, and alert and laughed a lot, having a tendency to garrulity, giddiness and even wantonness. Concentration was not their strong point. But God decided they should be the flowers that would hold the key to spring. The primroses left heaven in a rush of delight in their divinely appointed responsibility, but with terrible carelessness they left the key behind. The Lord laughed and returned it to his pocket. The primroses fell to earth and were very happy to be in the place they had been created for, but when the time came for spring to be unlocked, they were at a loss. They searched the streams because they thought the key could have fallen into one of them. But to no avail. And to this day they can be seen dotted around the vicinity of water looking for the key, which the Lord has entrusted to other more sensible flowers. I have two or three naturalized clumps of primrose, and the one by the pond symbolic of baptism is the largest and healthiest They all bloom for a long period and so I have plenty of time to notice them and to reflect on the symbolism of the Flemish story.

Readings and other suggested plants and their meanings
1 Pet. 2:9–10: You are a chosen race, a royal priesthood (Pennyroyal).
St Augustine, from 'Sermon 8 in the Octave of Easter': The newly baptized are 'the flower of our honour, and the fruit of our labour' (Blackcurrant, redcurrant, gooseberry).
John 20:19–31: Thomas doubts (Snapdragon, 'No').

Intercessions
For the newly baptized and for their catechists; for sufferers from rheumatism, gout and nervous tension.

For those who are careless with the gifts God has given them, and that we may all value and develop the ones we ourselves have been given.

For the grace to grow old with serenity and detachment.

Place of spiritual retreat
With Jesus and Thomas, as in John 20.

EASTERTIDE WEEK TWO

TREE OF LIFE *Thuya occidentalis; Arbor-vitae*

Cultivation notes
This evergreen tree is hardy to −50°F. and likes deep moist soil in a sheltered sunny position. It can reach a maximum of 60 feet in height but if kept trimmed makes a fine dense hedge or windbreak. If the foliage is scorched, remove while the damage is minimal, otherwise unsightly gaps will be left, spoiling the appearance of the hedge. There are numerous cultivars, varying in size and colour and therefore the Tree of Life is

versatile in garden planning. The species is a narrow conifer with reddish bark and small scaly leaves which sometimes turn bronze in winter. The whole plant is beautifully aromatic when brushed or cut. Of the many varieties *T. occidentalis* 'Rheingold' is probably the most popular, as its golden foliage can be relied upon to appear in winter.

History and lore

The aromatic qualities of the Tree of Life led to its use by the ancient Greeks as a purification element in sacrificial ritual, and indeed the name *Thuya* is from the Greek *thujo*, meaning sacrifice. As the Latin and English names suggest, the tree symbolizes immortality, and the Catholic Church consecrated the tree on the feast of the Immaculate Conception, 8 December, in 1862. In parts of northern Germany it often replaces the cypress or yew in cemeteries. European explorers of the eastern part of North America found the tree, and it was one of the first to be introduced to Europe from there. It arrived in Britain about 1596; the herbalist John Gerard had one in his garden. M. de Cleene and M. Lejeune record it being grown in Paris as early as 1553 (*Compendium of Symbolic and Ritual Plants of Europe*, Vol. 1, Man and Culture Publishers, Ghent 2003). The Tree of Life was important to many native North Americans, its timber being used to make bows, canoes, baskets, rope and roofing. Medicinally they used it to treat menstrual problems, headaches and heart disease. North American loggers made twigs into an anti-rheumatic tea, and it was listed in the US *Pharmocopoiea* (1852–94). The timber is light, soft and sweet-smelling, and before the introduction of glass fibre was frequently used in Canada in the construction of lightweight boats. In modern herbalism it is combined with Virginian witch hazel to make a lotion for weeping eczema, warts and muscular pain. Collect and dry the bark and leaves as needed for making liquid extracts.

Note: Use internally only under instruction from a qualified medical practitioner. It is not given to pregnant women. The leaves are toxic if eaten and may irritate some skins.

Towards meditation

'Listen to what the Spirit is saying to the churches. To everyone who conquers, I will give permission to eat from the tree of life that is in the paradise of God' (Rev. 2:7). From now until the end of the fifth week of Eastertide the first Office readings will take us through the book of Revelation. This week we read of John's encounter with the Son of Man and the messages to the seven churches. He then sees the worship in heaven in direct contrast to the imperfect condition of the earthly Church, and his vision continues with the beginnings of the revelation of future events that must come about as a result. Only Christ can set them in motion, not through his power as a 'lion', but through his sacrificial death on the cross as 'the Lamb'. Christ himself is the Tree of Life, whose fruit of immortality we may not taste unless we too are 'conquerors'.

Five of the early churches show features that prevent them from achieving this goal. Surely no one living in the developed world can fail to draw modern parallels. At Ephesus there is a lack of love for Christ, and of others; at Pergamum the church has made a brave start but is allowing false teaching and pagan practices to creep in; at Thyatira there is compromise with immorality; at Sardis apathy, indifference and self-satisfaction; and at Laodicea many of the Christians are tepid, complacent and completely blind to their faults. They share their town's pride in the production of fine clothing and in the wonders of its medicines. Only at Smyrna and Philadelphia do the churches meet with Christ's approval and receive his encouragement. In them we find the character we must emulate in our desire for the Fruit of the Tree of Life. At Smyrna the church is small and poor, but rich in spirit. Christ assures its members that their sufferings will be limited and promises them eternal life. The church in Philadelphia receives no blame either. Outwardly unimpressive and lacking in prestige, it is an example of effective work being done for Christ, not by the strong but by the faithful.

The motif of Christ as the Tree of Life runs through this week, but on Friday in the second Office reading St Theodore the Studite (759–826) meditates on the cross of Christ itself as the tree of life. Referring to the expulsion of Adam and Eve from Paradise, he says, 'Of old we were poisoned by a tree, now we have found immortality through a tree'. The reading calls to mind the anonymous early ninth-century poem, *The Dream of the Rood*, which I shall be certain to read during Eastertide, praying as it does:

> ... May the Lord be a friend to me,
> he who suffered once for the sins of men
> here on earth on the gallows-tree.
> He has redeemed us; He has given life to us,
> And a home in heaven.
> > (trans. of Vercelle MS by Kevin Crossley-Holland,
> > in *The Anglo-Saxon World*, OUP, 1984)

Readings and other suggested plants with their meanings

Acts 4:32–7: Unity and common ownership (Scarlet verbena, Church unity).

Rev 2:1–3:22: Messages to the Churches. These are full of colourful motifs and images that highlight their spiritual importance, and if space allows one could devote a corner of the garden to plants whose colours evoke the symbolism of this text. For example: silver (Artemisia); fire, polished brass and spiritual gold (*Acer brilliantissimum*); white stone (White stonecrop); morning Star (yellow Ixia); inheritance ('Heritage' rose); clean white clothing (Daphne *mezereum*); rainbow (Multi-coloured sparaxis); emerald (Euonymus); lighted torches (yellow irises); crystal sea ('Cristata' rose). Rev 5:1–4: Blood of the Lamb, rose 'Crimson Glory'.

Intercessions

For those suffering from conditions Thuya is traditionally used to treat.

For the help of the Holy Spirit to make our churches strong in those characteristics that Christ wishes to see, so that he may grant us, too, permission to eat of the Tree of Life.

Places of spiritual retreat

Monday, Tuesday and Wednesday: with Christ and Nicodemus, as in John 3:1–21.

Thursday: with John the Baptist and his disciples, as in John 3:31–6.

Friday: in the crowd at the feeding of the five thousand, as in John 6:1–15.

Saturday: with the disciples seeing Jesus walk on the lake, as in John 6:16–21.

EASTERTIDE THIRD SUNDAY AND WEEK

CORNFLOWER *Centaurea cyanus*; Bluebottle; Break-your-spectacles (*Casselunettes*); Hurtsickle

Cultivation notes

This ancient flower of the field is an annual and blooms from June to September. Two types are available for garden planting. The tall varieties, such as 'Blue Diadem', grow to 3 feet in height, while the dwarfs, such as 'Jubilee Gem', reach 9 to 12 inches. Sow seed in March or April in a sunny, well-drained position. The grey-green foliage makes an attractive contrast in mixed borders. To save the trouble of planting or sowing each year, try the perennial *C. montana*. This grows to about 2 feet and produces white, purple or pink flowers from May to July. Plant in groups from October to March in sun or light shade. Mulch with well-rotted compost in late spring; cut the stems down to ground level in autumn and divide every few years from October to March. Both annual and perennial cornflowers benefit from deadheading and need staking if their height is more than 2 feet.

History and lore

Cornflowers are known to have grown among grain planted by the Bronze Age people who lived near the Swiss lakes, and the blue of those found in the tomb of Tutankhamen had hardly faded since being put there in about 1550 BC. *C. cyanus* is native to Europe and western Asia and is so called from the legend of Chiron the centaur who was renowned for his knowledge of herbs. When wounded by an arrow poisoned with the blood of the Hydra, he covered his wound with cornflowers and was healed. *Cyanus* is from the Greek for blue. The legend is that a youth named Cyanus, who worshipped Chloris (Flora), the goddess of flowers, died while gathering blue flowers for her altar. She turned him into one and named them after him in honour of his love and sensitivity toward her. This legend is probably the reason why the traditional significance of cornflower is that of delicacy and sensitivity. Certainly there are many European folkloric practices that associate the plant with love. It is also symbolic of fidelity, propriety and hope. The juice of the flowers mixed with alum water has been used by watercolour artists, and to the Dutch painters of the Middle Ages the cornflower was a symbol of the modesty of the Blessed Virgin Mary.

'Hurtsickle' comes from the fact that its tough stems blunted reaping tools and therefore it was unpopular with farmers, who also disliked it because it took the soil's goodness from the cereal crops among which it likes to grow. Until the early twentieth century it was still a common sight in cornfields, but it has now been greatly reduced through modern farming methods. The pagan significance of the cornflower became Christianized throughout Europe, where many traditions developed in connection with it. For instance, if storms threatened, the flower was burned during a prayer for the protection of one's house; it was believed that holding the flower would stop heavy bleeding, particularly from the nose; and people covered their eyes with cornflowers in confidence that their sight would be strengthened. In Bohemia, for the same purpose, girls would look at St John's Fire (see the Birthday of St John the Baptist, 24 June, in Part 3) through wreaths of cornflowers. After this they would no longer need spectacles; the practice is almost certainly the origin of the English folk name, 'break-your-spectacles', and the French equivalent for the plant. In Renaissance herbals the cornflower is indeed mentioned as a disinfectant for eyes. Culpeper writes, 'the juice dropped into the eyes takes away heat and inflammation of them' (*Complete Herbal and English Physician Enlarged*, 1653). In folk medicine a tradition developed of making a rinse to combat eye infections and cataracts, and there was a French eyewash, *Eau de Casse-lunettes*, made from cornflower petals. Not surprisingly, tradition held that treatment with cornflower was particularly good for blue eyes. The plant is still used today to ease conjunctivitis, and to give colour to pot-pourri. Harvest and dry the flowers as they open.

Towards meditation

I have chosen the cornflower this week because of its connection with eyes. Sunday's Gospel is Luke's account of the two disciples' experience of recognizing the risen Jesus in the breaking of bread with them at Emmaus (Luke 24:13–35), and the first reading at Mass on Friday is the description in Acts 9:1–20 of the conversion of St Paul, which left him temporarily blind. Both texts provide rich food for meditation on the days in question. But the liturgy this week is particularly marked by its use of gardening terms to express spiritual truths. Tuesday would be an ideal day to do some seed sowing and at the same time to reflect on the second Office reading, in which St Augustine addresses us as 'holy seeds of heaven, you who have been born again in Christ' He encourages us to '"Sing to the Lord a new song!" but make sure your life sings the same tune as your mouth.' If you live good lives, he says, you yourselves *are* his praise. On Friday we could be accompanied among the seedbeds by St Ephraem, (*c.* 306–*c.* 379), who meditates in the Office on Christ's cross as the salvation of the human race. Addressing our Lord he says, 'Your murderers handled your body like farmers: they sowed it like grain deep in the earth, for it to spring up and raise with itself a multitude of men.' As we sow the cornflower seed we may see it as representative of that multitude, which will grow up into a people of vision, sensitivity, propriety, love and hope. And those gardeners who are advanced enough to do grafting will be interested in St Ephraem's image of Christ as the sweet shoot being grafted onto the bitter wood of the cross.

A check for garden pests on Wednesday could encourage a consideration of the first Office reading (Rev. 9:1–12), in which the locusts are 'told not to harm the grass or the trees, or any other plant; they could harm only the men who did not have the mark of God's seal on their foreheads'. They are allowed to torture these men for five months (the average lifespan of a locust), but not to kill them. But, as we shall see on Thursday (Rev. 9:13–21), even in the face of dire warning people will not listen. They live in a world that ignores God, makes its own idols and refuses to stop its wrongdoing and cruelty. Once again it is hard not to draw parallels. The very least one can do is have 'a pest check' on one's soul and avail oneself of the Sacrament of Reconciliation. On Thursday too, the first Mass reading (Acts 8:21–40) tells of Philip baptizing the Ethiopian. This will remind me, as I water my new seedbeds, to pray for people who suffer in countries where there is drought and to thank God again for my own baptism. On Saturday, time may be spent on planting and meditating on St Cyril of Alexandria's (376–444) *Commentary on St John's Gospel*. Speaking in the second Office reading of Christ's life-giving death, he says that through his body Christ 'planted life among us again'.

Reading and other suggested plants with their meanings
Readings from Revelation continue all week from 6:1 to 9:42 and as before offer much inspiration in theme and colour for the creation of commemorative garden borders and corners.

Acts 6:8–15: Stephen speaks; and Acts 7:51–8:1 Martyrdom of Stephen (Stephanandra).

Acts 8:24–40: Philip and the Ethiopian (Rose 'Philippa').

Acts 9:31–42: Peter cures the paralytic and raises Tabitha (Cowslip, also called Herb Peter and Peter's Keys).

Intercessions
For cereal farmers; for those suffering from eye complaints and those who care for them; for the physically and the spiritually blind; for light to see our faults, and for strength to mend our ways; for the conversion of those in deep sin; for those who have forgotten God, and those who worship false gods.

For ourselves, that we may be part of that multitude, sown with Christ in death but springing up to life in him, with him and in him.

Thanksgiving for the cross of Christ.

Places of spiritual retreat

Sunday: with Christ and the two disciples at the breaking of bread in Emmaus, as in Luke 24:13–35.

Days of the week: with Jesus as he successively teaches the crowd, the arguing Jews and his own complaining followers, as in John 6:22–69.

EASTERTIDE GOOD SHEPHERD SUNDAY AND FOURTH WEEK

DAY LILY 'GENTLE SHEPHERD' *Hemerocallis*
STRAWBERRY *Fragaria*

Cultivation notes

Day lilies are not true lilies and their common name comes from their lily-like flowers, which usually last only for a day. 'Gentle Shepherd' has creamy yellow flowers with darker yellow centres and slightly crinkly-edged petals. It may reach a height of 3 feet and the luxuriant foliage is excellent for smothering weeds. The plant should bloom in summer for up to six weeks in any soil except badly drained clay, and will produce its best if it is in sun for at least half the day. Divide in early spring.

Dean Hole once asked a boy what a garden is for. 'Strawberries!' the boy replied, without hesitation. And indeed they are probably the most widely grown fruit in domestic gardens, the only drawback of the popular summer varieties being the brevity of their cropping season. One flush is produced and picking lasts only for a couple of weeks in June or July. However, if you plant a few of several varieties strawberries will be in crop from May until the first frost of autumn. With a heated greenhouse you can prolong the supply until Christmas. I would suggest ten each of the following, more if you have room. Cropping times are given in brackets: Honeoye (May); Elsanta (late May to late June); Cambridge Favourite (mid-June to mid-July); Pegasus (mid to late July); Aromel (perpetual fruiting – several flushes are produced between August and October, more if you protect under glass). All these varieties have good resistance to botrytis, mildew and vericillum wilt. The secret is to plant from late summer, and no later than mid-September, so that the plants have a good start before the onset of winter, and when the fruit begins to swell to mulch with straw, or commercially produced mulch mats. I make my own from empty compost sacks cut to the required size. The insides of these are usually black and the plastic is stronger than ordinary black polythene. This recycling is an economical way of keeping down weeds round any newly planted subjects, especially fruit bushes, shrubs and tomatoes. After fruiting cut the leaves to 3 inches above the crown, but with perpetuals merely remove old leaves. In June or July, to raise new plants, secure a strong runner from each plant with a hairpin pressed into the ground, and nip off the runner beyond its plantlet. About six weeks later cut the runner between parent and plantlet and remove the hairpin. After a week, dig up the new plants and plant as required. Perpetual varieties do not produce runners and are propagated by division in early September. Plants deteriorate and need replacing after a few years. Where space is at a premium, grow strawberries in traditional pots with spirally arranged holes around the sides. Except for the necessity of frequent watering, this is a labour-saving method. Fruit is out of reach of slugs, mulching and hoeing are not needed and a net draped over the pot will protect your fruit.

History and lore

The Latin *fragaria* is thought to be a reference to the flavour and aroma of the strawberry. The English word is from Old English *strea(w) berige* but the *Shorter Oxford Dictionary* tells us that the reason for the name is unknown. However, I first saw strawberries growing in quantity on my great-aunt's farm in Wisbech and I cannot have been more than eight when she explained the straw in the berry's name. She said it was from the (barley) straw traditionally used as a mulch, having, as it did, the fourfold benefit of keeping weeds down, discouraging slugs (who do not like prickly things), preventing the fruit from making contact with wet soil in heavy rain and allowing it maximum exposure to the ripening strength of the sun. The strawberry is ancient and findings in Swiss pile-dwellings have shown that its popularity dates back to the Stone Age. Later it was dedicated to the Germanic goddess Frigg, guardian of marriage and motherhood. In Christian lore it thus became an attribute of the Virgin Mary, and de Cleene and Lejeune (*op. cit.*) record a tradition that St John the Baptist ate wild strawberries in the wilderness. If Bavarian children were picking strawberries and passed a cross or chapel they would make an offering of three fruits, and in other parts of Germany and Estonia the strawberry was believed to be the prerogative of the Blessed Virgin Mary. It was not to be eaten before St John's day, particularly not by pregnant mothers, who might then be punished by having their children barred from paradise. This supposed vengefulness would seem to hark back to the pagan goddess Frigg and to accord more with her character than with that of Our Lady.

Wild strawberries (*F. vesca*) are native to woods and grasslands in Europe, western Asia and North America. They and the French *F. moschata* were the only strawberries known in Europe until after the seventeenth century, when the ancestors of our large garden strawberries were introduced from America. These are thought to have been a cross between *F. virginiana* and *F.chiloensis*. Linnaeus believed that the berries were a cure for gout, and Polish peasants followed the 'Doctrine of Signatures' and used wild strawberries to treat erysipelas, one of the symptoms of which is a red flush on the skin. Culpeper recommends the strawberry as a remedy for 'wheals and other breakings forth of hot sharp humours in the face and hands ... and to take away any redness in the face, or spots, or other deformities in the skin, and to make it clear and smooth' (*Complete Herbal*, 1653). The nineteenth-century Dr Losch recommended strawberry tisane as a convalescent tonic and gave some delectable descriptions of the ways in which *fraises des bois* were eaten in France, with wine and cream, or with orange juice and champagne. In modern herbalism infusions of the astringent leaves are used to treat mild diarrhoea, and a decoction of the roots is given to patients with urinary tract inflammation. Strawberry tea makes a good gargle for a sore throat. The fruit is rich in vitamin C and iron and is an enjoyable dietary supplement for anaemia sufferers. Collect leaves in summer, and lift roots in autumn to use dried in infusions.

Towards meditation
The Day Lily 'Gentle Shepherd' is an obvious choice for Good Shepherd Sunday, which in its turn is named from its Mass Gospel, where Christ speaks of himself as 'the gate of the sheepfold' (John 10:1–10). And

21

Monday's Gospel continues the discourse of Jesus on the theme of the Good Shepherd (John 10:11–18). However, as we move on into the week a new theme takes over, namely that of the fruits of the spirit, and I have chosen the strawberry because it has come to represent these in Christian symbolism. In the language of flowers it indicates excellence and perfect goodness, in art it is a symbol of righteousness, and when illustrated with other fruits it refers to the good works of the righteous person. In the second Office reading on Monday St Basil (330–79) meditates on life in the Spirit and on fruit borne in holiness; on Wednesday St Peter Chrysologus (d. *c.* 450) reflects on the results of service; and on Saturday St Cyril of Alexandria (*c.* 376–444) exhorts us all to that service. When depicted with violets, strawberries may represent the humility of the true believer, but conversely in art they sometimes signify the temptation of worldly pleasures, as Hieronymus Bosch graphically represents in his *Garden of Delights* (*c.* 1500). And there is an old legend that the strawberry was originally white but then became very proud of itself and its flavour. When it repented of this vanity it began to blush in shame, and it has continued to do so until this day. The first Mass reading on Monday reminds us that God gives repentance and life to all, both Jew and gentile alike (Acts 11:1–18), and on Saturday St Cyril comments on the great truth that God's mercy is for all. Thanks to St Paul (Gal 5:22–4), we are able to measure ourselves by asking the question, 'How loving, joyful, peaceful, patient, kind, good, faithful, gentle, and self-controlled am I?' And we can also be reminded that 'those who belong to Christ have crucified the flesh with its passions and desires'.

Another significance of fruit and harvest is introduced in Wednesday's first Office reading (Rev. 14:14–15:4) about the Harvest of the Earth, the first fruits being that part of it that belongs to God in the last days. The sharp sickle with which this harvest is cut and put into the wine press of the wrath of God will almost certainly lead to a meditation on the Last Things. (And on a literal level to doing some tool maintenance before the gardening season really gets too busy to find time for it.) Finally, a glance at the tripartite shape of the strawberry leaves will act as a harbinger of Trinity Sunday, now only a month away.

Readings and other suggested plants
Rev. 12:1–18: the sign of the Woman in Heaven with the sun and moon under her feet (Sundew, Sunspurge, White moon-flower; Moonstones houseplant).

Rev. 15:5–16: seven angels in white shining linen (Flax).

Intercessions
For strawberry growers and their crops; thanksgiving to God for the fruits of the earth.

For convalescents and sufferers from complaints which the strawberry is used to treat.

For strength to resist the lure of earthly pleasures at the expense of our Christian priorities.

For repentance of pride and vanity; that we may grow in humility, and that our works and service may bear fruit to the eternal harvest.

Places of spiritual retreat
Listening to the words of Jesus as in the week's Gospel texts:
John 10:1–30: I am the gate of the sheepfold; the good shepherd lays down his life for his sheep; the Father and I are one.
John 12:44–50: I the light have come into the world.
John 13:16–20: Whoever welcomes the one I send welcomes me.
John 14:1–6: I am the Way, the Truth and the Life.
John 14:7–14: To have seen me is to have seen the Father.

EASTERTIDE FIFTH SUNDAY

RUNNER BEAN *Phaseolus coccineus*; Scarlet runner

Cultivation notes
This is the vegetable which for me above all others evokes long, hot English summers of yesteryear, but one which I have found difficult to grow in France. In England there should be no problem. Choose a sunny sheltered site in autumn and dig in well-rotted compost, but not too much or the plants will produce luxuriant foliage and the flowers will fail to set. If your soil is very acid, work in some lime during the winter. In crop rotation runner beans can follow onions, brassicas or potatoes, although they don't like to be grown next to the last. Some spearmint nearby will help to discourage aphids, and the proximity of celeriac is also beneficial. Make sure your supporting rows of canes or wigwams are really firm in the ground. The bean row will then make a strong windbreak and provide shade for summer catch crops of lettuce, spinach and radishes. The

common structure for supporting beans is a double row of poles leaning toward each other with horizontal cross poles tied at the top. Netting is then secured along the length and height of each side. Poles should be 18 inches apart with 12 inches between pairs in the row. Sow the beans so that each plant will ultimately have a pole of its own to climb. According to Sutton and Sons (*The Culture of Vegetables and Flowers*, 1904), 'It is seldom profitable to sow runner beans before the month of May is fairly in, for they are less hardy than the dwarfs; but as late supplies are everywhere valued, it is of great importance to sow again in June and July.' (Our French season tends to be a month ahead, so to anyone gardening south of Angoulême I recommend a first sowing as soon as the danger of frost is over, usually in mid-April.) Bearing in mind the traditional habit of farmers and gardeners, always sow more than you need thus allowing a percentage for the birds:

> One for the rook, one for the crow,
> One to die and one to grow.
> Plant your seeds in a row,
> One for the pheasant, one for the crow,
> One to eat and one to grow.
>
> (traditional rhyme)

Keep the soil friable and weed-free, and water thoroughly in dry spells, giving an occasional liquid feed once flowering starts, as this extends the cropping period. Pinch out growing points when the tops of the supports are reached. Do not lift the roots immediately after harvesting. Left awhile they increase nitrogen in the soil.

Note: By the time I came to prepare the final manuscript of the present volume for my editor, my heart had been warmed indeed, and my patience and determination rewarded. We did .in fact have a crop of scarlet runners that summer. The foliage and flower were superb, just as I imagined them in Yeats's glade on Innisfree, the bees seeming to have overcome their reluctance of years in eager and persistent visiting. It was not a heavy crop, but oh, the joy of that first 'boiling'! Now I knew how to raise the runner bean in France, and my only adjustments in future years would be to sow a whole month earlier, and perhaps not to prepare the ground quite as richly.

History and lore

The Latin *phaseolus* is named after a small bean-shaped boat (*olus* meaning vegetable), and *coccineus* for red, either from the flower or the bean itself, and the name certainly smacks of Linnaean erudition, imagination and wit. Even though it was unheard-of in Europe until it came here from South America in the seventeenth century, I still think of it as a peculiarly English vegetable, so widely is it grown in gardens and allotments up and down the land. I spent several childhood summers with my uncle in 'Metroland' and his bean row is indelible on the landscape of memory. Runners were the only vegetable he grew, and always 'Scarlet Emperor', and in this he did better than his horseradish-limited mother in Sheffield. I still conjure the flavour, texture and aroma of those beans and maintain that they are never replicated in the bought equivalent. One of the joys of gardening in Devon was that for several years I enjoyed them again.

The thought of beans growing and cropping reminds me of summer and of Yeats. I am sure he was writing of runners in his 'The Lake Isle of Innisfree', a poem that yearns for summer in a place of solitude. My French garden is my Innisfree, and 'while I stand on the roadway,/or on the pavements gray' of London, I long for it just as Yeats did for his. It is my 'bee-loud glade', and my evenings are full of swallows', not linnets' wings. I have no hive for the honey-bee, and a pond instead of a lake, but like Yeats, all the way through June and most of July, I yearn for its peace and 'hear it in the deep heart's core'.

Towards meditation

I chose a climbing plant for today, and moreover one that gives food, to remind me of the second Office reading on Sunday. This is from a sermon of St Maximus of Turin (d. *c.* 467). In it he reflects that through Christ's resurrection hell is opened up so that its dead may enter heaven; the earth is renewed and produces the crop of those who are risen; heaven is open to receive them as they ascend; the good thief is promised paradise; the saints enter the new Jerusalem; and earth sends its dead to heaven to be presented to God. Through Christ's passion, death and resurrection, all is raised from the depths, lifted up from earth and placed on high. In Christ's resurrection, he writes, 'all the elements tend upward'. It is a simple and obvious analogy that most plants climb upward to a greater or lesser extent, but it is fundamentally important in our whole approach to gardening. At whatever stage of a plant's life, our business with it is to encourage it to grow up and, annual or perennial, it *will* grow upward again somewhere. The analogy continues if we consider that all plants grow towards the light. So whatever I'm doing with plants, and whatever day of the year it is, I am reminded of St Maximus's simple truth. He goes on to think about Christ as 'The Day', that is, the light. Christ is light without end, a light that cannot be overcome by any sin or darkness. Though we are sinners, we know from the experience of the 'good thief' that we can be forgiven and that as our plants grow toward natural light, we, while on earth, can grow toward Christ the Light, and after death can at last ascend into that light for eternity.

Readings and other suggested plants with their meanings

Acts 9:26–32: The Church grows in the Holy Spirit (Angelica, plant of the Holy Spirit); Paul and the Apostles (climbing rose 'Paul's Scarlet Pillar').

1 John 3:18–24: Love one another (tomato, other name 'Love Apple' – see also Week 12 of Ordinary Time).

Rev. 18:21–19:10: The wedding feast of the Lamb (Meadowsweet, traditional bridal flower – see also Week 17 of Ordinary Time).

Acts 14:19–28: Paul and Barnabas persecuted (Snakeshead Lily, persecution).

Rev. 19:11–21: Flame of Justice (German iris, flame).

John 14:27–31: My own peace I give unto you ('Peace' rose; Peace Lily).

John 15:27–31: I am the vine, you are the branches (Grapevine).

Rev. 21:9–27: The New Jerusalem. This is another passage that lends itself to the creation of a special 'four-square' bed to commemorate the jewels that adorn the walls of the heavenly city, using flowers of appropriate colour to represent them.

The angel's gold measuring stick (Goldenrod). The twelve gates of pearl always open to those whose names are in the book (Floribunda rose 'Pearl', medium pink; Shrub rose 'Pearl Drift', white or light, soft pink).

Rev. 22:1–9: The Tree of Life (*Arbor-vitae*, tree of life, or *Ailanthus altissima*, tree of heaven).

Acts 16:1–10: Paul meets Timothy (Timothy grass).

Rev. 22:10–21: The foundation of our hope (hawthorn or almond, hope); Christ, the bright Morning Star (morning glory).

Intercessions

Thanksgiving for home-grown and commercially distributed food crops; that we may work to distribute them more fairly throughout the world.

For the health of our soil and plants, and that we may work harder to reduce pollution of the earth.

For spiritual growth.

Place of spiritual retreat

All week: listening to the teaching of Christ, as in John 14 and 15.

EASTERTIDE SIXTH SUNDAY AND ROGATIONTIDE

MILKWORT *Polygala vulgaris*; Rogation-flower

Cultivation notes

The *Polygala* genus consists of around 500 species of annual or perennial shrubs and trees found almost the world over. *P. calcarea* is a carpeting perennial that grows to 3 inches in height with a spread of 12 inches. Its bright blue flowers appear from May to August. Plant one-and-a-half-inch basal shoots with a heel in a mixture of peat and sand in a cold frame from June to August. Pot on, and overwinter in the frame. Plant out the following spring. This plant likes moist, well-drained soil in full sun. *P. chamaebuxus*, however, favours partial shade. It is a small evergreen shrub that grows to 6 inches in height and spreads for 12 inches. It produces cream or yellow flowers from April to June. Both these *Polygala* make good rockery plants. Common Milkwort (*P. vulgaris*) is the only one to produce white flowers, but the related Heath Milkwort (*P. serpyllifolia*) can produce pink, mauve or blue ones. In 1913 H. Essenhigh-Corke (*Wild Flowers as they Grow*, Cassell), wrote that milkwort 'clothes large areas of the Downs as the spring of May gives way to the summer of June'. And he quotes a contemporary writer, Maurice Hewlett, who had earlier written, 'Then

for a shelf among rocks the milk-worts,
the sky-blue, the white and the
pink; with these I float out
May like Fra Angelico.'
Essenhigh-Corke comments,
'As one recalls the tender
reds and blues of the
great Italian painter
the simile seems very apt.'
Indeed, but have
you visited the Downs
in spring recently?

History and lore
The Latin name is
from the Greek *polygalon*,
from *polu*, 'much', and *gala*,
'milk', and is probably a
reference to the plant's
abundant white sap. The
English milkwort is given its name for the same reason, and the ancient
Greek belief that it aided milk production in cattle and in human mothers
hung on in British folklore. *P. senega* was named after the north American
Seneca people who used it to treat rattlesnake bite, the symptoms of which
are similar to pleurisy and fatal pneumonia. Its efficacy in the treatment of
bronchitis and coughs was discovered about 1753 by the Scotsman John
Tennent, and by 1740 it was being cultivated in Europe for this purpose.
P. vulgaris has similar but less powerful properties. Lift and dry the roots in
autumn for making liquid extracts and decoctions.

Rogationtide and the milkwort
The word Rogation comes from the Latin *rogare*, 'to ask', in a supplicatory
or prayerful sense. Rogationtide seems to have been instituted in France in
477. Following a series of natural disasters in Dauphiny, St Mamertus,
bishop of Vienne (d. *c.* 475), ordered a solemn penitential procession on
the three days preceding the Ascension to entreat God's protection of the
crops. The penitential aspect led to these days also becoming known as
'Little Lent'. In 511 at the Council of Orleans the procession was ordered
for the rest of France and soon spread throughout the Universal Church.

Milkwort appears to have been carried in the processions in many countries and certainly in England, since Gerard wrote that in the days of 'good Queen Bess' they were the 'floures the maidens which use in the countries to walk the Procession, do make themselves garlands and nosegaies'. In England the blessing of the fields was often accompanied by the beating of the parish bounds, and as recently as 1998 several such ceremonies were still taking place, notably at Leicester, Cannington (Somerset), Richmond (Yorkshire), Hever (near Lichfield), Wishford Magna (near Salisbury) and Leighton Buzzard (Bedfordshire). In London on the Manor and Liberty of the Savoy (the area between the Strand and the Embankment) twelve boundary markers survive from the thirteenth century, and the Court Leet meets once every five years to appoint a jury to beat the bounds. They are accompanied by the choir of the Queen's Chapel of the Savoy, and at each marker a chorister is up-ended and bumped on a cushion. No political correctness here! To find out how much praying is done one should consult the Reverend Bill Scott, who is the present chaplain. The up-ending of choirboys also went on at Plymstock in Devon and there is an undated photograph in Day, *A Chronicle of Folk Customs* (Hamlyn, 1998) of a helmeted 'Bobby' doing the honours. But Rogation Days should, strictly speaking, remain a time for asking God's blessing on the whole life of the Church, as well as a time of prayer for the fields, livestock and a good harvest of crops. The singing of the *Litany of Saints* has given its name to these three days of public intercession, but they became known as the *Lesser Litanies* because there was already a similar procession on 25 April at Rome. This in itself had replaced a pagan ritual of the god Robig, who was believed to protect crops from 'red rust'. There was a time when participation in the Rogation procession was considered to be so important that anyone who missed it and who was bound to recite the Breviary, was bound also to pray the Litany of the Saints in private.

Towards meditation
Milkwort is among the most unusual of British wild plants. The flower has three tiny green outer sepals and inside the flower the stalks of the eight stamens are joined together to form a tube. United with this tube, one on each side, are two small petals. On the lower side of the flower lies the third larger and fringed petal, it too joined to the stamen tube. The leaves tend to grow in groups of three spaced at intervals up the stalk. And so Milkwort is a suitable choice for Rogationtide, not just because of its

history, but because its very structure reflects the Trinitarian character of the Rogationtide liturgy. In the first Mass reading of Sunday, God the Father is mentioned as having no favourites (Acts 10:25–48), and in Wednesday's second Office reading (1 John 2:12–17) we are reminded of the importance of attachment to God's will. In Sunday's first Office reading (1 John:1–10) the Word is characterized as life revealed in the Incarnation; and in the second Office reading St Cyril of Alexandria reflects on the conferring on us of the ministry of reconciliation. Later in the week, on Wednesday, we shall be enjoined in the second Office reading to be vigilant against the enemies of God the Son (1 John:18–29), who is, as we are reminded by St Cyril on Tuesday, the bond of unity. On Monday there is emphasis on the Holy Spirit: in the Gospel (John 15: 26–16:4) Christ tells us that the Spirit of Truth will be his witness; and in the second Office reading Didymus of Alexandria dwells on the way in which the Holy Spirit makes us new in Baptism. In Tuesday's Gospel (John16:5–11) our Lord makes it clear that unless he ascends and leaves the disciples, the Spirit, the Advocate, cannot come to them; and on Wednesday (John 16:12–15) we are promised that the Spirit will lead us to the complete truth.

Readings and other suggested plants
Acts 10:25–40: Peter and Cornelius (Cornelian cherry).
Acts 16:11–15: Conversion of Lydia, the dealer in purple cloth (indigo plant).
Sermon 1 of St Leo the Great on the purpose of the days between the Resurrection and the Ascension:
> They bring freedom from fear ('Peace' Rose, Peace Lily)
> They assure immortality (Amaranth, eternal life)
> The Holy Spirit breathed on Peter (Angelica, in France plant of the Holy Spirit)
> The flame of faith was received and scripture unfolded (German Iris, flame)
> Jesus is truly risen (miniature rose 'Easter Morning)
> Strength is gained from the appearances of the Risen Lord (Cedar, Fennel, strength and power).

Intercessions
For cattle farmers and all who work in the milk industry.
> For nursing mothers and their babies.

For more equitable husbandry of the earth's resources, and for God's blessing on our labours on farm and garden.

For those who suffer in countries where the harvest fails.

For sufferers from bronchitis, pneumonia and pleurisy.

For the people of the towns and villages where Rogationtide ceremonies still take place; for the Queen's Chapel of the Savoy, her parishioners, chaplain and choir.

Thanksgiving for the life and writings of St Leo the Great.

Thanksgiving for the resurrection of our Lord Jesus Christ, for the peace and the promise of immortality that it brings, for our faith and the strength it gains from reading of his risen appearances, and for the Advocate and Comforter whose sending we will shortly be celebrating.

Place of spiritual retreat

All week, listening to the teaching of Jesus, as in John 15:9–16:15.

ASCENSION DAY
Thursday of Week Six in Eastertide

A SELECTION OF ROSES Climber 'Excelsa'; floribundas 'Pink Parfait', 'My Joy', 'Perfect Day'; hybrid tea 'Joy'

Characteristics and history

'Excelsa' was introduced in 1909. Its small rosy-crimson, slightly scented double flowers are borne in profuse clusters in midsummer on long, easy to train, pliable and strong shoots. It is vigorous and suitable for pergolas in an open position where mildew is less likely to attack. 'Pink Parfait' was introduced in 1959. The hybridizer Herb Swim saw a bed of it in London's Regents Park and said that it was easy to understand its popularity. 'A soft pink, it made the most effective bed in the park ....' The fragrant blooms are a clear pink, which softens with age. Flowers are cup-like and produced in number. The form is bushy and the foliage bright green. There seems to be general agreement that its attributes remain unmatched. 'My Joy' is also sweetly scented and has medium pink blooms, while 'Perfect Day' bears fragrant, light yellow flowers. To the fragrance of 'Joy' is added a range of colour from ivory to light apricot. (The general history and lore of the rose is dealt with in more detail under 8 December in Jane Mossendew, *Gardening with God: Light in Darkness*, Burns & Oates, 2001.)

31

Towards meditation

> Hail the day that sees him rise, Alleluya!
> Ravished from their longing eyes; Alleluya!
> Christ, awhile to mortals given, Alleluya!
> Enters now the highest heaven! Alleluya!
>
> There the glorious triumph waits;
> Lift your heads, eternal gates!
> Wide unfold the radiant scene;
> Take the King of Glory in!
>
> Him though highest heaven receives;
> Still he loves the earth he leaves:
> Though returning to his throne,
> Still he calls mankind his own.
>
> Lord beyond our mortal sight,
> Raise our hearts to reach thy height,
> There thy face unclouded see,
> Find our heaven of heavens in thee.
> (Charles Wesley, 1707–88; Tune, Llanfair)

The liturgical keynotes today are praise, joy and eternal perfection. Evening Prayer on Ascension Eve begins with the hymn 'The Lord goes up with shouts of joy, while trumpets all his triumph tell'. The first psalm at the Office of readings (Ps. 113) is an exhortation to praise God, followed by Psalm 68, which is descriptive of solemn procession and festive gathering. In the second Office reading, which is from a sermon on the Ascension, St Augustine expounds the reason for our joy, the nub of which is that 'because of the unity between us and himself, for he is our head and we are his body', when Christ ascended into heaven, he did not leave us orphans. It is he alone who has ascended, 'but the body in its unity is not separated from its head'. At Morning Prayer the passage from Hebrews (10:12–14) refers to Christ's one sacrifice for sins and that by virtue of it he has achieved the eternal perfection of those he is sanctifying. At Mass the responsorial Psalm 47 is again one of joy, praise and celebration: 'God goes up with shout of joy/The Lord goes up with trumpet blast'.

Here I have to fight nostalgia for Dom J. E. Turner's motet *Ascendit Deus*, which was *de rigueur* on the Ascension days of my choir years. And indeed it is a shout of joy, and thoroughly stirring and enjoyable to sing and listen to. Turner may be out of choral fashion now, and I shall probably never hear the motet again, but every year I do hear it with the ear of memory. Opening with a theatrical two-page solo into which the chosen bass can really put his heart and show his range, it is a setting of the first two lines of verse 5, but the whole psalm enjoins us to sing praise to God with all our skill, and with Father Turner's help we did just that.

The Office during the day continues with psalms of praise 8 and 19, while at Evening Prayer Psalm 47 is repeated and the canticle (Rev. 11:17–18, 10b–12a) emphasizes the reason for our joy and praise. God has taken his power and begun to reign; the salvation, power, kingdom and authority have come; the enemy is conquered by the blood of the Lamb. At this time of year there will still be much seed to be sown. Aside from the beans of yesterday there are usually salad crops and annual herbs to be put in – chervil, dill, parsley, coriander – all good companion plants in the garden and well worth their place. I usually begin my gardening each day after Morning Prayer. But wherever I am I will begin work with the Ambrosian Lauds hymn on my lips and in my heart, probably the version of the old Latin Mattins. And simply because I *am* going to work, the tune Duke Street normally used for 'Fight the Good Fight', seems appropriate:

> O thou pure light of souls that love!
> True joy of every human breast,
> Sower of life's immortal seed,
> Our Maker, and Redeemer blest.
>
> Be Thou our Guide; be Thou our Goal;
> Be Thou our Pathway to the skies;
> Our Joy when sorrow fills the soul;
> In death our everlasting prize.
>
> (Rev. E. Caswall, 1824–71)

Reading
Acts 1:6–11: He was lifted up and a cloud took him from their sight.

Intercessions
For rose breeders and growers, and thanksgiving for the results of their work.

For gardeners in public parks and spaces, and that more people may benefit from them as oases of peace in busy, crowded cities.

Thanksgiving for the music of Dom J. E. Turner and for the hymns of Charles Wesley and Reverend Caswall.

That we may rejoice fully in the Ascension and in the knowledge that our Lord has not left us orphans.

Place of spiritual retreat

With the disciples as they return to Jerusalem in great joy after the Ascension of the Lord, as in Luke 24:50–2.

FRIDAY AND SATURDAY WEEK SIX TO PENTECOST EVE
Friday and Saturday after Ascension and Week Seven of Eastertide

SHEEP'S RED FESCUE *Festuca rubra*

Cultivation notes

This perennial grass grows in dry sunny places, has reddish panicles and flowers in May and June. It is used for lawn grass mixtures and, like ordinary Sheep's fescue (*F. ovina*) is a popular grass for sheep grazing. Unlike the latter, however, it spreads by creeping rhizomes and forms thick carpets. Some strains do not like close mowing, so if you require a fine lawn, special combinations of other grasses are available for the purpose, as are mixtures for different types of soil and site. Most of us will probably want a utility lawn that will stand medium to hard wear and will not be finely mown. Mixtures for this type of lawn are usually a combination of at least four of the following: sheep's red fescue; rye grass (*Lolium perenne*); crested dog's tail (*Cynosurus cristatus*); smooth and rough stalked meadow grass (*Poa pratensis* and *P. trivialis*); and Chewing's fescue (*F. rubra-commutata*).

History and lore

Festuca is the Latin word for grass or straw stalk, so the English name is a direct translation. In ancient times grass was a symbol of the occupation of land after a victory. Pliny (d. AD 77) records the practice of giving a crown of grass as a sign of gratitude for the release of the besieged and mentions the custom of the vanquished offering a handful of grass to their conquerors, symbolizing the surrender of their land. In Europe,

34

Christianized pagan myths and customs include the suggestion that God made Adam's hair from grass; that the souls of the dead are sent into certain grasses and these must not be uprooted; that blood will flow from grass mown on feasts of the Virgin Mary; and that hay should be placed in a shoe for St Nicholas's horse on the eve of 6 December. In England there was the peculiar practice of stealing hay for the cows on Christmas day in the belief that this would keep them healthy for a year. Butter made from the milk of cows that had been fed on churchyard grass was used to counteract enchantment, and in Carmarthenshire in 1848 a woman bitten by a donkey was sent to eat the grass in the churchyard as a cure. There was also a conviction that grass will not grow where ghosts have passed, or where a crime has been committed – not without foundation, as shown by several documented events. At Amersham in Buckinghamshire a site where martyrs had been burned for their beliefs remained bare. Grass would germinate and then die. In Montgomeryshire, a young man condemned to death for highway robbery maintained his innocence until executed in 1821. He had sworn that his grave would remain bare for a generation as a sign of the miscarriage of justice. In 1852 a Reverend R. Mostyn Price wrote, 'The grass has not covered his grave.' Nothing would grow there until at least 1886.

W. E. Shewell-Cooper (*Plants, Flowers and Herbs of the Bible*, Keats Publishing, 1988) maintains that grass is mentioned fifty-eight times in the Old and New Testaments, often in a rhetorical way, as in 'does the ass bray over its grass?' (Job 6:5), or comparatively: 'The grass withers ... but the word of our God will stand forever' (Is. 40:1). It frequently signifies the shortness of human life: 'As for mortals their days are like grass' (Ps. 103:15), and this is echoed in the New Testament: 'All flesh is grass' (1 Pet. 1:24). In art it represents human weakness, as in the 'Haywain Triptych' by Hieronymus Bosch. The Hebrew words translated as 'grass' are *deshe*, meaning 'tender', and *yereq*, meaning 'green'. *Eseb* or *asab* is 'herb', and the Greek *chortos* 'fodder'. Some scholars believe that Sorghum grass (*S. vulgare*) was used to make brushes, so it would have been appropriate in sprinkling or cleansing rituals. In *The Language of Flowers* grass represents purpose and obedience, and in modern herbalism decoctions of Dog's grass are sometimes used to soothe cystitis, gout and rheumatism.

Towards meditation

The paschal candle is extinguished after the Gospel on Ascension Day, thus symbolizing Christ's departure from the Apostles. In spite of our joy and praise of yesterday, and our understanding of the reasons for them, when that light goes out it is hard not to experience a stab of loss and to feel for the 'men of Galilee' who stood looking up into heaven (Acts 1:11). During the next few days the Church seems to sense that we may yet feel a very human sense of deprivation, and she fills the liturgy with texts that speak of the shepherd-like love and care that God holds out to us in the Persons of his Son and his Holy Spirit. For this reason, these days before Pentecost are very comforting and their readings are ones to which we can turn for solace in difficult times whatever the season.

On the day after the Ascension Christ promises us that no one will take our joy from us (John 16:20–3), and John reminds us that we are God's children (1 John 3:1–10). On Saturday Jesus assures us that we are beloved of God for loving him and believing in him, and John underlines that the new law is a law of love. The day's second Office reading is from St Augustine's *Homilies on St John's Gospel* and sets forth the truth that features of our earthly life are all to be changed when we reach heaven. In exchange for pilgrimage we will have an eternal home; in exchange for toil, rest; for work, reward; and for action, contemplation. Peter, he says, shows us what our actions should be, and John points the way to the growth of contemplative life. But on Sunday John too reminds us that our love must be real and active. In the Gospel Jesus prays for the disciples, and therefore for us, and comforts us with the promise that he will not leave us orphans (John 17:11–19). On Monday he tells us to be brave, for he has already conquered (John 16:29–33), and John states that God loved us first (1 John 4:1–10). On Tuesday he iterates that God is love (1 John 4:11–21). Wednesday's first Mass reading (Acts 20:28–38) strengthens us as we remember God has power to build us up, and in Thursday's first Office reading John's prayer for sinners is also a statement of confidence in Christ's love and protection. The second reading is a reflection by St Cyril of Alexandria on Christ's statement that if he did not go the Counsellor could not come to us. And so with Pentecost only a few days away, as I drain and clean my pond, I will be thinking of the living water of the Holy Spirit. But it is Friday's gospel that above all made me choose Sheep's Fescue as the main plant for these pre-Pentecost days. In it Christ characterizes us as his sheep and lambs, and thrice makes it clear to Peter that if he loves Jesus he must show it by tending his flock. Peter here is surely a type of the Church herself, of all good Popes, of every bishop, priest, minister and pastor, and indeed of us, for although we are the flock, we too become shepherds in the love we show to each other in Christ:

'Feed my lambs. Look after my sheep. Feed my sheep.' God grant that we may do the bidding of the supreme Good Shepherd.

Readings and other suggested plants with their meanings

1 John 3:1–10: We are God's children (Daisy, other name Bairnswort).

Acts 18:23–8: Priscilla and Aquila (Aquilegia).

Acts 1:13–26: Matthias chosen to replace Judas (Peach, immortality; dedicated to the apostle by the Church, one of the conditions of his election being that he had witnessed the resurrection of Christ. See also in Part 3, 14 May).

St Cyril of Jerusalem from *Instructions to the Jerusalem Catechumens* on the living water of the Holy Spirit (Watercress, cleansing).

John 17:1–11: Father, glorify your Son (Roses 'Gloria Mundi' and 'Crowning Glory').

St Basil the Great from his *Treatise on the Holy Spirit*. Have your thoughts fixed on heaven, dance with angels, have unending joy and perseverance (Rose 'Heaven Scent'; 'Yellow Archangel').

1 John 5:11–12: Victory over the world – our faith (Rose, 'Faith').

Second Vatican Council, 'Dogmatic Constitution on the Church', 4, on the Mission of the Holy Spirit within the Church; distribution of charisms as the Holy Spirit wills (Rose 'Charisma').

Acts 22:30; 23:6–11: Now you must bear witness in Rome (Borage, courage; Rose 'Courage').

2 John: To be faithful is to have the Father and Son with us (Rose, 'Faithful').

St Hilary of Poitiers, *Treatise on the Holy Trinity* (Trillium, Trinity flower, see also Part 2, Trinity Sunday).

3 John Let us walk in truth (Bittersweet nightshade, truth; Lupin, veracity).

From a sermon by an unknown sixth-century African: The Church in its unity speaks in every tongue (Scarlet verbena, Church unity; *Arctotis grandis*, African daisy).

(As can be seen, it would be possible to make a rose bed dedicated to this period before Pentecost, infilled with the other flowers mentioned above.)

Intercessions

For shepherds, sheep farmers, and all who work in the wool industry; for agricultural seedsmen.

For victims of injustice who are punished for crimes they did not commit.

For gratitude, obedience and a sense of purpose.

Thanksgiving for the works of Hieronymus Bosch.

That in troubled times we may turn to the Word of God for comfort and strength.

That the leaders, clergy and people of Christ's flock may care for each other, and love one another as he wishes.

Places of spiritual retreat

From now until the Thursday before Pentecost, continuing to listen to Christ's teaching, as in John 16 and 17.

Friday before Pentecost, with Jesus and Peter, as in John 21:15–19.

Eve of Pentecost, with John as he hears Jesus speak of his future, as in John 21:25.

PENTECOST
(Whit Sunday)

CLIMBING ROSE 'DANSE DU FEU'

Cultivation notes

This rose was introduced in 1954. Its orange-red double flowers, which have little or no scent, are of medium size and produced in clusters. It is, however, repeat-flowering and may continue in bloom until autumn and produce flowers in its first season. The foliage is attractively dark and shiny.

Note on Whit Sunday

The term comes from the Anglo-Saxon *hwita Sunnaudaeg* and means 'White Sunday'. It has been suggested that this refers to the white robe of Baptism. For many centuries both Easter and Pentecost were the times when Baptism was administered, and in our cooler northern climate the latter may have been preferred for the reception of a rite that involved total immersion. If this was the case then Pentecost was 'White Sunday' and the day when baptismal robes were put on for the first time, not Low Sunday (the *Dominica in alba*) of warmer climes when they were worn for the last time.

Towards meditation

Scholars believe that for at least two centuries Easter and Pentecost were the only days to be kept as festivals. The ancient tradition that Pentecost happened on a Sunday is confirmed by John 18:28, for if the Friday on which Christ died was the eve of the Passover, then the fiftieth day after it must have been a Sunday. Pentecost is traditionally known as the birthday of the Church, and a friend of mine was once roundly ticked off by a bishop for suggesting that this is inaccurate. Surely, he maintained, the Church was already alive. Jesus himself had referred to it, when he instituted Peter as the rock on which it would be founded. Perhaps my friend's mistake was to overlook Christ's use of the future tense: 'On this rock I will found my Church'. In any case (and I stand open to correction by anyone, bishop or not) perhaps the point is that the Church was conceived in the mind of God since before time, just as was the Virgin Mary. In that sense there was never a time when the Church was not. Until Christ came among us she had no chance of conception in our human sense. And only with the coming of the Holy Spirit could she truly be born and be given the power to walk, talk, grow and thrive. The Gospel accounts of the resurrection and that of Pentecost in Acts 2 strike the soul with their simple yet powerful immediacy. In each case we are given detail. We know exactly who was there. Acts 2 gives the impression of a tight-knit group of believers that included Mary the Mother of Jesus (the last time she is mentioned by name in the New Testament). They are gathered together constantly in one place in a siege-like, yet expectant atmosphere, but followed everywhere by about 120 people. Acts 2:1 tells us 'they were *all* together in one place' (my italics) and this is the foundation of the tradition that Mary was present at the coming of the Holy Spirit. The appearance of the Holy Spirit as a dove at the Baptism of Christ would have been a recognizable symbol of peace, as would the mighty rushing wind to those who were familiar with the scriptures. But the tongues of fire that enabled the recipients to speak in tongues were a new and altogether different experience. Today the power of the Holy Spirit is made manifest. The crowd is 'astonished', 'amazed', 'perplexed'. This is very definitely the beginning of a new era. The tongues are seen as a symbol of the apostles' universal mission. All nations are now to hear the Good News. The curse and clamour of Babel is cancelled and all who have ears to hear can hear and understand. But together with this wider implication that the Holy Spirit is now to direct the Church's mission comes a more personal presence, making strong, eloquent, authoritative instruments out of the formerly confused, bereft, ineffectual 'men of Galilee'. They are transformed almost beyond recognition by the Holy Spirit. The Apostles and disciples are now the Church, full of life and power in him. And if anyone should doubt it, Peter, who has not exactly covered himself with glory during Holy Week, and who has not so far given the impression of being a good speaker, is now, imbued with the Holy Spirit, able to preach the first, and most excellent, sermon in the infant Church (Acts 2:14–36). As the old *St Andrew Daily Missal* puts it, 'The Sequence of the Mass and the Hymn at Vespers describe and invoke this penetrating action of the Holy Spirit in the hearts of the faithful.'

Pentecost Sunday usually finds me in France these days, and if I cannot attend Mass I spend some considerable time near my 'Danse du feu' with St Peter's sermon and with the Pentecost Hymn and Sequence. (The Mass Sequence *Veni Sancte Spiritus* came into universal use with the liturgical reforms of the Council of Trent; it was first used in France in about 1200 and is attributed to Stephen Langton, later archbishop of Canterbury, who was in Paris around that date. The Vespers Hymn *Veni Creator Spiritus* was once attributed to Charlemagne but is now thought to be the work of Rabanus Maurus, abbot of Fulda and archbishop of Mainz, who died in 856.)

Readings and other suggested plants

John 15:26–7: The Spirit of Truth (Lupin, veracity; Bittersweet night-shade, truth; Camellia 'Inspiration'; Angelica, in France the herb of the Holy Spirit; Climbing rose 'New Dawn').

Galatians 5:16–25: Live by the Spirit; Romans 8:5–27: Those who follow the Holy Spirit are all God's sons (Rose 'The Pilgrim').

St Irenaeus (*c.* 130–200): From his treatise *Against the Heresies*. On the sending of the Holy Spirit (Climbing rose 'Breath of Life', Columbine, from *columba* meaning 'dove', Windflower).

Intercessions

Thanksgiving for the writers of hymns and sequences that still enrich our prayer life in the liturgy.

That we may be less materialistic and fix our minds on the things of God.

Thanksgiving for the coming of the Holy Spirit and for his gifts.

For time to reflect on the significance of this great day and to rejoice in the birthday of the pilgrim Church.

Places of spiritual retreat

With the disciples as Jesus appears to them, as in John 20
and when Jesus speaks of the Advocate, as in John 15 and 16
and when he speaks of the Holy Spirit who will teach them everything, as in John 14 and 15.

The urge to sing with joyful, fearless, loving and astonished faith is stronger than ever today, and so my prayer of Pentecost, and Part 1 of this book, close with a favourite hymn from my girlhood:

> Our blest Redeemer, ere he breathed
> His tender last farewell,
> A guide, a comforter, bequeathed
> With us to dwell.
>
> He came in tongues of living flame,
> To teach, convince, subdue;
> All powerful as the wind he came,
> As viewless too.

He came sweet influence to impart,
A gracious, willing guest,
While he can find one humble heart
Wherein to rest.

And his that gentle voice we hear
Soft as the breath of even,
That checks each fault, that calms each fear,
And speaks of heaven.

And every virtue we possess,
And every victory won,
And every thought of holiness,
Are his alone.

Spirit of purity and grace,
Our weakness, pitying see:
O make our hearts thy dwelling place,
And worthier thee.

(Harriet Auber, 1773–1862)

Part 2

Solemnities of the Lord and Weeks 6–17 of Ordinary Time

SOLEMNITIES OF THE LORD

INTRODUCTORY NOTE

After Pentecost the liturgical cycle of Ordinary Time resumes with the Monday of the appropriate week. This depends on the date of Easter: in other words, it will be the Monday of the week that would have followed had Lent not begun when it did. Therefore week 6 is indicated as the earliest possible one for the recommencement of Ordinary Time. However, Trinity Sunday is always the first after Pentecost; Corpus Christi always the Thursday after Trinity, and the Sacred Heart of Jesus always the Friday after the Sunday after Trinity. Following the arrangement in Volume 2 of the Breviary these Solemnities of the Lord open Part 2 of this book.

SUNDAY AFTER PENTECOST
The Most Holy Trinity

TRILLIUM *Trillium erectum*; Birthroot; Squawroot
Trillium sessile; (syn. T. grandiflorum) Wake-robin; Toadshade; Wood Lily; Trinity Flower (not to be confused with *Tradescantia*, also called Trinity Flower)

Cultivation notes
T. erectum and *T. sessile* are both shade-loving rhizomatous perennials and therefore do well in woodland gardens. In late spring a solitary bloom appears at the centre of each cluster of three leaves. *T. erectum* has three pale green sepals and three maroon to white petals, and there is also *T. erectum albiflorum*. The white flowers of the latter are particularly eye-catching in a shady position. All three grow to a height of about 20 inches and spread for 2 feet. *T. sessile* has three maroon-brown petals and three brown-red sepals. The leaves are stalkless (which is what 'sessile' means). It reaches 12 inches in height and spreads for up to 18 inches. *T.*

grandiflorum has 2 to 3 inch wide white flowers which
turn pink with age. Other varieties
are: *T. cuneatum*, dark red with
mottled leaves; *T. luteum*, yellow;
T. undulatum, white-streaked
purple; and *T. recurvatum*, a
dark red dwarf for the
rockery.) From late
summer to March plant
all varieties in
groups at a depth
of 3 inches about
12 inches apart,
having first
enriched the soil
with leaf mould or garden
compost. In spring lightly

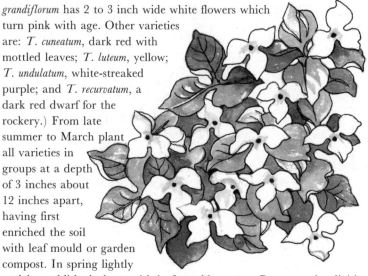

mulch established plants with leaf mould or peat. Propagate by division
when the foliage has died back. If grown from seed it may well be at least
five years before Trillium will flower, but leave it undisturbed and large
clumps will form in time.

History and lore

Trillium comes from the Latin *trilix*, indicating that all parts of the plants
are tripartite. It has three broad leaves, three small sepals and three large
petals surrounding the central group of gold stamens. According to
Maggie Campbell Culver (*The Origin of Plants*, Headline, 2001), *T.
cuneatum* (*T. sessile*) was introduced to Britain in 1673 from the southern
United States. *T. erectum* is mentioned in the *Medical Flora* (Philadelphia,
Atkinson & Alexander, 3 vols, 1828–30) by Constantine Rafinesque and
later listed in the *United States Pharmacopeia and National Formulary* (annual
from 1888, here 1916–17). It was used by Native Americans to ease sore
nipples and in their obstetric and gynaecological practices. *Culpeper's
Colour Herbal* (Foulsham, 1983) mentions birthroot (*T. pendulum*) as being
combined in an infusion with Dove's Foot (*Geranium molle*). In modern
herbalism this may be applied externally as a wash or taken internally in
the form of drops. Lift the rhizomes for drying when the leaves have died
back in late summer.

Trinity customs and history

Mystery Plays were probably often performed on Trinity Sunday in pre-Reformation times, and in some places the pews of the parish church were decorated with hay or flowers. Examples survive at Shenington (Oxfordshire) and at Clee-in-Grimsby (Humberside). The Southwold (Suffolk) Trinity Fair has moved to the first Monday in June, a fairly obvious result of the secularization of the late May holiday. On the Bank Holiday Monday there is a fair at Kirtlington (Oxfordshire, between Witney and Bicester). In former times, here, as at Eynsham (also Oxfordshire), things ranging from silly to cruel were done to sheep before they were slaughtered and eaten. One can see a connection with the second Person of the Trinity as 'a lamb to the slaughter', but the only acknowledgement of the other two Persons seems to have been in the form of a greenery bower shaped to symbolize the Trinity. Nowadays it appears that the original Christian reason for the celebration is almost completely lost.

According to John Sullivan, in *The Externals of the Catholic Church* (Longman, 1955), the celebration of Trinity Sunday was observed locally as far back as the tenth century but the date varied in different countries. Thomas Becket (1118–70) introduced it to England, and it was made universal in 1334 by Pope John XXII, who assigned it to its present position in the calendar. Scannell's *A Catholic Dictionary* (Virtue,1928) tells us that the feast was kept at Liège early in the tenth century, and it is mentioned as a common observance by Abbot Rupert in the twelfth. Tertullian (*c.* 160–220) apparently coined the word 'Trinity', but it was St Athanasius (*c.* 291–373; see also 2 May in Part 3), whose teaching on the nature of the Trinity was to become the foundation of the orthodoxy of those who came after him. (See 29 August, St Augustine of Hippo, and in other books of this series, 13 January, St Hilary of Poitiers, in *Light in Darkness*; 17 March, St Patrick; 21 April, St Anselm of Canterbury, in *Thorn, Fire and Lily*.)

Towards meditation

'The Trinity' has the reputation among lay folk of being an unpopular subject with those who preach sermons to them, and in some quarters is even regarded as a stumbling block to faith. Why? And how can the theologically untutored like myself, come to satisfactory and reasonable grips with it? Following St Patrick's example I think one may see the answer in the contemplation of any tripartite plant, in today's case using the Trillium. The flower says, 'I have three petals, three sepals and three leaves, all fulfilling the functions of petals, sepals and leaves, but they are all me. I do not have one circular petal, or round sepal and leaf. If I did I would not be a trillium.' One of Tertullian's opponents was a certain Praxeas, who belonged to a group of monotheists who got round the doctrine of the Trinity by saying, 'The Father is the Son, is the Holy Spirit', much as a human being can be a spouse, a teacher and a parent, but remain the one person. Tertullian refuted Praxeas by stating that God is one substance in three Persons. The petals, sepals and leaves of the Trillium are distinct but they are of each other and inseparable, comprising the whole plant. Were it not so it would not be a Trillium. Moreover, the Trillium of its very nature always has three petals, sepals and leaves: always has had, and always will have. There was never a moment in history when it had one petal, for instance, and then the others appeared out of nowhere. Nor indeed does each flower have three petals of different sizes. And so I remember that Origen (*c.* 185–*c.* 254), who was also a strong anti-monotheist, taught that the Son was not begotten at one particular moment in human time, but eternally being generated within the Trinity and integral to its nature. This was to become orthodox belief. The Trillium speaks again: 'One of my petals did not create the other two, nor is any one of them larger or more important in my nature than the other two.' Origen's Trinity was one of degree. For him the Father is greater than the Son, who is greater than the Holy Spirit. And in the century after Origen, Arius would conclude that only the Father is truly God and that the Son and the Holy Spirit are his creatures. St Athanasius spent his working life fighting the Arian heresy. He maintained that if Christ were not divine he could not save us. The Incarnation and the Cross were not inappropriate or degrading to the Son, as claimed by some Jews and pagans, but were essential and rational. Only the Creator could redeem and restore his creation, so if Christ is not divine there is no salvation, and no Christianity. Athanasius expounded this in *The Incarnation of the Word*. Little attention had been paid to the Holy Spirit before this (*c.* 359). Indeed the creed of Nicaea (325, and not to be confused with the Nicene creed, which came out of the Council of Constantinople of 381) has only the bald clause, 'And in the Holy Spirit'. Athanasius addressed this neglect in his letters to Bishop Serapion, who was having trouble with some Egyptians who believed in the deity of Christ but thought that the Holy Spirit was created out of nothing. These letters constituted the first fully Trinitarian theology and considered in full the status of all three Persons, arguing that the Holy Spirit 'proceeds from the Father' (John 15:26) – as the Son is eternally and continually generated, so does the Holy Spirit proceed from within the integrity of the Most Holy Trinity. Today's second Office reading is from the first letter, and in it Athanasius says of the Trinity 'Nor is it compounded of creator and created matter, but it is endowed with the complete power of creating and energizing; its nature also is consistent with itself and undivided and its energy and activity is one. God the Father makes all things through the Word in the Holy Spirit, and in this way the unity of the Holy Trinity is preserved.' Looking at the Trillium again, I wonder whether our problem is that we humans feel we must define, we must encapsulate God in words. And because of the limitations of language, unless we speak of the Holy Trinity, we must mention the Persons in a consecutive list, and this perpetuates Origen's idea of rank order. I think this is why we ordinary folk often feel that refutations of this are a mere playing about with words, a semantic game. But I do believe that if we look at the Trillium today, keep our mouths shut and try to stop formulating human phrases to express the inexpressible, we *can see* and wordlessly approach, if not understand, the nature of the Triune God. The other thing that perhaps goes unnoticed because of familiar usage is that to be grammatically accurate, we should say 'in the names of the Father, Son and Holy Spirit', but we use the singular 'name'. So for God in three Persons we have to break the grammatical rules of our language, which should remind us that God must not and cannot be restricted within human systems and constructs.

Readings
Exodus 34:4–9: A God of tenderness and compassion.
1 Corinthians 2:1–16: The Spirit reaches the depth of everything, even the depths of God.
2 Corinthians 13:11–13: The grace of Jesus Christ, the love of God and the fellowship of the Holy Spirit.
John 3:16–18:God sent his Son so that through him the world might be saved.

Intercessions
For women in labour and all with gynaecological and obstetric problems.
Thanksgiving for the writings of the Fathers, and for plants which help us to understand our faith.

Place of spiritual retreat
With Jesus and Nicodemus, as in John 3.

THURSDAY AFTER MOST HOLY TRINITY
(In USA, Sunday after Most Holy Trinity)
The Body and Blood Of Christ
(Corpus Christi)

ROSE 'REMEMBER ME'

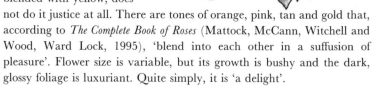

Cultivation notes

This hybrid tea rose was introduced in 1984. Its colour classification in many catalogues, copper or bronze blended with yellow, does not do it justice at all. There are tones of orange, pink, tan and gold that, according to *The Complete Book of Roses* (Mattock, McCann, Witchell and Wood, Ward Lock, 1995), 'blend into each other in a suffusion of pleasure'. Flower size is variable, but its growth is bushy and the dark, glossy foliage is luxuriant. Quite simply, it is 'a delight'.

History of the Solemnity

In 1246 the bishop of Liège instituted the celebration of Corpus Christi for his diocese at the urgent request of St Juliana, prioress of a convent on Mount Cornillon near the city. Pope Urban IV, a former archdeacon of Liège, later established it for the universal Church, probably in part because of his knowledge of Juliana, but also because of a current heresy that denied transubstantiation. Added to this, the laity had been showing signs of indifference to the Blessed Sacrament, and it was being neglected. The Pope asked St Thomas Aquinas to complete the Mass and Office, and in 1264 published a Bull commanding observance of the feast and its date (still observed today), but he died shortly afterwards. Succeeding popes took great pains to secure the celebration and the Council of Trent spoke of it as a triumph over heresy. Almost from the beginning the custom of carrying the Blessed Sacrament in procession was part of the ceremonial. The feast became popular, probably because this allowed the faithful to witness publicly to their belief in the real presence of Christ in the Blessed Sacrament, and to proclaim their gratitude to God for the spiritual benefits it brought to them. In medieval times Mystery Plays were often performed at Corpus Christi, and cycles are still performed at Chester,

York, Wakefield and Coventry, although not every year, and not necessarily at Corpus Christi. Before the Reformation there were many Corpus Christi fairs in different parts of England, but processions did not return until after the emancipation of Catholics and the restoration of the hierarchy in 1850. Sadly, to my mind, they have all but disappeared again. At my own church in central London, we still have a procession inside the church on the nearest Sunday, and the aisles are strewn with sweet-smelling herbs and other greenery. Personally I feel we would do better to have the procession out of doors, round the parish as an act of witness. As it is, the outside world perhaps cannot be blamed if it thinks that the Church has grown indifferent to the Blessed Sacrament, or even lost faith in it altogether, just as she was in danger of doing in the early thirteenth century.

Towards meditation

My choice of rose is an obvious reference to the words of Jesus at the Last Supper, 'Do this in memory of me'. But there is another reason: today's second Office reading is from the works of St Thomas Aquinas, reflecting on the nature of the Blessed Sacrament and its purpose and effect in the receiving soul. It contributes to salvation because it purges our sins, increases our virtues and feeds our minds with spiritual gifts. The Church offers it for the living and the dead so that all may benefit. Through it, says St Thomas, 'the sweetness of the Spirit is tasted at its source', and through it we celebrate the surpassing love for us that Christ showed in his passion. It is a fulfilment of the types in the Old Testament, and the continual and greatest miracle of Christ. Moreover he invites us, undeserving as we are, to witness this miracle every time we go into church and to Mass, and even to participate in it by receiving communion. Here is the ultimate consolation for the desolate and bereft, not only for the first disciples, but for all those who have loved and followed Christ down the ages to the present day. When I look at the rose 'Remember Me', its subtle blending of several tones reminds me of the different aspects of the Eucharist that St Thomas identifies. He twice uses the word 'delight': 'the Sacrament', he says, is precious, wonderful, 'and full of delight'; and 'No one is capable of expressing the delight of this sacrament.' *The Handbook of Roses* describes 'Remember Me' as a 'delight', and as a 'suffusion of pleasure'. If we reclaim the words from their earthly aesthetic sense they are free to attain a deep and full spiritual significance when applied to Holy Communion. Suffusion is an overspreading as from within, which seems to me an excellent description of the *effect* of Holy Communion, if not of its *nature*, which, as St Thomas himself says, no one can fully describe. However, in spite of himself, his own Sequence *Lauda Sion* and Vespers Hymn *Pange Lingua* are probably the noblest attempts in the Church's treasury. (Nowadays only the last four verses of the Sequence are used at Mass, but I find that the full version in my old *St Andrew Daily Missal* rewards a concentrated reading at some point during today.

Other suitable roses
Red floribunda 'Glad Tidings; pink floribunda 'Fragrant Delight'; crimson, splashed pink, gallica shrub 'Rosa Mundi'; orange/scarlet polyantha shrub 'Gloria Mundi'; pink prostrate shrub 'Holy Rose'; soft coral pink hybrid tea 'Blessings'; soft pink alba shrub 'Celestial'.

Readings
Genesis 14:18–20: He brought bread and wine.
Exodus 24:3–8: This is the blood of the covenant.
Deuteronomy 8:2–3,14–16: He fed you with manna.
Wisdom 16:20: The food of angels.
1 Corinthians10:16–17: There is only one loaf.
Hebrews 9:11–15: The blood of Christ can purify our inner self from dead actions.
1 Corinthians 11:23–6: Every time you eat this bread and drink this cup, you are proclaiming the Lord's death.
John 6:51–8: My flesh is real food and my blood is real drink.
Mark 14:12–26: This is my body. This is my blood.
Luke 9:11–17: They all ate as much as they wanted.
1 Corinthians 10:16–17: The cup of blessing.
Psalm 23: You have prepared a banquet for me.
Seqence *Lauda Sion*.
Vespers hymn *Pange lingua*.

Places of spritual retreat
Listening to Christ's teaching on the Eucharist, as in John 6.
At the Last Supper, as in Mark 14.

FRIDAY AFTER THE SECOND SUNDAY
AFTER PENTECOST
The Most Sacred Heart of Jesus

HEARTSEASE *Viola tricolor*; wild pansy; Love-in-idleness; Trinity Flower
(not to be confused with *Trillium* or *Tradescantia*)

Cultivation notes

Heartsease can be annual, biennial or short-lived perennial, and I have found it to be a delightfully incorrigible self-seeder and, as we shall see, with the help of bees and the structure of its flowers, the plant has a truly remarkable method of ensuring propagation. I noticed one in my courtyard about fifteen years ago and now it is prolific in my garden (about 30 yards from its original roothold) growing around the pond, along the Way of the Cross, and on the grave of a beloved cat, where it does indeed ease the heart's pain in his absence. (There is a saying that heartsease is the most faithful flower to plant on a grave, for you will find one in bloom every day of the year. In my experience this is almost true.) This year, when hoeing in the vegetable patch, I discovered a healthy heartsease among the carrots, and I let it be. The plant seems to thrive anywhere, in sun or shade and in poor or rich soil. Sow seed in spring or autumn if you need to introduce it to your garden. Deadhead to prolong flowering and, if necessary, propagate by division in autumn. Heartsease can reach a height of 12 inches and each stem bears several flowers, blooming from April to September. They are purple, yellow and white, hence the *tricolor* of the botanical name. The structure of the flower, and the way in which it attracts and accommodates the questing bees, are intricate and fascinating. First there are the five sepals that project backwards, seemingly to discourage small, creeping insects; then the five petals that form the 'face' of the flower. The largest petal has a spur running from its back, and a surface marked with lines that act as guides for the bees.

There are five stamens, two of which have small spurs carrying a nectar sac, which fits into the big petal spur and is protected by it. The five almost flat stamen heads, or anthers, form a cone round the ovary column, which has a kink at its base and which acts as a spring, while on top, touching the big petal, is its remarkable stigma. If touched with a bristle to simulate a bee's proboscis a minute skull-shaped stigma thrusts itself out from between the anthers. It has a mouth with a lip, and whiskers on either side. The only way to the nectar is beneath this stigma. When the bee comes away, pollen is scraped off by the stigma lip, but when the bee's tongue has become dusted with pollen and is being withdrawn, the slight pressure makes the lip close against its own pollen. The insect probing the flower knocks its head on the stigma and the kink spring in the column comes into action. This disturbs the already open anthers, and the pollen is revealed, lying loose around the style. This now falls onto the head of the bee, and dusts its proboscis as it is withdrawn. The structure and process are all the more remarkable because they take place in such a tiny flower.

History and lore

In modern herbalism the leaves and flowers are collected during flowering and dried or used fresh in decoctions and infusions. These are taken internally to ease bronchitis, whooping cough, rheumatism, weeping eczema and urinary problems, and applied externally in the treatment of varicose ulcers. The plant is laxative and diuretic, lowers fever, cleanses the system, reduces inflammation, relieves pain and promotes healing. All these qualities would perhaps explain its English name, but in fact this is connected with the folklore of love that surrounds the plant. It must have had such a connotation as early as Shakespeare's time, as he has Oberon squeezing the juice of the wild pansy into Titania's eyes so that she will fall in love with the first thing she sees upon awaking, famously Bottom wearing an ass's head.

A more spiritual allusion appears in Bunyan's *Pilgrims's Progress*, where Christiana and her children in the Valley of Humiliation hear a lad singing 'He that is down need fear no fall; he that is low no pride.' 'Then said the guide, "Do you hear him? I will dare to say this lad leads a merrier life and wears more of that herb called heartsease in his bosom than he that is clad in silk and velvet."'

'Trinity Flower' is possibly explained by an old German legend that the Heartsease began life with a perfume even more sweet than the violet. It grew on arable land and was so much prized that the crowds who came to gather it were trampling the crops. The Heartsease was upset at being responsible for this ruination and prayed to the Holy Trinity to have its perfume taken away. God granted its request, and that is why, says the legend, the Heartsease is scentless to this day. The name may also have come from the 'doctrine of signatures'. The plant is vaguely triangular, as is the human heart, and therefore was believed to be effective in the treatment of diseases of that organ.

History of the Solemnity

In 1671 Margaret Mary Alacoque (1647–90) entered the Visitation convent at Paray-le-Monial in France. During the year after her profession in 1672 she began to experience visions of Christ, which continued to 1675. She alleged that in these visions Jesus showed her his heart, pierced with a wound, encircled with a crown of thorns, surrounded by flames and surmounted by a cross. He asked for devotion to his Sacred Heart, because he wished that all people should receive his love and mercy and that they should love him. Initially her account met with incredulity, and she experienced many trials and difficulties within her convent. The devotion spread rapidly through France, and then through the world at large, but it did not immediately receive the approval of the Church. In 1765, however, some churches were given permission to celebrate the Sacred Heart as a feast, and in 1856 this was extended universally. In 1889 Leo XIII raised it to higher honour and the human race was consecrated to the Sacred Heart of Jesus. In 1929 Pope Pius XI raised the feast to the highest rank (which it retains as a Solemnity) with a new Mass and special Preface. He also ordered a public act of reparation in all churches on that day.

Towards meditation

June is dedicated to the Most Sacred Heart of Jesus, and the month is crowned with its Solemnity. In one sense it is the crown of the year of the title of this book (the other being a reference to Psalm 64, where God is thanked and honoured for crowning the natural year with his goodness). The Heart of Jesus our Saviour, considered as part of his sacred humanity and as the emblem of his infinite love, had been mentioned by writers as early as St Bonaventure (1221–74; see below). And indeed it seems to me that each day at Morning Prayer we refer to it in the *Benedictus* of Zachariah, which elsewhere I refer to as a blueprint of salvation:

To make known to his people their salvation
through forgiveness of all their sins,
the loving-kindness of the heart of our God
who visits us like the dawn from on high.

A Bull of Pius VI dating from 1794 explains the principle on which devotion to the Sacred Heart rests. The faithful worship with supreme adoration the physical heart of Christ considered 'not as mere flesh but as united to the Divinity'. They adore it as 'the Heart of the Person of the Word to which it is inseparably united'. This is by no means new but as old as the belief in the hypostatic union, as solemnly defined in 431 at the Council of Ephesus. If anyone should ask why the heart of Jesus should be singled out for particular devotion, *A Catholic Dictionary* (*op.cit.*) elucidates: 'The real and physical heart is a natural symbol of Christ's exceeding charity, and of his interior life. Just as the Church in the Middle Ages turned ... to the Five Wounds as a symbol of Christ's Passion, so in these later days she bids us have recourse to his Sacred Heart, mindful of the love wherewith he loved us even unto death. Devotion to the Heart of our Saviour is as old at least as the twelfth century while early in the sixteenth, the Carthusian Lansperg recommended ... devotion by using a figure of the Sacred Heart.' But because the 'Sacred Heart' came to popular prominence relatively recently, in many minds it smacks of a cloying nineteenth-century piety, an impression not helped by some rather lurid statues in Catholic churches. So every year I ask myself why I love it so much. Firstly I suppose because of nostalgia for the (perhaps) easy emotions stirred by the love and safety aspects of the devotion, for the incense of countless Benedictions and mawkish renditions of 'Soul of my Saviour'. But, more importantly, I love it as a devotion that can be understood by everyone, because the most common symbol for love, and for our deepest feelings and concerns, is the heart. But *most* important of all, perhaps, is that devotion to the Heart of Jesus is biblically supported, as today's liturgical readings show, both in types in the Old Testament and in Christ's fulfilment of them in the New. I have already referred to the *Benedictus*, which Breviary users say everyday, so it makes absolute sense that in today's Office of Readings we should find St Paul saying that nothing can separate us from the love of Christ, who died for us, who pleads for us. We conquer because of his love (Rom. 8:28–39), and 'God brought us to life in Christ when we were dead through our sins ... because he loved us with so great a love' (Eph. 2:5, 4, 7). And then in the second reading we find St Bonaventure saying, 'This blood, which flowed from its source in the secret recesses of his heart, gave the Sacrament ... power to confer the life of grace, and for those who already live in Christ, [it] is a draught of living water welling up to eternal life.' Here the saint becomes ecstatic, and after the reading it is hard not to answer him by joyfully singing the responsory instead of merely saying it: 'Bless the Lord, my soul, remembering all he has done for you; he rescues your life from deadly peril, crowns you with the gifts of his kindness and compassion. O taste and see that the Lord is good' (Ps. 103:2, 4; Ps 34:8).

And so, for me, the little heartsease is symbolic of our Lord. Its skull's head stigma is representative of Golgotha (Jn 19:17). That stigma is, for the bees, the only way to the pollen; the cross is, for us, the only way to eternal life. It is there we must drink, suffer love and conquer in the love of him who is our true Heartsease. Every Communion is a visit to this Flower, and from it we take into the world the spiritual pollen he has given us.

Readings

Psalm 103: The love of the Lord is everlasting.
Deuteronomy 7:6–11: The Lord set his heart on you and chose you.
Hosea 11:1–9: My heart recoils from it.
Ezekiel 34:11–16: I myself will pasture my sheep.
Jeremiah 31:2–4: I have loved you with an everlasting love.
1 John 4:7–16: Love comes from God.
Ephesians 3:8–19: The love of Christ is beyond all knowledge.
Romans 5:5–11: What proves that God loves us is that Christ died for us.
Romans 8:28–39: The love of God is revealed in Christ.
Matthew 11:25–30: I am gentle and humble of heart.
John 19:34: There came out blood and water.

Intercessions

For those suffering from complaints which heartsease is used to treat.

Thanksgiving for garden writers and the way in which their words lend themselves to spiritual interpretation.

Thanksgiving for the canticle of Zachariah; and for the lives and work of St Bonaventure and St Margaret Mary Alacoque, and for the Popes whose influence encouraged devotion to the Sacred Heart.

Places of spiritual retreat

Listening to Jesus' teaching about his Heart, as in Matthew 11.

At the foot of the cross when the soldier pierced the side of Jesus, as in John 19.

Listening to Jesus speaking the parable of the lost sheep, as in Luke 15.

WEEK SIX OF ORDINARY TIME

LINDEN *Tilia cordata* (Small-leaved Lime)

Cultivation, history and uses

Unlike other limes, *T. cordata* does not tend to be the subject of aphid attack. For this reason, and the fact that it will stand quite hard pruning, it is a good choice for the garden, even though left to itself it can reach a height of 30 feet in twenty years. The leaves are heart-shaped and are a glossy green with pale yellow undersides. Sweet-smelling ivory flowers are borne in midsummer, followed by small, round green fruits. These have nothing to do with citrus limes of course, but although some people say they are edible and taste rather like cocoa, I have never been tempted to try them. When introducing a Linden to the garden, buy a young bare-rooted transplant about 3 to 4 feet high.

The Latin *tilia* is connected with *tela*, meaning 'something woven', and Pliny refers to the fibrous inner bark, or bast (Anglo-Saxon *baste)* from which ropes and matting have been made over the centuries and in Sweden thread for fishing nets. The English 'Linden' is related to the German and Dutch *linde,* and the Swedish *lind.* The Swedish verb *linda* means 'to bind or wrap around', and the German *lind* means 'bast of Lime'; the Swedish *bastetrad* also means 'lime tree'. Welsh has *llwyf teil,* meaning 'lime-elm', and in Gaelic *teile* means 'lime tree'. The Swedish *lind* is the root of the name of Linnaeus (1707–78), arguably the greatest botanist of his century. Professor at Uppsala University, he brought structure to the chaotic world of plant classification (*Species Plantarum,* 1753*)* and was later ennobled as Carl von Linne; so, aside from other reasons, to have a lime tree in your garden would be a permanent way of honouring the great man. If you visit the Chelsea Physic Garden, you will be following in his footsteps, for he went there in 1736.

The Linnaeus, Lindelius and Tiliander families were all named after the legendary lime tree with three trunks that grew in Hvitarydssocken. When the Lindelius family died out, one of the main branches of the tree died; when the daughter of Linnaeus died, the second trunk ceased to produce leaves; and when the last member of the Tilianders died, the tree was left with no leaves at all. But as recently as 1938 the dead trunks were still being revered.

Lime timber is smooth, white and close-grained and is often used to make the keys and sounding boards of musical instruments. In stark contrast, it was also used in the construction of Mosquito fighter-bombers in the Second World War. It has been a favourite with wood-carvers at least since the medieval period. Grinling Gibbons (1648–1721) used it for carving many of his exquisitely detailed works, and one of the reasons for their perfect state of preservation is that lime wood is never worm-eaten. David Esterley, who restored Gibbons' work after the fire at Hampton Court Palace in 1986, refers (in Richard Mabey, *Flora Britannica*, Chatto & Windus, 1998) to the light, floating quality of the master's limewood leaves and flowers. Another example features on the fireplace in the state dining room at Chatsworth. How fortuitous for Gibbons that the lime tree grew prolifically in the Derbyshire Dales, where it can still be found. In St Paul's Church in Covent Garden, London, there is a Gibbons limewood carving of a wreath of flowers and fruits, some with stems less than an inch thick. (Limehouse in London was once 'Limehurst', from the Anglo-Saxon for a grove of limes.)

Theophrastus (*c*. 372–*c*. 287 BC) said that lime leaves were used for feeding cattle, and it is known that in Switzerland this practice continued for a long time. Pliny the Elder (AD 23–79) mentions the lime several times, but neither he nor any other classical scholar mentions the use of its blossom for making tea, and for centuries all its recommended uses seem to have been external. Culpeper is thought to have been the first to recognize its efficacy in treating apoplexy, epilepsy and palpitations. Dr Losch in the nineteenth century recommended a tisane of lime flowers for these conditions, and Pastor Kneipp, also in the nineteenth century, prescribed an infusion of the flowers for bronchial conditions and ordered flower baths for hysteria and nerves. Tea and honey made from lime flowers are popular nowadays and the tea aids digestion, quietens the nerves, promotes sleep and is thought to help vertigo sufferers. A very mild form can be used for infants, but in any case avoid the old flowers, as these can have an intoxicating effect. Harvest the flowers when first opened, and dry for use in infusions and tinctures. Lime-flower teas and honeys are not to be confused with those made from citrus limes. In modern herbalism infusions of lime flowers are administered internally in cases of hardened arteries, urinary infections, feverish colds, influenza and catarrh and combined with hawthorn for the treatment of high blood pressure. A pleasant cordial for easing the symptoms of the common cold can be made from lime flowers and Elderberry Rob (for Rob recipe see *Thorn, Fire and Lily*, p. 130).

Lore and liturgy

A great deal of pagan and quasi-Christian lore surrounds the lime tree but a brief journey through this week's liturgy will show how this is developed and superseded in the orthodox faith of the universal Church. In English lore the linden represents conjugal love. This most probably comes from the Greek myth of Zeus and Hermes, who when travelling one day were forced to lodge in the poor home of an elderly couple. They were so touched by the hospitality they received that when the couple died, the gods transformed the husband into an oak, and the wife into a linden. The trees grew side by side and their branches intertwined. This story is also reflected in Estonian and Lithuanian folklore, which encourages devotion to these trees for the purpose of bringing children and prosperity into the marriage. Monday's first Office reading is from Proverbs (3:1–20): as the old Greek couple gave to their pagan gods, so we read here:

> Honour the Lord with your substance
> and the first fruits of all your produce;
> then your barns will be filled with plenty,
> and your vats will be bursting with wine.

In parts of Germany it was customary to plant a lime at the birth of a baby girl, so that as the tree grew strong so would she eventually grow to marriageable age. And so, as the lime represents conjugal love, on Saturday we read Proverbs 31:10–31, which is a poem on the perfect wife. The second reading that day is from an address by Pope Pius XII, given to newly married couples on 11 March 1942.

As the Estonians and Lithuanians believed in the lime as an aid to fertility, so we, in the first Mass reading on Thursday, reflect that true fruitfulness in the physical and spiritual senses comes from God, who says to Noah, 'Be fruitful and multiply, teem over the earth (Gen. 9:1–13). The old Greek couple offered hospitality to the gods, and on Wednesday Procopius of Gaza (*c.* 475–*c.* 528), commenting on the book of Proverbs, reflects on the amazing hospitality of God towards us, in the Blessed Sacrament, prefigured in Proverbs 9:6–32: 'The Wisdom of God has mingled her wine and prepared a table for us.' The lime also came to represent love and friendship, and as Proverbs 15:17 reminds us on Friday: 'Better is a dinner of herbs where love is, than a fatted ox and hatred with it.'

In northern Europe particularly, judges would sit under lime trees to deliberate and pronounce judgment. One of the major liturgical themes this week is that of wisdom and so we have:

'The pursuit of Wisdom', from *Sermons of Saint Bernard* (Monday, second Office reading).

Proverbs 8:1–38: Praise of the eternal Wisdom (Tuesday first Office reading).

'The knowledge of the Father through creative Wisdom made flesh', from *The Discourses of Saint Athanasius* (Tuesday second Office reading).

Proverbs 1:1–19: Wisdom and foolishness (Wednesday first Office reading).

Proverbs 15: 8–33; 16:1–9; 17:5: The fear of the Lord is instruction in wisdom. Better is a little with righteousness than great revenues with injustice.

The lime also became associated with peace, and through the work of the medieval poet and troubadour Walther von der Vogelwide (d. *c.*1170) it came to represent the social community; a single lime leaf became an emblem of truth, and the tree itself was protective of the community and its gardens. In Tuesday's responsorial Psalm at Mass we turn to the Lord for *our* peace: 'May the Lord bless his people with peace!' (Psalm 29:11). And we are reminded here of Christ's words 'Peace I leave with you; my peace I give to you; not as the world gives do I give to you' (John 14:27). I note that last clause, and take it as a warning not to expect that the peace of Christ will always be of an outward or worldly kind, but more often, I think, of a deep, inner and spiritual peace, and indeed one that is often granted after self-denial and suffering.

There is a legend of St Odrada, who was Flemish and born in the seventh century. As a child she was made to ride a wild horse. She made the sign of the cross over the animal with a lime switch, and it immediately became docile. After she had mounted and ridden the horse, she planted the lime switch in the earth and it grew into a large tree. Later in her life Odrada is supposed to have caused a spring to flow, whose waters were particularly curative of eye diseases. In Wednesday's Mass Gospel Christ cures the blind man, and we learn that true healing comes only through faith in him (Mark 8:22–6).

To look upward at the sun through the leaves of a lime tree is to have one's eyes dazzled. How much more, then, would the disciples have been dazzled at the sight of their transfigured Lord as he gave them a glimpse of his glory? (Saturday Mass Gospel Mark 9:2–13)

Other plants appropriate to this week
Rose 'Thank you'; Ajuga 'Rainbow'; White Mulberry (wisdom – see also Week 9 of Ordinary Time); Aster 'Peace'; Eyebright; Rose 'Glorious'.

Intercessions
For those being treated with linden as a medicine.

For married couples; for those who offer hospitality in retreat houses and pilgrim centres.

That we may fully open our hearts to God and offer him our best efforts and 'fruits'.

For an increase in our faith, and that Christ may help in our search for true wisdom and inner peace.

For peace in war-torn areas of the world.

Places of spiritual retreat
Listening to Christ's teaching on marriage and divorce, as in Mark 5:17–37.
At the healing of the blind man, as in Mark 8.
With the disciples after the Transfiguration, as in Mark 9.
With our Lord in a reflection on the nature of his peace, as in John 14.

SUNDAY AND WEEK SEVEN OF ORDINARY TIME

WALLFLOWER *Cheiranthus cheiri*; Chevisaunce

Cultivation, history and uses
The wallflower normally reaches a height of about 2 feet and is usually grown as a biennial, but left to itself it will behave as a short-lived perennial. If sown late, say my old friends Sutton and Sons, wallflowers 'will present but a feeble show ... whereas they should in their season be little mounds of fire and gold, exhaling a perfume that few flowers can equal ... sow the seed in May or June, in a sunny place, on rather poor

but well prepared soil ... when the plants are two inches high transplant into rows six inches asunder, allowing three inches apart in the row. In about three weeks transplant again, six or nine inches apart every way, aiding with water when needful ... or lift every other row and every other plant, leaving the remainder untouched to supply flowers for cutting. When the beds are cleared of their summer occupants, they may be filled with the best plants of Wallflower, to afford cheerful green leafage all through the winter and a grand show of bloom in the spring, as frost will not hurt the single varieties, but the doubles will not always endure uninjured the rigours of a severe winter.' In south west France it is possible to sow as early as mid-April if danger of frost has passed, and pinching out the plants when they reach 6 inches aids branching.

The English common name comes from the fact that the flower grew on stones, rocks and walls, and clearly the latter habitat is the origin of our characterization of girls at balls whom no one asks to dance. There is a Scottish story that explains the name even further, and which certainly underlines its meaning in *The Language of Flowers*, which is 'Fidelity in adversity': A laird's daughter was betrothed to a prince, but was in love with a chieftain. Disguised as a minstrel, this chieftain sang underneath the tower where her father had imprisoned her. Possibly because troubadours often wore the flower in their caps, she threw him a wallflower and then tried to climb down the outer walls of her prison. The ladder broke and she fell to her death near the spot where the flower had landed. The grieving chieftain vowed to remain faithful to her memory and took the wallflower as his emblem.

The Latin is thought to derive from the Greek for hand, because the flower was often carried in the hand in bouquets. Until the seventeenth century 'chevisaunce' meant comfort and was another common name for the wallflower. There is an old legend that the wallflower sprang from drops of Christ's blood as they fell to earth from the cross. In any case, since it is now grown in gardens and not necessarily on or near walls, 'Comfort Flower' would perhaps be a more attractive name, if only for its lovely perfume and velvety petals.

Culpeper advocated its use for inflammations and swellings, but it is little used in modern herbalism and is not recommended for domestic use. Unsurprisingly, the essential oil is used in the perfume industry.

I have to admit to being very emotional about wallflowers because they provided my first experience of flower scent, probably when I was about three or four years of age. The memory is indelible and is bound up with

63

the happiness of carefree and innocent childhood and love of the parents who ensured it. The scent of wallflowers always evokes the Botanical Gardens in Sheffield, where even in the mid- to late 1940s, with the war hardly over, the municipal gardeners managed to produce a magnificent late spring display of them. There was a terrace of huge glasshouses on the north side of the gardens, empty of plants because of the Blitz. I knew what that word meant but had no concept of what should have been in the glasshouses, or of how important the word 'botanical' would become for me in later life. I would run along jumping on and off the terrace, and when I was tired of that game, my parents would take me to the wallflower beds to the south of the gardens, where there is a statue of Peter Pan. After the first time, I would always ask to go there. To my child's senses it was paradise. I do not visit my home city very often and think I last saw the gardens in 1988. I walked in astonishment round the restored glasshouses full of tropical plants. And then to my delight found that the descendants of those immediately post-war gardeners had kept up the tradition of the wallflowers. There they were, and I stood with my mother (my father being dead by then) and wept paradoxical tears of gratitude for the happiness of the past, and of yearning regret that it can never be regained.

At least 850 years before my first encounter with the Sheffield wallflowers, their ancestors had arrived in Britain from France. It is thought that William the Conqueror was responsible, though almost certainly unwittingly, for bringing the wallflower to England. When he began to build castles here, he preferred to use stone imported from the continent rather than material from our native quarries. This imported stone carried the seeds of the wallflower and the pink (*Dianthus*), both known to have grown on the walls of Caen in Normandy. *Cheiranthus cheiri* came originally from southern Europe, and this name was retained until 1980, when the entire genus was re-allocated and is now more correctly known as *Erysmum cheiri*. The first part of the name comes from the Greek for 'blistercress', and indeed the plant does sometimes suffer from white fungus blister.

Lore and liturgy

There is much in this week's liturgy that chimes with features of the lore surrounding the wallflower, but two themes stand out for me. The first of these is 'vanity'. This is a word that has become synonymous with conceit in one's own attractiveness, much as the girl left at the side of the ballroom might feel humiliation in her dented pride. But to take this as the whole meaning of the word is surely wrong. In fact, her hurt feelings are only one type of vain human reaction: vain, that is, in its full meaning of 'useless', 'futile' or 'in vain'. And I think of this fuller meaning when reading the week's liturgy. Sunday's first Office reading is entitled 'All is vanity' (Ecc. 1:1–18); and second reading is from *The Four Centuries of Charity* by St Maximus the Confessor (*c*. 580–622) entitled, 'Without charity all is vanity of vanities'. On Monday a further reading from Ecclesiastes 2 and 3 speaks of the vanity of pleasures and human wisdom; on Wednesday, in Ecclesiastes 5, we must face up to the vanity of riches. St Jerome (*c*. 345–420) tells us on the same day to seek the things that are above, and on Thursday we are warned in Ecclesiastes 6 and 7 against intellectual vanity. This is pressed home in Saturday's Mass Gospel when Christ tells us that anyone who does not welcome the kingdom of God like a little child will never enter it (Mark 10:13–16).

The wallflower has the meaning of faithfulness in adversity, and this is another important liturgical theme this week. On Tuesday the first Mass reading warns us to prepare for an ordeal if we aspire to serve God (Ecc. 21:1–11) and in the face of this knowledge exhorts us to sincerity and steadfastness. But the responsorial Psalm 37 assures us: 'Commit your way to the Lord; trust in him, and he will act', and, 'The salvation of the righteous is from the Lord; he is their refuge in the time of trouble.' But it is in Monday's Mass Gospel, when the convulsive boy is healed (Mark 9:14–29), that we see an example of faith in adversity, of the order God wishes to see in us. Jesus tells the father of the boy that anything is possible for someone who has faith, and the father cries out, 'I do have faith. Help the little faith I have.' It may be a much-used prayer, but it is an excellent one, and although it may be a cliché, I still find that the best way to get my own problems into proportion is to remember the terrible things that other people have to bear.

The wallflower is the flower of comfort, but the first Office readings during the latter part of the week (Ecc. 8 to 12) rub our noses in the fact of our mortality. So where shall we find comfort, where is our 'chevisaunce'? The answer is of course that Christ himself is our true chevisaunce, and our true light. This is borne out by the second Office readings of Friday and Saturday, both from St Gregory of Girgenti's (d. *c*. 638) commentary on Ecclesiastes, the first entitled, 'My spirit exults in the Lord' and the second, 'Come to the Lord to be enlightened.'

Intercessions

Thanksgiving for our happy memories.

That we may work to rid ourselves of pride, conceit, silliness and wrong priorities.

For an increase in faith.

Thanksgiving for the Light of Christ and for the comfort he gives us.

Place of spiritual retreat

At the healing of the convulsive boy, as in Mark 9.

SUNDAY AND WEEK EIGHT OF ORDINARY TIME

ERIGERON *Pulicaria dysenterica* (small fleabane); *Erigeron acer* (blue fleabane); *Conyza canadensis* (Canadian fleabane); *Erigeron speciosa* (garden fleabane)

Cultivation, history and uses

Garden fleabane produces clusters of single or double flowers that may be violet, pink, blue or lavender. They resemble Michaelmas daisies but bloom earlier, from June to August, when they are excellent for cutting. Plant in groups in a sunny site from October to March, preferably in well-drained soil that has been enriched with peat or garden compost. Mulch in early spring, support with sticks, dead-head to encourage continued flowering and cut to ground level in autumn. Propagate by division from October to March.

Wild fleabane was used by ancient Arab doctors to treat dysentery and ulcers. For centuries its dried leaves, when burned, were thought to drive fleas away. Hence *Pulicaria*, from the Latin word for flea, *pulex*. Even the fresh leaves are supposed to deter fleas and other insects. The smell, said Culpeper, 'is supposed delightful' to them, 'and the juice destructive to them, for they never leave it till the season of their deaths'. He refers to the use of small fleabane in the treatment of dysentery and to the blue fleabane for chest complaints, but he is otherwise uncomplimentary, describing the plant as 'an ill-looking weed'. Perhaps because of his influence, and the plant's unpleasant taste, it has never found popularity in English herbalism. Canadian fleabane is sometimes used, but even that is taken in drop form on a sugar cube. Fleabane is not recommended for domestic use.

Lore and liturgy

It has been suggested that the name erigeron comes from the Greek *eri* 'early' and *geron*, 'old man'. It would therefore seem an apt choice for a liturgical week that takes us through the book of Job. Job is early, in the sense that his experiences are recounted in the Old Testament, and since he had ten adult offspring by the time his troubles started, he can hardly have been in the first flush of youth. Possibly to counteract the poor reputation of wild fleabane and its unpleasant flavour, garden varieties of Erigeron have been given names such as 'Dignity', 'Serenity' and 'Felicity'. Job loses all three when his possessions and his children are taken away. But he does not curse God: ' "The Lord gave, the Lord has taken back. Blessed be the name of the Lord." In all this Job did not sin or charge God with wrong' (Job 1:21b–22). Fleabane was once used to treat ulcers but when Job is stricken with them from head to toe, he still does not blame God: ' "If we take happiness from God's hand, must we not take sorrow too?" In all this misfortune Job uttered no sinful word' (Job 2:10). But Job's faith is shaken, and he cries to God in his weariness of suffering. His plight is made worse when one recalls that the theology of his time did not include an assurance of life after death. There was no dignity in a miserable death, and no promise of eternal serenity or felicity after it, however good one had been on earth. Job's belief system dictated that justice would be done to a man while he lived. Goodness would be rewarded with prosperity, evil with calamity. So those debating Job's predicament assume that he must have been wicked. Job knows this is untrue and questions God as to why misfortune has come upon him. His question is probably as old as humanity (and known in theology as the problem of 'theodicy'). If God is good and fair, why does he let innocent people suffer? The last word on my own father's lips, a moment before cancer killed him, was that one word, 'Why?' Why the pain and indignity of disease, why the innocent victims of war, terrorism, drought, famine and other disasters? Why my neighbour's child dying of leukaemia (see *Gardening with God*, 18 February)? Why the appalling suffering and loss of life caused by the 2004 Tsunami in Asia? Pope Gregory the Great and Augustine of Hippo, extracts from whose works form the second Office readings this week, interpret the book of Job in the light of those under the new covenant, and on Saturday Zeno of Verona (d. 371) sees Job as a type of Christ, who 'at his resurrection held out to those who believe in him, not merely health, but immortality, and took back to himself dominion over all nature.' But it is still a hard answer for the believer's 'Why?', and not an answer at all to that of the unbeliever.

The readings at Mass on Sunday penetrate to the heart of all our anxieties and fears. Here, and during the rest of the week we find the light, hope and fulfilment that are the Christian response to the gloom, despair and frustration of the book of Job. As the unpleasant flavour of fleabane is counteracted by the names of its cultivated cousins, so I understand that the redemption wrought for us by Christ, if I truly believe in him, will counteract all my painful experiences and all my worst fears.

Readings

Sunday: Isaiah 49:14–15: I will never forget you; Psalm 62: In God alone is my soul at rest; 1 Corinthians 4:1–5: The Lord will reveal the secret intentions of men's hearts; Matthew 6:24–34: Do not worry about tomorrow.

Monday: Sirach [Ecclesiasticus] 17:24–9: Return to the Lord and leave sin behind; Psalm 33: Rejoice in the Lord, exult you just; Mark 10:17–27: Sell everything and follow me.

Tuesday: Sirach 35:1–12: Follow the commandments; Psalm 50: God's salvation to the upright. Mark 10: 28–31: You will be repaid with eternal life, but not without persecutions.

Wednesday: Sirach 36:1–17: Let the nations know; Psalm 79: Have mercy on us Lord. Mark 10:32–45: The Son of Man is about to be handed over.

Thursday: Sirach 42:15–25: The work of the Lord is full of his glory; Mark 10:46–52: Lord, let me see again.

Friday: Psalm 149: The Lord takes delight in his people; Mark 11:11–26: Have faith in God.

Saturday: Sirach 51:12–20: Glory be to him who has given me wisdom; Psalm 19: The precepts of the Lord gladden the heart; Mark 11:27–33: Nor will I tell you my authority for acting like this.

Other plants suitable for this week

Scabious, 'I have lost all'; Heliotrope, 'I turn to thee'; Briar rose, 'I wound to heal'; Aspen, lamentation; Aloe, acute sorrow; Plum tree, fidelity; Rudbeckia, justice; Lily of the Valley, return of happiness; Masterwort, power and authority; Hawthorn, hope; Amaranthus, immortality; Pinks, 'Joy' and 'Happiness'; White mulberry, wisdom (see also Week 9 of Ordinary Time); Roses 'Sweet Repose', 'Sight Saver', 'Ray of Hope', 'Faith'.

Intercessions

For all who suffer in body, mind or soul.
    For those tempted to despair, and who suffer unjustly.
    For serenity, dignity and joy, and for an increase in faith.
    Thanksgiving for our redemption.

Place of spiritual retreat

Resting with Jesus in the Gospel of each day.

SUNDAY AND WEEK NINE OF ORDINARY TIME

WHITE MULBERRY *Morus alba;* **BLACK MULBERRY** *Morus nigrum*

Cultivation, history and uses

Whichever mulberry you grow, it is, like the lime, perhaps best as a single specimen at the centre of a large lawn. It can, if not checked, grow to a height and spread of 20 feet, reaching about half this within ten years. (*Morus alba* 'Pendula' may be an option as it grows only to 10 feet and spreads for 15.) Self-fertile ball-rooted mulberry seedlings are available about 3 feet in height. Be careful when planting, as the roots are vulnerable and easily broken. Stake, and take care with training for the first two years. Pruning or pollarding can keep the crown small, or the tree can be trained against a stout pergola. Prune only in winter, when the tree is fully dormant, and ideally prune dead wood only. Growth is slow at the beginning, and it may take up to eleven years before the tree produces its first luscious harvest. This is easy to gather. In August or September, when the mulberries are beginning to fall naturally, spread a sheet under the tree and gently shake the branches. The fruit is tartly sweet and is usually eaten fresh or mixed with other fruits in puddings and desserts or made into excellent preserves or wine. It is fairly well known that white wine, if applied immediately, will remove red wine stains. Similarly the red stains of mulberry can be removed by washing with the juice of the unripe berries, a trick referred to by Pliny.

Mulberry leaves are famous as the food of silkworms, and James I encouraged black mulberries in England in an attempt to start production of silk, but silkworms prefer white mulberry, native to China, so the enterprise came to nothing, except for the legacy of a few ancient trees and a belief that once the mulberry is in leaf there will be no more frost.

Black and white mulberry are considered equally efficacious medicinally, and *M. alba* has been used in Chinese medicine since the mid-seventh century. Recent research has shown that injections of the leaf extract are helpful in the treatment of elephantiasis, and internal doses of the sap mixed with sugar are an aid to the treatment of tetanus. In modern herbalism the leaves are used for colds, eye problems, stress and tension – the branches for rheumatism; the foot bark for asthma, bronchitis, oedema and diabetes; and the fruits for incontinence, tinnitus, greying hair and constipation. For medical use collect leaves after the first autumn frost, branches in early summer, roots in winter and fruits when nearly ripe. Before drying the fruit, blanch to lengthen storage time.

Lore and liturgy

There is a theory that *morus* comes from *demoror*, Latin for 'delay', and this *is* more satisfactory than the usual explanation that it is from *morus*, meaning 'silly', since, as Pliny said, the plant displays caution and wisdom in not forming buds until after the frosts of winter are safely over. For this reason he said it was called *sapientissima arborum*, 'the wisest of the trees'. Its flowers are late, but fruits still ripen on time and it drops its leaves early in the autumn. Although originally applied to black mulberry, this symbolism of wisdom came to be regarded as an attribute of all mulberries. In any case it is surely the sensible growth habits of both trees that have led to them being emblematic of wisdom throughout European folklore. The mulberries of the King James Version of the Bible (2 Sam. 5:23–4 and 1 Chron. 14:14–15) are almost certainly not mulberries at all. On the other hand the sycamore of Luke 19:4 *is* thought to have been a mulberry (see F. Nigel Hepper, *The Illustrated Encyclopedia of Bible Plants*, Inter-Varsity Press, 1992). We know the tree was grown for its fruit in the Holy Land at the time of Jesus. (I am rather pleased about this, because it means I do not need a sycamore to represent

Zacchaeus in a garden where space is at a premium. And the symbolism of wisdom and fruitfulness attached to the mulberry makes it a more apt tree for Zacchaeus to have climbed in order to get a view of Jesus, and from which to come down in order to welcome Wisdom into his house.) The theme of the search for wisdom and its nature has been central in the liturgy since we resumed Ordinary Time, and it continues this week in the Office of Readings with the completion of Job's story in Job chapters 28 to 42: *Sunday*: Wisdom rests with God alone (28:1–28); *Monday*: Job's lament (29:1–10; 30:1, 9–13); *Tuesday*: Job's appeal to his upright life (31:1–8, 13–23, 35–7); *Wednesday*: The Mystery of God (32:1–6; 33:1–22); *Thursday*: God confounds Job (38:1–30); *Friday*: Job submits to God's Majesty (40:1–14; 42:1–6); *Saturday*: Job's fortunes are restored (41:7–17).

As during last week, these readings are paired with interpretative passages from the early Christian Fathers, thus: *Sunday*: St Augustine speaks of our hearts being restless until they rest in God; *Monday and Tuesday*: St Dorotheus of Tyre (d. *c.* 362) gives the refusal to take blame on oneself as the reason for all disturbances and warns against false peace of soul; *Wednesday and Thursday*: St Gregory the Great tells us that sound teaching, to be found in the Church, which rises like the dawn, helps us to avoid the sin of pride; *Friday*: Baldwin, archbishop of Canterbury (d. 1190), reflects that much as God knew everything that was going on in Job's mind, so he scrutinizes the thoughts of all our hearts; *Saturday*: St Thomas Aquinas concludes the week with an exposition of the way to reach true life.

The children's rhyme 'Here we go round the mulberry bush' is strange because the mulberry is very definitely a tree, but it is supposed to have been planted in prison yards where the prisoners took their daily exercise around it. Perhaps it was stunted to a bush in that environment. This leads me to reflect further that Job was in a prison of ignorance, pride in his righteousness, false peace and an unwitting attempt to cut God down to size in order to understand divine actions. As the mulberry takes several years before bearing its first fruit, so Job took a long time to come to terms with the fact that it is not his place to ask questions of God but to listen instead to the questions God is asking him. And through these questions Job finds that his opinion of himself shrinks, as his concept of God becomes altogether greater. God, he realizes, is of incalculable magnitude. There is no longer any question of putting his case and pleading his cause. His questions remain unanswered, but now he can trust where he cannot understand. He can accept, and he can regret his complaints; he can worship God and see himself and his problems in perspective. Is this the answer to our 'Why?' of last week? If so, it is still a hard saying but one that may help us to understand a little better what is required of us. I feel that if I do not open my mind to it, then I will remain spiritually stunted and locked in my 'prison', just as was Job until near the end of his story.

As we shall see, Job's lesson is one that must be learnt by rich and poor alike. Sunday's Mass readings advocate rock-like faith as an antidote to all our troubles and temptations. Mulberry leaves are used to treat eye problems and stress, and at Mass during the week, as if to underline the truths we have learned from Job, we follow the story of Tobit, who feared God more than he feared the king. He was struck blind, but he did not complain against God and prayed in lamentation. In European art the black mulberry may represent suicide: Sarah, who was to become Tobit's daughter-in-law, was tempted to this because of wrong accusations against her. But instead she prayed that God would let her die. God hears the prayers of both Tobit and Sarah and sends the angel Raphael to bring them relief. Sarah then marries Tobit's son Tobias, and, under instruction from Raphael, Tobias removes the film from his father's eyes, 'so that he might see God's light with his eyes' (Tobit 3:17). Even if one does not accept the book of Tobit as inspired by God, it is perhaps easy to see why the Church includes it this week while we are concentrating on Job. Job was rich before his misfortunes began. Tobit was poor. Job did not curse God, but he certainly complained. Tobit does not complain; Sarah does not commit suicide because it would bring disgrace on her father. Both pray. Perhaps we are being told that even the poor must suffer seeming unfairness, sickness, disability, disaster and persecution. But Tobit and Sarah, though they may lament, pray to God for death rather than blame him for their problems.

The branches of the mulberry bleed when they are cut: the shedding of Christ's blood is figured in the Mass Gospel on Monday when Jesus speaks the parable of the vineyard owner's son. 'They seized the beloved son, killed him, and threw him out of the vineyard.' The chief priests, scribes and elders knew the parable was aimed at them and about Jesus himself, and they would have liked to arrest him there and then, 'but they were afraid of the crowds. So they left him alone and went away' (Mark 12:1–12).

Other suitable plants
Rock rose; Bittersweet nightshade (trust); Bluebell (constancy); Lucern (life, see also Ordinary Time, week 13); Lemon blossom (fidelity in love);

Wallflower (fidelity in adversity); Everlasting sweet-pea (eternal life); Rose 'Blessings'; Orange tree (generosity).

Readings

Sunday: Deuteronomy 11:18, 26–8: I set before you a blessing and a curse; Psalm 31: Be a rock of refuge for me, O Lord; Matthew 7:21–7: The house built on rock.

Monday: Psalm 112 1–6: Happy the man who fears the Lord.

Tuesday: Psalm 112 1–2, 7–9: With a firm heart he trusts in the Lord.

Wednesday: Psalm 25: I trust in you, let me not be disappointed; Mark 12:18–27: God of the living, not the dead.

Thursday: Psalm 128:1–5: Blessed are those who fear the Lord; Mark 12:28–34: The commandment of love.

Friday: Psalm 146:7–10: The Lord keeps faith for ever.

Saturday: Tobit 13:2, 6–8: Blessed be God who lives for ever; Mark 12:38–44: The widow's mite.

Intercessions

For those being treated for elephantiasis and tetanus.

For the blind; for patients with cataracts, and for the surgeons, doctors and nurses who treat them.

For victims of bullying and persecution; for the stressed, anxious, and depressed; and for those tempted to suicide.

That we may fear and trust God and offer thanksgiving for his constant love; that we may not fall victim to false peace of soul; that rich or poor we may turn to God in our troubles; for less concern about material things, and for more about the things of God.

For greater generosity.

Place of spiritual retreat

Throughout the week: listening to the teaching of Jesus, as in Matthew 7 and Mark 12.

SUNDAY AND WEEK TEN OF ORDINARY TIME

PARSLEY *Petroselinum hortense crispum (sativum)*

Cultivation and uses

Parsley is a biennial and is usually sown successively from spring to autumn in order to ensure year-round supply. It likes rich, moist, neutral to alkaline soil in sun or part shade. *Crispum* is Latin for 'kinky' or 'curled', and *hortense* and *sativum* indicate a cultivated rather than wild plant. Curled parsely seems to have first made its appearance as early as AD 42 Until recently it has perhaps been more popular in Britain that its cousin *P. crispum* 'Neopolitana', also known as 'Italian' or 'French' parsley. This can reach a height of 2 feet, has flat leaves, and sometimes has an even stronger flavour than curled parsley. In my view it is rather an untidy and space-consuming plant, and I prefer the dense, compact versatility of curled parsley. This grows to a maximum of 12 inches and makes an attractive border edging, or it can be cultivated in pots and window boxes, as well as in traditional rows in the vegetable garden. Both types have a notoriously long germination period, usually of about a month. Country lore maintains that this is because the seed has to go down to visit the devil, and in Devon they say it must do this seven times before showing itself above ground level. Another tradition has it that one should laugh while sowing parsley, and perhaps this is connected with the old belief that the devil does not like being laughed at. In the Erz Mountains of Germany there is an old custom of sowing parsley on the feast of SS Peter and Paul, possibly because the Latin root of its name, *petro*, means rock. The English word 'parsley' is a contraction of the old English *petersilic*, which is a straightforward translation of the Latin name.

Parsley is a good companion plant to tomatoes, and if grown under roses it will help to repel aphids. It is rich in iron, calcium, phosphates, antiseptic chlorophyll, vitamin D and pro-vitamin A. Thirty grams will supply your daily requirement of vitamin C (containing three times as much as an orange), more goodness being concentrated in the stems than in the leaves. It is quite safe in the amounts normally used, but is toxic if taken to excess. In the past it was given, like dill water, to calm teething and fretful babies ('the frets' is an old term for 'wind'). The roots and seed were also given to aid lactation and contract the uterus after childbirth. Wild parsley has been successfully used in the treatment of anaemia, rheumatism, sciatica, jaundice, tumours and boils. All varieties are good for the complexion, and eating them after onion or garlic will remove the smell of the latter from your breath. Harvest the leaves before flowering, and lift the roots in late autumn of the first year or spring of the second year. Always harvest stems from the outside of the plant to enable the growth at the centre to flourish. Collect the seed when ripe.

St Hildegard of Bingen (1098–1174; 17 September), abbess, mystic, poet, composer and musician, was also a herbalist and left a recipe for parsley honey wine, an excellent tonic for the heart: take 8 to 10 parsley sprigs and stems. Boil for five minutes in 2 pints of (additive-free) red or white wine with two tablespoons of wine vinegar. Add three quarters of a cup of honey and reheat for a further five minutes. Skim, strain and bottle. Take one to three tablespoons daily. St Hildegard recommended the mixture for convalescent heart patients, and as a remedy for gout.

Parsley has an unassailable place on my shortlist of favourite herbs, and in my opinion no herb or vegetable garden is complete without it. I do not feel secure unless I have a strong row of it growing all year round. For me, it is the culinary 'salt of the earth', the essential garnish in presentation, and parsley sauce has been *de rigueur* from childhood with Friday's traditional meal of fish. I have also found that chewing a sprig of parsley allays nausea.

Note: *Parsley is not given medicinally to pregnant women, or to patients with kidney problems.*

Lore and liturgy

The folklore of parsley is particularly well documented and the plant has multiple significances, some of which are self-contradictory. However, a great deal of it is relevant to this week's liturgy.

The ancient Greeks esteemed parsley as having sprung from the blood of Achimonus, the forerunner of death, and it was therefore strewn over the dead and used to decorate graves: Monday's first Mass reading draws our attention to the fact that any lasting comfort we receive in our troubles (including bereavement), comes from God (rather than from funeral sprays and wreaths). Moreover, this comfort is given so that we may comfort others in their sorrows (2 Cor. 1:1–7). The Greeks also used the plant on festive occasions, and bridesmaids wore it at weddings. Victors at the Isthmian Games in Corinth were crowned with parsley wreaths: Sunday's first Office reading is a paean in praise of Joshua and Caleb, mainly in terms of their physical strength and prowess as military defenders of God's people (Sir. 46:1–10). Then, in a reading from the letter of St Ignatius of Antioch (d. 107) we understand that it is not men we should want to please or impress, but God. Thursday's account of the siege and victory over Jericho (Jos. 5:13–6:21) is followed by an interpretation by Origen, who takes it as a type of Christ's conquest of the world. And so the two paradoxical uses of parsley by the Greeks are matched by the salvific paradox at the heart of our faith, namely that through death, death itself is changed to life. Christ completes the law (Wednesday's Mass Gospel, Matt. 5:17–19), and as he rose from the dead so we too shall be raised with him (Friday's first Mass reading, 2 Cor. 4:7–15).

The Greeks recognized the medicinal properties of parsley, and it seems that the Romans were the first to use it as food. They too wore wreaths of it on festive occasions, in the belief that it would increase conviviality or help to control any subsequent intoxication. Perhaps this is the foundation for its signifying entertainment and celebration in art and in the 'language of flowers'. In the latter it also means 'useful knowledge': in Wednesday's first Office reading (Jos. 3:1–17; 4:10–12) Joshua exalts the Lord, and the people pass through the Jordan and celebrate the Passover in the plains of Jericho. The very next day the manna that had sustained them ceased, and they 'ate the fruit of the land'. How much more should we exalt the Lord in celebration, we who through Christ's cross will also 'pass through the Jordan' and until then be fed by him in word and sacrament. The connection of parsley with entertainment and knowledge reminds me of the young nun in Rumer Godden's novel *In This House of Brede*, who is astonished and incredulous when the novice-mistress tells her that the Liturgy entertains as well as being a deep well of spiritual knowledge. Stories and poems came partly from the human need for entertainment, and celebration. The Old Testament is full of them, and of course our Lord himself used parables and poetic figures in his teaching: the second Office readings on Friday and Saturday, from the writings of St Ambrose of Milan (*c.* 340–97), single out the Psalms for their brilliance and the sheer delight they afford. But he celebrates them for much more than these. He describes them as 'medicine for . . . spiritual health', a remedy to cure wounds caused by our own faults. From the Psalms, at any time, we can choose the one best suited to our particular need. And in the Psalms the life, passion, death, resurrection and ascension of Jesus are all prefigured. They also provide a marvellous range of celebratory praise and thanksgiving to God. As St Ambrose continues on Saturday, 'The psalm is the musical instrument of virtues, which the holy prophet played with the help of the Holy Spirit, making the earth resound with the delightful melody of heavenly music.' So, he concludes, we should follow David and sing praise in our hearts, and with St Paul 'sing with the spirit and the mind also'.

During this week's celebration of the Psalms my mind is bound to turn in gratitude towards the countless much-loved hymns of praise and celebration learned from the Anglican treasury of my formative years, many whose words and tunes are indelibly printed in my memory.

And so I leave a favourite and healthy herb with a favourite and gentle hymn that meditates on the action of the Word of God in our lives:

> Lord, thy word abideth,
> And our footsteps guideth;
> Who its truth believeth
> Light and joy receiveth.
>
> When our foes are near us,
> Then thy word doth cheer us,
> Word of consolation,
> Message of salvation.
>
> When the storms are o'er us
> And dark clouds before us,
> Then its light directeth
> And our way protecteth.
>
> Who can tell the pleasure,
> Who recount the treasure,
> By thy word imparted
> To the simple hearted?
>
> Word of mercy, giving
> Succour to the living;
> Word of life, supplying
> Comfort to the dying.
>
> O that we, discerning
> Its most holy learning,
> Lord, may love and hear thee,
> Evermore be near thee.
>
> (H. W. Baker, 1822–77; tune 'Ravenshaw')

Readings and other suitable plants

Matthew 5:1–12: Happy the poor in spirit (Sweet vernal grass, 'Poor but happy').

Matthew 5:20–6: Anger with brothers (Phlox, unanimity, see also Week 16 in Ordinary Time).

Matthew 5:27–32: Adultery and Divorce (Linden and Meadowsweet, traditional marriage plants).

Matthew 5:33–7: I say to you, do not swear at all (Fool's parsley, silliness; Willow, candour, plain speech).

Intercessions

For nursing mothers, nannies and child minders, and the well-being of their charges.

For more efficient distribution of food to underdeveloped countries. That we may help these countries with sensitive and effective programmes of training in the principles of sound agriculture and nutrition.

For health, and for a sensible use of plants for food and medicine.

Thanksgiving for the life and work of Hildegard of Bingen.

For heart patients and those who treat and care for them.

For athletes, and for the armed services.

For the bereaved and for undertakers.

For the souls of the faithful departed.

For those preparing for marriage, and their families and friends.

Thanksgiving for our salvation, and for the Word and Sacraments.

For greater appreciation of the Psalms, and that we may with their help be full of joy and praise of God, and that through them we may be helped to meet Christ.

Thanksgiving for the life and work of St Ambrose, and of Rumer Godden.

For spiritual health.

For church musicians, choristers and the composers and authors of hymns.

Thanksgiving for the Word of God as found in the Bible.

Places of spiritual retreat

As before, listening to the teaching of Jesus in any of the week's Gospels, or a week for finding him in the Psalms: Psalm 34: Taste and see that the Lord is good; Psalm 119:129–33, 135: Let your face shine on your servant; Psalm 85:8–14: A voice that speaks of peace; Psalm 116:10–18: Precious in the eyes of the Lord is the death of his faithful; Psalm 103:1–12: Great is his steadfast love.

SUNDAY AND WEEK ELEVEN OF ORDINARY TIME

HYDRANGEA *Hortensia*

Cultivation, history and uses

The name, given by Linnaeus, is from Greek *hydor*, 'water' and *angos*, 'jar' (the fruit of the shrub is cup-shaped). Both parts of the derivation speak of the hydrangea's need to be kept well-watered in dry weather and to be fed regularly. Its popularity is probably due to its long flowering season, from July to September (it is usually still happily blooming when most other summer perennials have died back), and also to the fact that even its faded blooms continue to provide muted colour as autumn sets in. Two main types are normally found in gardens, both more or less hardy in the south and west of Britain but best grown in shelter in areas accustomed to heavy frosts. The familiar mop-headed type arrived from China in about 1753, and lace-cap hydrangeas were discovered in Japan by Charles Maries (*c.*1851–1902). Plant in compost-enriched soil in October or November, or in late spring, where young shoots will not scorch in morning sun after a frost. In warm areas prune after flowering, but protect new growth; in cool regions do not deadhead. During the first spring after planting cut out all but three or four of the strongest stems and prune these to no less than 10 inches. In subsequent years cut out a couple of older branches to ground level; shorten flower stems to pairs of buds; and remove any spindly stems altogether, unless there are strong-looking buds lower down; if there are, prune to these. Hydrangeas are supposed to grow to a maximum height of 6 feet, and the lace-caps growing in our London courtyard are approaching that height. The massive banks of mop-heads that I saw growing around the 'chines' on the south coast of the Isle of Wight (in 1971) had definitely exceeded it. There are climbing hydrangeas, the most popular being *H. petiolaris*, and if you lack space on the ground for the rampancy of the shrub form, this may be a good choice on a north-facing wall or trellis. It will climb to at least 6 feet in light shade, and in June will produce large white lace-cap flowers, but these last for a shorter period than the shrub type. It will need no formative pruning and, when established, only minimal seasonal pruning. As the plant climbs into its allotted space, shorten over-lengthy shoots by cutting back to a healthy bud. Older plants tolerate hard pruning, but this may reduce flowering for a couple of seasons, so it is best to stagger pruning over the same length of time.

H. arboresens is the only hydrangea used medicinally. It is sometimes grown for its foliage and for its large flower heads. Native Americans used its roots to treat urinary stones and this practice was adopted by early European settlers. It is still used in modern herbalism for related problems but is not recommended for domestic use.

Note: Excessive use can cause dizziness and bronchial trouble.

Lore and liturgy

I have been unable to find any reason why the hydrangea is nicknamed 'The Boaster' in English folklore, and can only suppose it is a reference to the fact that in spite of its showy rampancy, the plant is without fragrance. I have chosen it because, in the Old Testament readings at least, this week's liturgy presents a depressing account of humanity's bias towards wrongdoing of every kind and then, after the act, towards self-justification and gloating boastfulness.

After the death of Joshua, 'There arose another generation who did not know the Lord or the work which he had done for Israel' (Judg. 2:10), and in readings from Judges chapters 2 to 9, 13 and 16 we learn of the attitude of that generation and its doings. This people turn from God and worship the Baals; God raises judges to save them from the power of their enemies but they will not listen to the judges and do not abandon their idolatry or stubborn ways. And so God allows the surrounding nations to remain as a test for his people and to see if they will turn to him. The Philistines are among these opponents, and as introducers and controllers of the iron industry they have good reason to boast of their superior weaponry and chariots. On Monday we read the horribly graphic account of the murder of Sisera by Jael while Deborah is judge over Israel and Barak their military leader; on Tuesday and Wednesday we have the story of Gideon, in whom we see a glimmer of God-fearing decency and obedience, but whose victory over the Midianites is not really his but God's; Thursday's first Office reading tells how Abimalech, one of Gideon's seventy sons, becomes king after his father through treachery, bribery and murder, and we read the prayer and prophecy of Jotham, the only son of Gideon to survive the massacre of his sixty-eight brothers. The week ends with

Samson, who although dedicated to God from birth and endowed with strength from God for a particular purpose, leads a life of moral laxity and allows himself to be robbed of both spiritual and physical power, symbolized in his blinding and capture by the Philistines. Before dying he finally turns to God, but then only with a prayer that he avenge the loss of his eyes. God restores Samson's great strength and he is able to bring down the building on himself and his tormentors. Since he was supposed to be entertaining the crowd, I have often wondered whether Samson's feat is the origin of our theatrical phrase 'to bring the house down'. In any case it must have been a huge edifice since there were about three thousand people on the roof alone.

The book of Judges records an age of religious decline in which the people appear to have forgotten their Covenant with God. I found it difficult not to draw modern parallels when reading the book of Revelation during Eastertide, and the same is true here. The Church is strong in many ways but lives in an age of declining belief, and even in nominally Christian countries the New Covenant is not kept. Everyone feels free to criticize and comment, often from a standpoint of ignorance, as when a certain 'quality newspaper' recently equated the consecration of bread and wine at Mass not only with its administration but also with its reception by the faithful – and then felt itself qualified to report on the subject of 'lay presidency'. For comfort and relief in the depressing scenario of the book of Judges and of our own times, we now turn to the New Testament readings of this week:

Each sorry episode in the first Office readings is matched by extracts from *The Treatise of St Cyprian on the Lord's Prayer*. St Cyprian (*c.* 200–58) draws our attention clause by clause to the way in which, if we pray the Lord's Prayer aright, our behaviour will become the exact opposite of that displayed by God's people under the Judges.

Further antidotes to the wretchedness of the people in the book of Judges are to be found in the week's Mass readings. On Sunday Romans 5:6–11 and Matthew 9:36–10:8 speak of our reconciliation with God through Christ, of his compassion towards us and his authority over us. In the Gospel he sends out the twelve to go first 'to the lost sheep of the House of Israel'. They are to 'cure the sick, raise the dead, cleanse lepers, cast our devils'. Well, we may not be able to raise the dead …. Modern science may attempt it but, one fears, largely out of pride in human ingenuity and cleverness, not in the name of Christ. We boast of our technology, our medical knowledge, even interfering with God's creative process and attempting to replicate it. Some of us may, like the hydrangea, be in rude health and materially successful but have nothing of the odour of sanctity in our lives. During the week the Mass readings from 2 Corinthians 6, 8, 9, 11 and 12 and from Matthew 5 and 6 highlight the following antidotes to the way of sin, pride, decadence and unbelief:

> action to prove we are servants of God
> love of our enemies and those who hurt us
> cheerful giving
> unostentatious good deeds and private prayer
> free preaching of the Word
> being at peace with God
> having and showing concern for the Church
> trusting in God
> prayer in word and deed

And then, although in the eyes of the world all this may make us weak, even though we are made so by individual weaknesses and temptations, we may say with St Paul, 'I will boast all the more gladly of my weakness, so that the power of Christ may dwell in me... . I am content with weakness, insults, hardships, persecutions, and calamities for the sake of Christ; for whenever I am weak, then I am strong' (2 Cor. 12:9b–10).

Intercessions
Thanksgiving for the work of botanists who have brought plants from abroad.

For those who glory in the wrong kind of strength.

For the physically and spiritually blind and imprisoned.

For a lack of vengefulness; for less pride in worldly achievement.

For those who, from a standpoint of ignorance, criticize and comment on the behaviour of others, and who thus spread and perpetuate false impressions.

That the nations may turn to the way of Christ and acknowledge the authorship, authority, power, love, compassion and justice of God.

Places of spiritual retreat
Listening to Jesus teaching on prayer, as in Matthew 6, and meditating on the Lord's Prayer with St Cyprian.

SUNDAY AND WEEK TWELVE OF ORDINARY TIME

TOMATO *Lycopersicum esculentum*; Love-apple

Cultivation, history and uses

The tomato arrived in Europe from South America in 1597, and it seems that its English name, which is derived from the Mexican *tomatl*, was first used in the United States in 1604. The botanical name originally applied to an Egyptian plant was later transferred to the tomato and is derived from the Greek *lykos*, 'wolf', and *persicon*, 'peach'. The tomato did not gain popularity as a food until the end of the nineteenth century. The fruit was considered harmful, particularly to women, possibly because of its reputation as an aphrodisiac. Only a few people, usually men, ate it as a dessert – for the same reason, one is tempted to think. It was normally grown for ornamental purposes, and Sutton and Sons speak at some length in 1904 of its use as a table decoration. We have come a long way from this to the discovery that tomatoes actually take up antibiotics from the soil. Perhaps when the efficacy of commonly used antibiotics is exhausted we will find ourselves taking tomato tablets instead of penicillin to control infection. Nowadays, it is difficult to imagine culinary life without the tomato. Versatile in its uses when fresh, it is also amenable to preservation in the form of sauces, jams, chutneys and concentrated juice in its association with vodka, or without it, in that concoction known to bartenders and recovering alcoholics as a 'Virgin Mary'. It is of course an essential ingredient, with basil, in Mediterranean cooking. And every French cook I know has his or her own version of *Charens du midi*. Strictly a lunchtime dish, as the name suggests, it is delicious and quick to make at any time. Skinned tomatoes are chopped and mixed with partially fried courgettes and garlic. These are then layered and seasoned in an oven-proof dish and covered with a gratin of crème fraiche, a sprinkling of parsley and basil, and often topped off with a *chapelure* of fresh breadcrumbs. (The dish freezes well, and I often make several in rigid foil containers during the tomato glut period, adding the toppings when unfrozen and just before cooking in a moderate to high oven for a maximum of 45 minutes.)

I wrote in the first book of this series that I found the leek a most satisfying vegetable to plant. To my mind the tomato is among the most satisfying of fruits to harvest. Ten or a dozen plants will supply the average family for the summer months, with more than enough for the preserving cupboard and freezer, even after many pounds have been given away to friends and neighbours. In common with many gardeners I buy plants in late spring, growing from seed being impossible because I am not usually in France at the right time. But in the second half of May the carefully chosen specimens from the local market are planted immediately after purchase, in ground that has been composted the previous autumn, usually in an east to west line, against 4-foot stakes that have been driven in beforehand. The tomato is closely related to the potato and should be kept apart from it. Nor is it happy in the company of fennel, wormwood, brassicas and kohlrabi, and apricots are uncomfortable with tomatoes. However, it is friendly with alliums, marigolds, nasturtiums and gooseberries and helps to prevent blackspot in roses. It is effective against asparagus beetle, and asparagus reciprocates by killing *Trichodorus,* a nematode to which tomatoes are vulnerable. I surround each plant with its own mulch mat to keep down weeds and plant the same number of basil plants in the row next to them. Tomato without basil is like blackberry without apple, raspberry without redcurrant, lamb without mint, beef without horseradish, and – as we shall be considering spiritual love and friendship this week – like St Francis without St Clare, St Vincent without St Louise or St Francis de Sales without St Jane.

Lore and liturgy

The name love-apple was given by the Spaniards, who introduced the tomato to Europe from South America, because of its alleged aphrodisiac effects. In Friday's first Office reading, although conjugal love is clearly implied in David's wooing of Abigail 'to make her his wife', it is plain that he has been as much impressed by her character and actions as by any (unrecorded) physical attractions she may have had. However, this week the companionability of the tomato calls to my mind not married love but rather the phenomenon of spiritual friendship as exemplified in Wednesday's Office readings and their responsories. The first of these records the friendship between David and Jonathan and the latter's unswerving loyalty and love for his friend in the face of dire and abusive threats from his father, Saul (1 Sam. 19:8–20; 20:1–17). The responsory hails this as a sign of the true love of a brother. 'A friend loves at all times, and a brother is born for adversity' (Prov. 17:17). The second reading is an extract from the treatise *On Spiritual Friendship* by St Aelred of Rievaulx (1110–67), who concentrates not only on Jonathan's unshakeable devotion to David but also on his putting David before himself in succession to the kingship. Whoever finds a friend like this 'has found a rare treasure' (Sir. 6:14). We are not often called to give up our own preferment for a friend, but the least we can do is to give our time and concern to them and to speak out for them when they are unjustly criticized. Spiritual friendships are a wonderful feature of Christian life, not least because being a Christian can be a lonely business in the modern world, and to have even one spiritual friend is a precious gift from God and one of his ways of supporting and sustaining us. But I think the second parts of the responsories today really hit the mark as to why and how these friendships exist: 'For he who loves is born of God, and knows God' (1 John 4:7) and 'Whoever fears the Lord directs his friendship aright; for as he is, so is his neighbour also' (Sir. 6:17). So this week I offer heartfelt thanks to God for the friends he has sent me, particularly over recent years when my need has been great, some from within the Church and some from outside it. I think especially of Sue who always comes with me to select my tomato plants and who understands what I'm trying to achieve, both horticulturally and spiritually. Moreover, as the years have passed, in spite of frequent separation she and I have done our best to be mutually supportive in times of hardship, difficulty, illness and stress. I have believed in her work and she in mine. And this year a Christian friend whom I had not seen for thirty-four years because she had been living in Tasmania for most of that time came to stay. How wonderful it was to have a sowing, weeding and planting companion who also approaches gardening as prayer; how amazing the reward of being able to speak quite naturally of our shared faith as we worked together, and to feel the beginnings of healing as we listened to the joys and tragedies that had marked our lives during the years of separation. But of course Miriam and I did not do the healing. God did that by using as his instrument Russell, our mutual priest friend who had put us in touch after so many years. (Certainly a case of 'By their fruits shall ye know them': Wednesday's Mass Gospel; Matt. 7:15–20.) Yes, I thank God for these three and pray for his continued blessing on their lives.

But of course we know that friendships go wrong, often out of misunderstanding or the jealousy of one of the parties. This is the case with Saul and David in Tuesday's first Office reading (1 Sam. 17 and 18), but on Friday we read of David's forgiveness of Saul (1 Sam. 26:5–25), showing that God *can* be found in a person's heart. In the week's Mass readings we find how God will come to be present in ours. Monday's Gospel tells us that we should always examine our own culpability before falling out with each other (Matt. 7:1–5); and here I remember another woman friend, this time a colleague. In the stresses of school Margaret and I have occasionally offended or annoyed each other, but somehow at the earliest opportunity afterwards we have fallen over ourselves to admit our own fault and be friends again. Thus in a small way we show Christ in our lives and are acknowledging the statement in Tuesday's first Mass reading that there should be no continued disputes (Gen. 13:2–18) and the one in the Gospel of the same day that we should behave toward others as we would wish them to behave toward us (Matt. 7:12–14).

Left to themselves, tomatoes will sprawl and in the end produce an inferior harvest, and so when training and pinching them out, I reflect (as I do when pruning any plant) that God trains us in a similar way, so that the fruit we bear will be of the best and most abundant. Away from the garden, and in the vicissitudes of my relationships with others, I will try to remember the main points of the Gospel that begins the week: I am not to be afraid, every hair on my head has been counted. God knows when a sparrow falls to the ground, and I am worth more to him than hundreds of sparrows. And moreover, if I declare for Jesus in my life and love others, he will declare for me in the presence of the Father (Matt. 10:25–33). This sounds very like 'tit for tat', but I must understand that Jesus is speaking of divine and not human reciprocity and that therefore it is of the utmost importance. For underneath his words is the astonishing fact of God's love for us. The highest, deepest, noblest, most loyal, forgiving and enduring love that humans are capable of bearing toward each other, is a mere shadow of God's love for us. And it is this love above all that the humble tomato helps me to celebrate this week.

Intercessions
Thanksgiving for love in all its senses, but mostly for our friendships in Christ, and for God's love for us.

For God's blessing on our friends.

Thanksgiving for the fruits of the earth.

That we may bear fruit to the eternal harvest.

For healing and forgiveness when there are rifts in our relationships.

For a deep and constant awareness of God's love for us.

Place of spiritual retreat
Resting in Christ's words, as in Matthew 10:26–33.

SUNDAY AND WEEK THIRTEEN OF ORDINARY TIME

LUCERN *Medicago sativa;* Alfalfa

Cultivation, history and uses

The word *Medicago* means a crop plant and is derived from the Greek *medike*, so the botanical name is tautological. The plant is thought to have originated in central Asia and to have been introduced to China two thousand years ago. It reached Greece in the fifth century BC and arrived in Africa and Spain during the eighth century AD where it was known by its Arabic name, *alfalfa*. The term 'lucern' dates back to 1626 and seems to be from the French for glow-worm, *ver luisant*. This is thought to be a reference to the plant's shiny seeds, but the white stems that go deep into the ground also have a luminous tinge. A tasty garnish can be grown in the kitchen. First soak the seed in a clean jam jar, cover with muslin secured with an elastic band, drain off the water and lay the jar on its side on the windowsill. Dampen and drain the seeds daily and the seeds will germinate in under a week. Grown outdoors, lucern likes light, well-drained to dry, neutral to alkaline soil in a sunny position. It will grow up to 3 feet in height with a spread of 2 feet. The leaves can be cooked as a vegetable, but excess can have an adverse effect on liver function and the production of red blood cells. Modern herbalism uses it to treat anaemia and haemorrhage, PMT, fibroids and hormonal imbalance. Sow seed in autumn or spring and cut before flowering. (*Note: Lucern is not given to patients with rheumatoid arthritis.*)

Lucern is a valuable fodder plant, being rich in vitamins and protein.

It can be cut up to five times a year and has naturalized in Britain near fields where it has been farmed. It is an upright, bushy plant with pea-like flowers at the top of the stems. These are usually purple, occasionally yellow and appear in June and July. The pods are coiled and spiral in form and contain many seeds. Bees set off a fascinating mechanism when pollinating lucern (somewhat similar to that of heartsease). When a bee lands on the flower, the stigma is released and taps the bee's head so that it drops pollen picked up from another lucern flower. The stamens dust the bee with more pollen, which it then takes to the next plant. Excellent honey is produced from bees whose hives are close to lucern fields. The roots of the plant have small nodes that give it the ability to take nitrogen from the air and convert it into plant food. In this way it improves the agricultural potential of poor pasture. As the result of the educational work of the Henry Doubleday Research Association (HDRA), an increasing number of gardeners are using green manure to replace soil nutrients, increase humus content, hearten the soil of tired gardens and set new ones off on the right foot. The nitrogen taken in by lucern is released into the soil when the plant is cut down and turned in to the top six inches of soil. It is very deep rooting and brings trace elements to the surface. Sow for green manure from April to July, turn under in autumn or leave to overwinter. Allow at least a month between digging in and using the plot. (An excellent, economically priced booklet, *Gardening with Green Manures* is available from The Organic Catalogue, Chase Organics, Riverdene Business Park, Molesey Road., Hersham, Surrey KT12 4RG; email: *enquiries@chaseorganics.co.uk*; Online: www.OrganicCatalogue.com.)

Liturgy and lore
In the language of flowers lucern represents 'life', and this is no surprise, given the benefits it brings to livestock and soil. I have chosen it this week because, as it feeds animals, so are we fed by the Word; as the bees drink of its nectar, so we drink of the Fountain of Life; and as the bees transfer its pollen to other flowers, so we receive the precious dust of the Good News, fertilizing it with our faith and works in order to sow seed for the eternal harvest; as the word lucern comes from the glow of a worm in the dark, so Christ lightens our darkness, and we in our turn try to dispel darkness from the lives of those around us; as the plant dies and is dug into the ground, enriching it with valuable nutrients, so we know decay, but through our Christian lives try to enrich those of the others and after death shall rise again in Christ. Lucern is deep-rooted, as we pray our faith

should be. Lucern is long-lived. Through Christ we have the promise of *eternal* life. This week's Old Testament liturgy concentrates on death, sin and darkness, and this is answered and balanced each day by readings from the New Testament and the Fathers that emphasize light, goodness, life and the way in which Christ fulfils prophecy and as the Good Shepherd makes all things new and brings us to life in him. Thus:

Death, Sin and Darkness	Life, Goodness and Light
Sunday	
1 Samuel 28:3–25: Saul consults with the witch of Endor.	Sermon of Paul VI, Manila, 1970: We preach Christ to the ends of the earth.
1 Chronicles 10:13–14: Saul paid with his life for his unfaithfulness; he resorted to ghosts for guidance, instead of to God.	2 Timothy 1:10; 1 John 1:16; Colossians 1:16-17: Christ has broken the power of death and brought life and light; through him we have received grace upon grace; all things are held together in him.
2 Kings 4:8–17: Elisha is welcomed by the Shumanite couple and prophesies a son for them.	Matthew 10:37–42: Anyone who welcomes you welcomes me; he who loses his life for my sake will find it.
Monday	
1 Samuel 31:1–4; 2 Samuel 1:1–16: The death of Saul.	St Augustine: *Sermon 47:* He is our God and we the sheep of his *flock*.
Genesis 18:16–33: God spares Sodom and Gomorrah for the sake of the just.	Matthew 8:18–22: Follow me and leave the dead to bury their dead.
Tuesday	
Genesis 19:15–29: God destroys Sodom and Gomorrah but spares Lot.	Matthew 8:23–7: Jesus calms the tempest.

Wednesday
2 Samuel 4:2-7:
David becomes king and captures Jerusalem.

St Teresa of Avila: 'Thy Kingdom Come' from *The Way of Perfection*, chapter 30.

Genesis 21:5, 8–20:
Hagar and Ishmael are sent away.

Matthew 8:28–34:
Jesus casts out devils.

Thursday
2 Samuel 6:1–23:
The Ark of the Covenant is taken to Jerusalem.

St Jerome, *On the Newly Baptized*: They long for the wonderful Tabernacle, the fountain of baptism in the Holy Spirit.

Genesis 22:1–19:
The near sacrifice of Isaac by Abraham.

Matthew 9:1–8:
Jesus heals the paralytic; the Son of Man has the power to forgive sin.

Friday
2 Samuel 7:1–25:
Nathan's messianic prophecy.

St Augustine: *The Predestination of the Saints*, chapter 15; Galatians 4:4–5; Ephesians 2:4; Romans 8:3:
God has sent his own Son into the world in the likeness of sinful flesh to redeem those under the law.

Genesis 23:1–24; 24:1–8, 62–7:
Isaac loves Rebecca and is consoled in the loss of his mother.

Matthew 9:13:
It is not the healthy that need a doctor; I want mercy not sacrifice.

Saturday
2 Samuel 11:1–27:
The sin of David.

St Cyril of Jerusalm: *Instructions to Catechumens*:
Make your confession at the accepted time.
Proverbs 28:13; 1 John 1:9:
He who confesses and renounces his sins will find mercy; if we acknowledge our sins God will forgive us.

Genesis 27:1–29:
Jacob takes his brother's birthright
and supplants him.

Matthew 9:14–17:
Put new wine in a new skin and
both are preserved.

Intercessions

For stock farmers and their animals; for those who suffer from complaints
that lucern is used to treat; for the work of the HDRA, and all who seek to
treat the earth with greater respect and kindness.

That we may bring light into the lives of those around us, and that we
may not go before the Lord with hands empty of harvest; that our faith
may be deep-rooted and unassailable; that we may welcome Christ and
his little ones and preach him to the ends of the earth in whichever way it
is our calling to do; that more people may acknowledge Christ as having
the power to forgive sins and as the source of light and life.

Thanksgiving, joy and praise to God for our salvation.

Places of spiritual retreat

At any of the scenes of Christ's demonstration of his power over nature
and over human disease, as in the week's Gospel readings from Matthew,
chapters 8 and 9.

SUNDAY AND WEEK FOURTEEN OF ORDINARY TIME

SOLOMON'S SEAL *Polygonatum multiflorum*

Cultivation, history and uses

This perennial grows to a height of 3 feet, spreads for at least 2 feet, and
produces fragrant, white, green-tipped flowers in early summer. These
hang from arching stems and are a graceful addition to flower
arrangements. Solomon's seal can be found growing wild in woodland,
particularly in the south of England. The related angular Solomon's seal,
whose stems are angular instead of round, is more rare, but garden
Solomon's seal is usually a hybrid of the two types and is stronger than
both. Plant in groups in a shady border or woodland garden between
September and March. The soil should be moisture-retentive and have
been enriched with garden compost. Mulch annually, water in dry spells

and cut back to ground level in autumn. Propagate by division from then until late winter.

The first part of the botanical name is derived from Greek and means 'having many small joints', a reference to the swellings on the plant's roots; the second is Latin, meaning 'many-flowered'. The origin of the English name is uncertain, although there are two popular theories. One is that the scars on the underground rhizomes resemble document seals, and the other that the plant has the ability to 'seal' wounds and broken bones. John Gerard wrote, 'the root of Solomon's Seale stamped while it is fresh and green and applied, taketh away ... any bruise ... gotten by falls, or women's wilfulness in stumbling upon their hasty husbands' fists.' (I cannot forbear to comment on this as a masterstroke of transferred guilt!) In modern herbalism the root is used fresh in tinctures and ointments, and dried for decoctions and powders. These are given internally for coughs and gastric upsets and externally for bruises, broken noses, haemorrhoids and dislocated joints. The rhizomes are harvested in autumn.

Note: All parts of the plant, especially the berries, are harmful if eaten, and it should not be confused with Polygonum *(Bistort).*

Liturgy and lore

The liturgical themes suggested by lucern continue throughout this week, and so I have chosen Solomon's seal, because in Friday's Office of readings David designates Solomon as his successor (1 Kgs 1:11–35; 2:10–12). And on Saturday we have a short history of Solomon's gifts and achievements – his wisdom and building of the temple, for instance. But we read also of his failings which led to his son Rehoboam, who was 'broad in folly and lacking in sense', becoming king after him, with the result that the kingdom became divided (Sir. 47:12–25). This is followed by an extract from St Augustine's *Discourses on the Psalms*, in which he describes the temple built by Solomon as a type of the Church and Solomon, whose name means 'peacemaker', as a prefigurement of Christ, the true peacemaker and builder, who is the cornerstone joining together the two 'walls' of the circumcised and uncircumcised. Augustine then refers to the fact that 'unless the Lord build the house, they labour in vain who build it' (Ps. 127:1). We may work with Christ on his 'building', but he is the Architect and Master Builder, in charge of operations. We are inwardly built by him; he opens our understanding and 'directs our minds to faith', so that we may fittingly become his apprentices. And although our pastors may notice how we respond to their teaching, and how we are functioning as members of the workforce, Christ is the Head Quality Controller, and the only one who can rightly assess our performance and contribution to the building and maintenance of his temple.

I once had occasion to interpret this verse from Psalm 127 in a way connected with the atmosphere in a physical church building. After the departure of a beloved and spiritual priest and an equally beloved and spiritual parish administrator, and during the long interregnum that followed, I gradually became aware that the profound atmosphere of prayer that had dwelt in the building was palpably beginning to seep away, and division rose to the surface in the community. When I mentioned this to another priest friend, he said 'The underpinning of prayer and love is lessening. What you feel is the Holy Spirit withdrawing.' A cold chill ran up my spine and I was shaken to the core. The humble apprentices who had sought to organize things *under* Christ, rather than attempting to do them *for* him, had gone. And it made me realize again how hard we should pray for our priests and for all who hold responsibility in our parishes. For indeed, 'Unless the Lord watches over the city, the watchman stays awake in vain' (Ps. 127:1b).

Readings

From *The Letters of Pope St Clement to the Corinthians* (Letter 46): Let each fix his eyes on the good of the whole community.

Matthew 9:32–8: The harvest is rich but the labourers are few.

2 Samuel 24:1–25: David's census and the building of the altar.

From an ancient work, *The Teaching of the Twelve Apostles* or *Didache*: 'The Eucharist'.

Matthew 10:1–7: Go to the lost sheep of the house of Israel.

1 Chronicles 22:5–19: David prepares for the building of the Temple.

From St Ambrose's discourse on Psalm 118 (9): God's temple is holy, and you are this temple.

Matthew 10:16–23: The Spirit of the Father will be speaking in you.

From *The Letters of Pope St Clement* (Letter 50): Keep God's commandments in true loving comradeship.

Another reading and plant

Genesis 28:10–22: He saw a ladder, the angels were going up and down it, and God was speaking. Jacob's Ladder.

Intercessions

For abused wives; for all recovering from broken bones and the complaints that Solomon's Seal is used to ease.

For the priests and people of God.

For peace in our communities.

For peace in Iraq and in the Holy Land.

For a deepening of prayer and love in our communities, and within the wider Church.

That the Holy Spirit may not be taken from us.

For wise management under Christ of the material resources of our churches, and that we may not lose sight of ourselves as apprentices of Christ, the Master Builder; for parish administrators and councillors, church wardens, vergers and sacristans.

Places of spiritual retreat

With the disciples when Jesus speaks to them, as in Matthew 9:32–8: The crowd was like a flock of sheep without a shepherd; and Matthew 10:7–15: You received without charge, give without charge.

SUNDAY AND WEEK FIFTEEN OF ORDINARY TIME

MASTERWORT *Astrantia major; Astrantia maxima;* Black masterwort; Hattie's Pincushion; Melancholy Gentleman (also applied to common masterwort, i.e. *Peucedanum imperatoria*, as in Culpeper)

Cultivation, lore and uses

Astrantia is the masterwort grown as a garden plant. It is perennial and produces papery long-lasting flowers for cutting in June and July. *A. major* grows to a height of 2 feet, spreads for 18 inches, and has greenish-pink flowers surrounded by white-green bracts. *A. maxima* reaches similar proportions but has shell-pink flowers and bright green, three-lobed leaves. Plant in groups from October to March in moisture-retentive soil, preferably in shade. (In sun the soil must be kept moist.) Mulch annually, keep well-watered and support with sticks in exposed areas. Cut back to ground level after flowering and propagate by division from October to March. Both plants are native to damp meadows and woodland, *A. major* in mountainous regions of central and eastern Europe, and *A. maxima* in southern Europe to the Caucasus. *Astrantia* is a medieval name, possibly from *magistrantia*, derived from Latin *magister*, 'master', or *aster* 'star'. The name Masterwort seems to have appeared in the English language about 1548 from the German *meisterwurtz*. *A.major* is thought to have arrived in Britain about 1596, and Gerard acquired it from Austria. According to Culpeper 'Common Masterwort' (*Peucedanum imperatoria*) was used as a pot-herb and in medicine. In modern herbalism a decoction is made from the root and taken to ease asthma, flatulence, and delayed menstruation.

Note: *Masterwort should not be taken during pregnancy.*

Towards meditation

This week I have identified the mastery of God over all things as a salient theme, and therefore Masterwort is appropriate because of its name alone.

Sunday

1 Kings 16:29–17:16: In the land of Baal, through Elijah, God demonstrates control over the elements, and this is particularly appropriate since Baal was worshipped as a weather god. The miracle through which the jar of meal is not spent and the cruse of oil does not fail means that Elijah, the widow of Zarephathe and her son are able to live on them for several days and is further proof of God's power over his creation.

Titus 3:3, 5: God in his mercy saved us through the water of rebirth and the renewing power of the Holy Spirit.

Isaiah 55:10–11 The rain makes the earth give growth.

Monday

1 Kings 18:16b–40: Elijah overcomes the priests of Baal through God's power over the element of fire.

Isaiah 44:3–4: Through the Spirit we shall grow like poplars by running streams.

Tuesday

From St Ambrose's treatise *On the Mysteries*: St Ambrose reflects that every event and character in the Old Testament prefigures something or someone in the New Testament. For instance, baptism is prefigured by God's use of his mastery over water at the crossing of the Red Sea, and the swallowing up of error by the drowning of the pursuing Egyptians. Similarly the God-given power of Moses to change the water of the fountain at Marah from bitter to sweet prefigures the water that has been 'consecrated by the mystery of the saving cross'. When Naaman the leper is healed, God shows his power over disease, and the healed man understands that it is not by water, but by grace that we are cleansed.

Wednesday

Matthew 11:25–7: Here Christ speaks of his mastery: 'Everthing has been entrusted to me by my Father. No one knows the Father except the Son, and those to whom the Son chooses to reveal him.'

Thursday

Exodus 3:13–20: 'I Am who I Am. I Am has sent me to you.'

Friday

Again, in his treatise *On the Mysteries*, St Ambrose reflects on God's provision of manna as daily food in the wilderness as a prefiguring of the Eucharist, 'the bread that came down from heaven, so that whoever eats it shall never die, for it is the body of Christ', who continually exercises his power over the creatures of bread and wine at every Mass. For God's people in the wilderness, water flows from the rock; for us, blood flows from Christ. Manna and water provide temporary relief from physical hunger and thirst, but whoever partakes devoutly of the Eucharist will never hunger and thirst again. The manna and water were symbolic; the Eucharist is reality.

Matthew 12:1–8: The Son of Man is master of the sabbath.

Saturday

St Ambrose continues to reflect that Elijah had power to bring down fire from heaven. In the Eucharist Christ has power to change his own created elements.

2 Kings 2:1–15: Elijah went up by a whirlwind into heaven. God alters the natural order and at the same time prefigures the ascension of Christ.

Intercessions

For asthmatics; for healers, the healed, and the unhealed.

That we may acknowledge the Blessed Trinity as having mastery over the world, nature, and our souls and bodies.

For greater faith and trust in God, and for less worship in our society of the gods of materialism, superstitious prediction and self.

Thanksgiving for our baptism, and for the Eucharist.

Place of spiritual retreat

With Jesus and the disciples in the cornfields, when he tells the legalistic Pharisees, 'The Son of Man is master of the sabbath', as in Matthew 2:1–8.

SUNDAY AND WEEK SIXTEEN OF ORDINARY TIME

PERENNIAL PHLOX *P. maculata* 'Alpha'; *P. maculata* 'Omega'

Cultivation and uses

P. maculata 'Alpha' has rose-pink flowers, *P. maculata* 'Omega' white with a lilac eye. Both grow to a height of 3 feet and spread for 18 inches. Other usual colours are various shades of pink, violet and purple. *P. paniculata* 'Eventide' is lavender blue. The maculatas bloom in summer and the paniculatas in late summer. Their showy flowers are produced in large trusses and are good for cutting. Plant, maintain and propagate as for Masterwort. The name 'Phlox' is Greek, meaning 'flame', and also Greek for a plant with flame-coloured flowers. Our modern phloxes are native to the eastern United States and were brought to Britain from there in the early eighteenth century. The paniculatas quickly became popular because their late blooming added colour to the garden when many other summer flowers had faded.

Lore and liturgy

I have chosen the Phlox this week for three reasons: first, because the named varieties 'Alpha' and 'Omega' call to mind the eternal sovereignty of God; second, because 'flame' has connotations with the flame of faith, the new Fire of Easter, which is Christ, and with the tongues of fire of the Holy Spirit at Pentecost; third, because in the language of flowers the Phlox represents unanimity. The aptness of the plant is clearly demonstrated by the week's liturgical readings, any one of which could be taken as a springboard for meditation day by day:

Sunday

Wisdom 12:13, 15–19: Your sovereignty over all makes you lenient to all. You show your strength when your sovereign power is questioned.

Romans 8:26–7: The Spirit expresses our plea in a way that could never be put into words.

Monday

Exodus 14:5–18: The Egyptians will learn that I am the Lord.

Matthew 12:38–42: The Pharisees spoke up: 'Master,' they said, 'we should like to see a sign from you.'

From *The Letter of St Ignatius of Antioch to the Magnesians*: One united supplication, one hope in love and innocent joyfulness.

Tuesday

Exodus 14:21–15:1: The Lord overthrew the Egyptians in the midst of the sea.

Exodus 15:8–10: You blew with your breath, the sea closed over them.

Matthew 12:46–50: Anyone who does the will of my Father … is my brother and sister and mother.

St Ignatius of Antioch (*op. cit.*): You have Jesus Christ within you.

Wednesday

Exodus 16:1–5, 9–15: I will rain down bread from heaven.

From Thomas à Kempis's *The Imitation of Christ*: The kingdom of God is peace and joy in the Spirit.

Thursday

Exodus 19:1–20: The Lord descended on Sinai in the form of fire.

From St Ambrose, *Discourses on the Psalms*: The light of your countenance is imprinted in us.

Friday

Psalm 19:8–11: The law of the Lord is perfect.

John 6:68: Lord, you have the message of eternal life.

2 Corinthians 5:1–21: The ministry of reconciliation.

From *The Confessions* of St Augustine, Book 10: Christ died for all.

Saturday

Psalm 50: The God of gods, the Lord has spoken and summoned the earth.
Proverbs 10:12: Hatred stirs up strife, but love overlooks all offences.
From St John Chrysostom (347–407), *Homily 13*: Like St Paul we have opened wide our hearts in love of our brothers.

Intercessions

Thanksgiving for the flowers in our domestic and public gardens.

That the sovereignty of God may be more widely acknowledged and revered in the world he created.

That the flame of faith may burn strongly in us.

That the flame of the Holy Spirit may inspire and unite us.

That the flame of Christ's love may be shown in our love for him, and in our love for our brothers and sisters.

Place of spiritual retreat

Among the crowd, listening to Jesus when he told them that anyone who does God's will is a close member of his family, as in Matthew 12:46–50.

SUNDAY AND WEEK SEVENTEEN OF ORDINARY TIME

MYRTLE *Myrtus communis*; Bridal myrtle; Jew's myrtle

Cultivation, history and uses

This evergreen shrub, which is native to the Mediterranean and south-western Europe, is erect in form and can be grown as a single specimen or, in mild areas, as a dense, windbreak hedge. As a shrub it will grow to a height and spread of 10 feet. It has lustrous leathery leaves with oil-producing glands that emit a juniper-like scent when crushed. The flowers are white and fragrant with golden stamens. These appear in spring and summer and are followed by blue-black berries. The cultivar *M. communis* 'Floro Pleno' is similar in habit but its double white flowers last longer and it can reach 15 feet in height. *M. communis* 'Tarentina' is a compact variant that reaches a height of 3 to 6 feet. This has narrow leaves and produces smaller, pink-tinged flowers in late summer and autumn, followed by white berries. Myrtles appreciate well-drained, neutral to alkaline soil in sun and, if given protection, they may survive a winter temperature as low as −10 degrees Celsius. Trim in spring and remove any damaged shoots.

The Greeks attributed a cleansing power to myrtle and placed it with their dead. Medicinal use of myrtle goes at least as far back as Dioscorides, who prescribed the berry juice with wine for stomach upsets. From Pliny we learn that all parts of the plant were used to treat a host of injuries, minor complaints and life-threatening diseases. The plant has mildly disinfectant and astringent properties, and these were known during the Renaissance. Rembert Dodoens, in his herbal of 1554, recommended dried myrtle leaves to treat infected nails, and as an anti-perspirant. In modern herbalism the fresh or dried leaves are used to make douches. Myrtle is also given internally for bronchitis, sinusitis and cough and externally for gum infections and haemorrhoids. The distilled oil is used to treat acne. Harvest leaves as needed and fruit when ripe.

Myrtle (Hebrew *hadas*) is mentioned six times in the Bible: in Isaiah's vision of the messianic future he saw myrtle growing where previously there had only been thorns (Isaiah 11:19; 53:13). Certainly to the Jews, myrtle became a symbol of peace and reconciliation, hence the English alternative name. (In Wales, until quite recently, to kill a myrtle plant signified the killing of love and peace.) The Arabic word for fresh myrtle is *astur* and from this comes the name of the beautiful biblical Queen Esther. Myrtle wood has sometimes been used to make incense, and it is recorded in Vaz, Switzerland (1885), as having been used on Palm Sunday instead of palm.

Lore and liturgy

I have chosen myrtle this week mainly because of its marriage symbolism (see below), but first there are several other resonances in its lore, which will lead us into the liturgy:

Magistrates and judges in Athens were crowned with myrtle wreaths after having been sworn in to office, and it therefore became a symbol of authority and wise judgement. In 1 Kings 3:5, 7–12 Solomon asks for, and is granted, 'an understanding mind ... able to discern between good and evil'. Tuesday's responsorial Psalm at Mass speaks of God's justice: 'The Lord works vindication and justice, for all who are oppressed (Psalm 103:6); and Friday's Mass Gospel finds the people reacting to the deeds of Jesus with astonished curiosity: 'Where did this man get this wisdom, and these mighty works? Is not this the carpenter's son?' (Matt. 13:54–8).

Pliny refers to two special myrtle bushes in Rome, one representing the

Plebeian, and the other the Patrician sections of Roman society. Depending on which one flourished or ailed, the respective power of the two groups was indicated, and therefore the state or destiny of the people was prophesied. In scriptural prophecy, Zechariah sees the angel of the Lord standing among the myrtle trees (Zech. 1:11). Here, through the angel, God speaks of his anger but assures his prophet of eventual mercy and compassion. However, Tuesday's Mass Gospel is in stark contrast. Here Jesus himself prophesies, through the parable of the weeds, the most important aspect of the future for all mankind. Afterwards he privately uncovers its symbolism to his disciples: 'The one who sows the good seed is the Son of Man; the field is the world, and the good seed means the sons of the kingdom; the weeds are the children of the evil one, and the enemy who sowed them is the devil; the harvest is the close of the age, and the reapers are angels' (Matt. 13:37–9).

Myrtle leaves and flowers are used to make *eau d'ange* ('angel water'), a preparation for purifying the skin. Tuesday's Gospel continues with Christ's elaboration of the role of the angels at 'the close of the age'. Certainly they will not be concerned with the purity of anyone's outward complexion! 'The Son of Man will send his angels and they will gather out of his kingdom all causes of sin and all evil doers and will throw them into the furnace of fire, where there will be weeping and gnashing of teeth. Then the righteous will shine like the sun in the kingdom of their Father' (Matt. 13:41–4). These are they who will have become true images of his Son, as he intended. 'For those whom he foreknew he also predestined to be conformed to the image of his Son, in order that he might be the first-born among many brethren'(Rom. 8:28–30).

In antiquity the myrtle had more to do with erotic love and fertility, than with the Christian married love, compassion, or the self-control and chastity it later came to symbolize. Its leaves were used to decorate the temple of Aphrodite, a practice continued by the Romans for whom the myrtle was sacred to Venus. They crowned her with it and she was sometimes known as Myrtilla. Monday's responsorial psalm speaks of other gods that cannot save: 'They made a calf at Horeb and worshipped a molten image. They exchanged the glory of God for the image of an ox that eats grass. They forgot God their saviour.' The only difference between the Romans, and the Israelites is that the people of the One God should have known better. There is an ancient Arab legend that narrates how Adam brought a sprig of myrtle with him from Paradise to remind him of the bower where he had declared his love to Eve. At Mass on

Monday, the gospel reminds us that all knowledge is in Christ: 'I will proclaim what has been hidden from the foundation of the world' (Matt. 13:31–5).

In Christian art and symbolism the myrtle may signify love, or it may refer to those who have been converted by Christ. Sometimes it may represent compassion for the distress of others. Two important first Office readings this week relate to this: on Sunday we have 2 Corinthians 7:2–16, in which St Paul begs that they 'make room for us in your hearts' and then goes on, 'I have great pride in you; I am filled with comfort. With all our afflictions, I am overjoyed.' On Tuesday, in 2 Corinthians 9:1–15, he writes of the spiritual benefits that will be received by those who have contributed to a collection he has raised for the Christians of Jerusalem. Using farming imagery he says: 'The point is this: he who sows sparingly will also reap sparingly, and he who sows bountifully will also reap bountifully.' We should not give reluctantly or under a feeling of compulsion, 'for God loves a cheerful giver'. Giving of this kind will be rewarded with 'every blessing in abundance', and 'you will be enriched in every way'. We must show compassion and love for others in the same way that God shows them to us: 'The Lord is abounding in steadfast love' (Tuesday's responsorial: Ps. 103:8).

The scriptural myrtle is *M. communis*, which still grows to a height of 20 feet on Mount Hermon and on the slopes of Mount Carmel. This reminds me of another great biblical mountain, Sinai, on which Moses was with the Lord for forty days and nights. 'And he wrote on the tablets the words of the covenant, the ten commandments' (Exod. 33 and 34; Tuesday, first Mass reading). We know from Nehemiah 8:15 that myrtle was used to cover the huts during the Feast of Tabernacles (booths). And the institution of this and other solemn festivals is recorded in Friday's first Mass reading (Leviticus 23:1-37). 'On the fifteenth day of this seventh month ... there shall be a festival of booths to the Lord' (23:34). This, together with Thursday's reading from Exodus, where 'The Glory of the Lord filled the Tabernacle', is for Christians a clear prefiguring of the Blessed Sacrament.

In Britain there are many old superstitions about the growing of myrtle, one being that one should plant it with a proud look on one's face, and another that it should be watered daily, and have great pride taken in it by its owner. The correct focus of pride is pointed out by St Paul in Wednesday's first Office reading, 'Let the one who boasts, boast in the Lord' (2 Cor. 10:1–11:6).

Pliny mentions marriage wreaths, whose myrtle leaves were reputed to encourage the growth and longevity of the love between the newlyweds. In ancient Palestine brides and bridegrooms wore crowns of myrtle and roses, and as recently as 1965 young brides in the Mediterranean region are known to have worn or carried myrtle. In Britain in Victorian times it was popular as a bridal flower and, although it has fallen from general favour, all brides of the British royal family are reputed to carry a sprig in their bouquets, either from the tree in the Royal Lodge garden at Windsor or from the one at Osborne on the Isle of Wight. In Lent in Tuscany lovers would wear myrtle or box to reveal their love. They would then embrace on Easter Sunday and be married in July. And so the myrtle became a symbol of spring and, because of its white flowers and fragrance, also came to represent beauty, youth, chastity, charm and purity. The direct opposites of the latter three virtues feature in Monday's Mass Gospel, where we read of the unholy alliance between Herod and Herodias, which results in the gratuitous execution of St John the Baptist (Matt. 14:1–12).

It is above all Thursday's second Office reading that guided my choice of myrtle as this week's plant, as a prime example of how secular myth, custom and even superstition can lead to spiritual considerations. In this extract from *The Instruction to Catechumens*, St Cyril of Alexandria meditates on the Church as the bride of Christ. The Church as Christ's bride 'fulfils the type and carries out the pattern of the Jerusalem which is from above, which is free and the mother of us all. Though she was at first childless, she is now the parent of a mighty family, in which are to be found apostles, prophets, teachers, workers of miracles, healers, helpers, administrators, speakers in various languages; and every type of virtue: wisdom, intelligence, self control, justice, mercy, humanity, and invincible endurance in persecution.' This is the list against which we must measure ourselves and our church communities, to find out whether we are truly a part of this 'Bride of Christ'. We have come a long way from the love bower of Adam and Eve, from Athenian magistrates and from the temples of Aphrodite and Venus.

Intercessions
For those suffering from conditions that myrtle is used to treat.

For peace and reconciliation between nations; for all who make incense, and that it may represent an ever-deepening prayer life in our churches; for recourse to the sacrament of Reconciliation and for peace of soul.

That those in authority may govern and judge wisely and with equity; for greater recognition that Christ is the true Wisdom and Equity, and for increased reverence for his presence in our tabernacles.

That we may be among the righteous who will shine like the sun in the kingdom of the Father.

Thanksgiving for our faith and salvation in Christ.

For all who will be married today, and for all engaged and married couples; for those in loving, faithful partnerships whose unions are unblessed by the Church.

For consecrated virgins and widows; for greater self-control.

For compassion and generosity toward others.

For less worship of the 'false gods' of our times.

For all who collude to harm and kill the innocent, and for their victims.

For time and space to meditate on the mysteries of faith.

For the Church, the 'Bride of Christ'.

Places of spiritual retreat

In the crowd listening to the 'kingdom' parables, or in the synagogue with the people who were astonished at the wisdom and power of Jesus, as in Matthew 13.

ENVOI

And so I leave Ordinary Time until the final book of the present series completes the church and gardening year, and I close this section with a poem/hymn that expresses what I have tried to do in many of its entries, particularly this last one, that is to show how the power of the Father, Word and Spirit can convert myth, superstition and misguided theories into the truth. Alchemy was the forerunner of modern science that sought the elixir of life and a formula for the conversion of base metal into gold. With delicate, kindly wit and humble faith, George Herbert here uses its terminology to show where the truth really lives:

'The Elixir'

Teach me my God and King,
In all things thee to see,
And what I do in anything
To do it as for thee.

A man that looks on glass,
On it may stay his eye;
Or if he pleaseth, through it pass,
And then the heaven espy.

All may of thee partake;
Nothing can be so mean,
Which with this tincture, 'for thy sake,'
Will not grow bright and clean.

A servant with this clause
Makes drudgery divine;
Who sweeps a room, as for thy laws,
Makes that and the action fine.

This is the famous stone
That turneth all to gold;
For that which God doth touch and own
Cannot for less be told.

(George Herbert, 1593–1633; Tune: Sandys)

Part 3

Solemnities and Saints' Days
28 April–1 August

INTRODUCTORY NOTE

Saints' days that occur in Lent before 26 April appear in *Thorn, Fire and Lily*, the Lenten book of this present series. Generally, as in that volume, I do not deal fully here with optional days. Exceptions are made occasionally for days that are particularly relevant to the Christian history of the English-speaking world, or for saints whose lives and attributes make them particularly helpful in deepening spiritual life through gardening. The optional celebration of the Immaculate Heart of Mary is a case in point. This is always celebrated on the Saturday following the Solemnity of the Sacred Heart of Jesus and, like the Sacred Heart, is dependent on the timing of Easter for its date in any particular year. It is therefore moveable, and it appears here as it does in the Breviary, between the Feast of the Visitation (31 May) and Justin Martyr (1 June). Other optional memoria days appear on the next pages with an assigned plant and its meaning. Unless otherwise stated, Places of Spiritual Retreat in this part of the book are normally in the Gospel of the day's Proper Mass.

OPTIONAL MEMORIA DAYS

April

28. Peter Chanel   1803–41   Priest and Martyr   Sorrel
Sorrel represents maternal tenderness, and sorrel tea eases both exhaustion and sunburn/stroke. During his missionary work on the island of Futuna (Australasia), St Peter worked to exhaustion-point every day and frequently suffered from the effects of the sun.

30. Pius V   1504–72   Pope   Chamomile
This Pope was renowned for his humility.

May

1. Joseph the Worker   First century   Foster-father of   Bee orchis
                                          Jesus

109

The plant symbolizes diligence and industry.

7. John of Beverley	d. 721	Bishop	All-Heal

St John is alleged to have worked miracle cures.

12. Nereus, Achilleus and Pancras	Second century d. early fourth century	Martyrs	Climbing 'Peace' rose
15. Pachomius Isidore the Farmer	d. 346 1070–1130	Religious	Egyptian privet Spanish onion
18. John I	d. 526	Pope	'Tuscany superb' rose

This pope was born in Tuscany.

20. Bernadine of Siena	1380–1444	Priest	Scarlet lychnis

St Bernadine is described as having had 'bright, beaming eyes' which is the plant's meaning in *The Language of Flowers*.

25. Gregory VII and Mary Magdalen of Pazzi	*c.*1028–85 1566–1607	Pope Mystic	Tulip 'Triumph'
30. Joan of Arc	1412–31		Crocus 'Joan of Arc'

June

2. Marcellinus and Peter	d. *c.* 304	Martyrs	Whitebeam

The place of their execution was later named 'White Wood'.

6. Norbert	*c.*1080–1134	Bishop	Rose 'Faith'

'Faith is Norbert's great quality' (from *The Life of St Norbert*, extract from proper Office of Readings)

8. William of York	d. 1154	Bishop	White rose
15. Vitus	d. *c.* 303	Martyr	Paeony

The plant is being researched for possible use in the treatment of convulsions.

17. Juliana Falconieri	1270–1341	Religious	Iris Florentina

St Juliana was born in Florence.

19. Romuald	d. *c.* 1027	Abbot	Rose 'Pearl Drift'

St Romuald is described as an abandoned pearl because of his holiness and lonely death (see proper Office reading, from the biography by St Peter Damian).

22. Paulinus of Nola   355–431   Bishop   Sweet William
St Paulinus was a poet, and the French for Sweet William is *Œillet de Poète*.

26. John Southworth   1592–1654   Martyr   London Pride
St John's body is in Westminster Cathedral.

27. Cyril of Alexandria   370–444   Bishop and Doctor   Tansy
History shows St Cyril to have been combative in his defence of orthodoxy, and Tansy has the meaning, 'I make war upon you'.

30. Martyrs of Rome   First century   Roman
    under Nero   pine

July

5. Antony Maria   1502–39   Priest   Million Bells
    Zaccaria
St Antony founded an Order of nuns and one of priests and, among many other achievements, instituted the practice of ringing church bells on Friday afternoons, in memory of the death of Christ.

6. Maria Goretti   1890–1902   Virgin Martyr   Lily
The plant symbolizes purity.

10. Oliver Plunkett   1625–61   Bishop and Martyr   Fleabane
St Oliver, the last Catholic to die for his faith at Tyburn, said of that death that it would be a mere 'fleabiting' compared with the suffering of Christ.

14. Camillus de Lellis   1550–1614   Priest   Nasturtium
St Camillus was a Capuchin friar, and the French for nasturtium is *Capucine*.

21. Laurence of Brindisi 1559–1619   Doctor   Nasturtium
St Laurence was also a Capuchin and so shares the nasturtium with St Camillus.

24. John Boste and   1597   Martyrs   Veronica
    other English
    Martyrs
The plant symbolizes fidelity.

30. Peter Chrysologus   380–450   Priest and Doctor   Olive
'For you the earth is embroidered with flowers, groves, and fruit; for you is created a beautiful, well-ordered and marvellous multitude of living things' (proper Office reading, an extract from St Peter Chrysologus, *Sermon 148.*)

APRIL

29 APRIL
St Catherine of Siena, Doctor (1347–80)

WELD *Reseda luteola*

Cultivation, uses and lore

Weld is biennial, producing long
wavy leaves in its first year and
elegant, curved spikes of small,
yellowish green flowers in its second.
In full sun and fertile, well-drained
alkaline soil it can reach up to
5 feet in height. The seed, which
stays fertile for years, should be sown
in late summer. The whole
flowering plant will give a
strong yellow dye for wool and
silk, which was known to the Stone
Age inhabitants of Switzerland.
Later, it was one of the three plants
used by medieval dyers, the
other two being woad for blue
and madder for red. It is a
native British plant but in the
Middle Ages demand by the
rapidly growing wool industry outstripped supply and it had to be
imported from France. (Up to 6 lb of weld plants are necessary to dye
1 lb of cloth.) Large-scale cultivation ensued in Kent, Essex and
Yorkshire, and weld continued to be used even after the introduction of
chemical dyes. Now it is an outcast in waste spaces, field edges and
limestone quarries. Like the sunflower, it is heliotropic; that is, its
flowers follow the daily course of the sun, facing east in the morning, but
by late afternoon turning to face the sunset. *Reseda luteola* derives from

Latin, *reseda* from the verb meaning 'to heal' or 'to calm' and *luteola* meaning 'yellow'.

St Catherine and weld

St Catherine is one of several saints usually depicted in art with a lily, and the primrose is also dedicated to her. But I have chosen weld, first because she was the daughter of a well-to-do Sienese dyer and would therefore probably have been familiar with it. She was a twin in a family of twenty-two children and apparently inherited great determination from her mother. Her childhood inclination towards ascetic prayer and penance was followed by a refusal to consider marriage, and she eventually became a Dominican tertiary. She seems to have spent long years in contemplative preparation before embracing the active life, nursing the sick during the famine of 1370 and the plague of 1374. At this time she met the men and women who would become her disciples and companions on her frequent journeys. They included Dominicans, Augustinians and an English Austin friar, William Flete. It is known that she was treated at home more like a skivvy than a daughter. Certainly she was not well educated as a child and did not learn to read and write until adulthood. One wonders if it was the 'disciples' who were called to sow the seeds of the orthodox theological insight and discernment she was later to display in *The Dialogues*, upon which her qualification as a Doctor of the Church largely rests. Feeling a call to preach, she was, as a woman of her time, reluctant to obey, but Raymund of Capua, her confessor and eventual biographer, encouraged her and she did indeed preach while continuing to work actively to combat poverty in society and abuses in the Church. She was filled with the love for others commanded by Christ and spent time and energy trying to bring peace among the City States of Italy and in defence of the papacy during its exile in Avignon. Before she was twenty-one she had lost two of her sisters, and she hardly ate after that. Later, as part of her struggles for the papacy she went on hunger strike, collapsed as a result and then would take only the host in Communion. She died at the age of thirty-three. This self-starvation has led to accusations that she was anorexic, and therefore caused her own death. Catherine, however, did not fast severely on account of the misperception, characteristic of anorexics, that she was too fat, but from a desire to control her will and so to draw closer to union with the suffering Christ. She may not be unique in that her mysticism was nourished by active works rather than withdrawal from the world, but she is certainly unique in that she is the only laywoman to have been made a Doctor of the Church in its entire history. That Church chooses a reading today from her *Dialogues* 'On Divine Revelation'. In it are found the other reasons why I have chosen weld for St Catherine's day. As weld turns to the light of the sun, so St Catherine constantly mentions light in this extract. She speaks of herself as eager in God's light to see him who is the light. And in the light of her understanding, in God's light she has tasted and seen the abyss that is 'the eternal Trinity', and the beauty of its creation. God, she says, is an ever-burning fire, never extinguished yet burning away the self-love of the soul and taking away coldness. 'By your light,' she continues, 'you enlighten our minds, as by light you have brought me to know your truth.' And in this light she knows him as supreme, blessed, incomprehensible, inestimable good and beauty, and wisdom beyond all wisdom and beauty, the food of angels given to us in the fire of God's love for us.

Readings
James 3:17–18: The wisdom that comes from above is marked chiefly by its purity.
Sirach 39:1–10: The wise man is wise through his study of the word of God.
Wisdom 7:13–14: What I learned without self-interest, I pass on without reserve.
Psalm 45: To the king I must speak the song I have made, my tongue as nimble as the pen of a scribe.
1 Corinthians 7:25–40: Christian virginity.
Song of Songs 8:7: Love is a fire no waters avail to quench.
Wisdom 8:21: I perceived that I would not possess wisdom unless God gave her to me.
Revelation 19:6, 7: The time has come for the wedding of the Lamb, and his bride has prepared herself for it.
Matthew 5:13–16: You are the salt of the earth.
Matthew 11:25–30: You have hidden these things from the learned and have revealed them to mere children.
Luke 10:38–42: Martha welcomed Jesus; Mary chose the better part.

Intercessions
For those who work in the textile and dyeing industries.
    For twins and members of large families.
    For greater determination, prayer and penance.
    For Dominicans and Augustinians.

For the people of Sienna.

For the illiterate, and for the educated; for theologians.

Thanksgiving for the lives and works of the Doctors of the Church and for those who teach and preach the faith.

For sufferers from eating disorders; for those bereaved of siblings.

Thanksgiving for the writings of St Catherine and all the other mystics.

For greater self-control and self-denial in the service of others.

For greater desire to see, know and love the Light of Christ.

For the priests and people of parishes and institutions under the patronage of St Catherine of Siena.

2 MAY
St Athanasius, Bishop and Doctor (295–373)

EGYPTIAN LOTUS *Nymphaea lotus*; sacred lotus; white lotus

Cultivation, history and uses

This aquatic perennial has tuberous roots and floating leaves. Its large fragrant flowers lie on the surface of the water and open at night and in the morning. The fruits, which contain many small seeds, ripen under water. The plant can spread for up to 5 feet, so if space is limited, a smaller white water lily will evoke a similar symbolism. *N. lotus* appreciates full sun, fairly rich soil in still water which is at least a foot deep, and a minimum temperature of 70° F. (In winter dormant tubers can be stored in moist sand.) If the water is too deep or the soil too rich the blooms may be inhibited. Sow seed under cover in spring or divide tubers in early summer. In the east the sacred lotus has been used in medicine for at least 1500 years. In modern herbalism the roots are made into decoctions for the treatment of a range of conditions from dyspepsia to insomnia. They are used either fresh or dried, and the fresh open flowers are infused to calm palpitations. In parts of India, Sri Lanka and China the roots are used as a starchy vegetable, and pickled fruits and seeds are an addition to curries. The crushed seed in water is an old remedy for diabetes.

Both parts of the botanical name are from Greek: *Nymphaea* means 'water nymph', and *lotus* is a Greek word thought to be of Semitic origin. However, the plant appears more often in Indian and Egyptian mythologies than in those of ancient Greece or Rome. To the Hindus the lotus symbolizes creation, spiritual flowering and self-awareness. The

Buddha draws an analogy from the development of the lotus: flowers that do not reach the surface are compared with people who are inward-looking; those that do not open, with people who try to open themselves to knowledge; and the fully open flower with those who open themselves entirely to knowledge and enlightenment. In China, before the advent of Buddhism, the lotus symbolized open-heartedness, purity, fertility and creative power. In ancient Egypt the lotus was dedicated to the sun god Ra, who was also the god of eloquence, and there is an Egyptian saying, still in use at the beginning of the twentieth century, that the more lotus plants there were, the richer the blessing. The Israelites encountered the lotus during their 430-year stay in Egypt, but they valued it for its beauty rather than for is 'sacredness'. The lotus appears as a symbol of purity in Indian Christian art. In the language of flowers a lotus in a bouquet represents eloquence and, in water, purity of heart.

St Athanasius and the lotus

Athanasius was born in Alexandria, hence the choice of an Egyptian plant to celebrate his day. But there are other resonances in the lore of the plant that chime with his life, character and work. His major concern, as we saw on Trinity Sunday (page 48), was with the purity of orthodoxy, particularly in connection with the divinity of Christ and the doctrine of the Holy Trinity. As the lotus loves the sun, so Athanasius uses the image of the sun in his argument: 'The sun's rays belong really to it and yet the sun's substance is not divided or lessened. The sun's substance is whole and its rays are perfect and whole. These rays do not lessen the substance of its light but are a true offspring from it. Likewise we understand that the Son is begotten not from outside the Father but from the Father himself. The Father remains whole while "the stamp of his substance" (Heb. 1:3) is eternal and preserves the Father's likeness and unchanging image' (*Orations againt the Arians: 2*). The Western Church in particular celebrated his eloquence and benefited from it. Besides *The Incarnation of the Word* and *The Letters to Serapion*, he also wrote 367 Easter letters to the Egyptian churches. These are important not only because they set out, for the first time, the New Testament canon more or less as we have it today but also because they are to some extent the fruit of his stay at Rome, where he both influenced and was influenced by the Church there. His *Life of Antony* (St Antony of Egypt, 251–356; 17 January) is the record of the lone fight of this hermit against the powers of evil and helped to spread the monastic ideal to the West, playing an important role in the conversion of St Augustine of Hippo (354–430; 28 August). As the lotus represents purity of heart and in Hinduism and Buddhism is used to represent spiritual growth and enlightenment, so St Athanasius makes it clear that asceticism, virginity and mysticism are the most effective means of restoring the divine image to humanity. It is this aspect of his writings and teachings upon which the Eastern Church has concentrated. The Jews came to know the lotus during their exile in Egypt. Athanasius was bishop of Alexandria for forty-six years, but 'the see-saw of imperial politics' (Paul Burns, *Butler's Lives of the Saints* (new concise edition), Burns & Oates/Liturgical Press, 2003) during his lifetime forced him to spend repeated periods in exile from Egypt until his last seven years. Immediately after his death Athanasius was venerated as a 'confessor' (that is someone revered as a saint even though he had not been martyred), and from early times he has been regarded as a Doctor of the universal Church.

Readings
Sirach 15:1–6: He will fill him with a spirit of understanding.
Sirach 19:1–10: The wise man is wise through his study of the word of God.
2 Timothy 1:13–14; 2:1, 3: Keep this precious thing with the help of the Holy Spirit.
Matthew 10:27: What I tell you in the dark, utter in the light.
Matthew 10: 22–5: If they persecute you in one town, take refuge in the next.

Intercessions
For sufferers from stomach disorders, insomnia, heart disease and diabetes.
For the peoples of Egypt, China, India and Sri Lanka.
For greater understanding, faith, spiritual growth and purity of heart.
For our priests and bishops. For eloquence when we speak of our faith.
Thanksgiving for spiritual writers in our own day, and for publishers who disseminate their works.
For the priests and people of churches and institutions under the patronage of St Athanasius.

3 MAY
Feast of SS Philip and James, Apostles (first century)

'THE LILIES OF THE FIELD'

The differences of opinion as to the identity of these plants are really rather irrelevant, for it is not what they were, but *how* they grew that was the point our Lord was making when he referred to them. However, the following have been suggested as specific contenders: crown marguerite (*Chrysanthemum coronarium*); white daisy (*Anthemis paleestina*); *iris*; *gladiolus*; and even martagon lily (*L. Martagon*), with its matt purple and dark spotted flowers. But the most popular candidate seems to be the poppy anemone (*A. coronaria*). Like most of its rivals, this plant grows wild in the Holy Land and its royally scarlet and purple flowers, when seen in drifts of natural colour, certainly challenge 'Solomon in all his glory'. But I prefer to think that Jesus was using the term lily in a general sense, to mean any or all of the spectacularly beautiful wild flowers of the Palestinian countryside of his time. Many still grow there and are beautifully photographed in *Illustrated Encyclopedia of Bible Plants* by Nigel F. Hepper (Inter-Varsity Press, 1992). Our own woodland or wild-flower meadow gardens cause the Matthew and Luke texts to spring readily to mind.

SS Philip and James and 'the lilies of the field'

For St Philip I could also have chosen horseradish or the horse chestnut tree, as his name means 'lover of horses', or the rose 'Philippa'; for St James I could have had Jerusalem cowslip (lungwort) or the rose 'The Bishop', since he is traditionally regarded as the first bishop of the city. Teasel would also be appropriate for him as he was supposedly beaten to death with a fuller's club. But I wanted something that would have been familiar to both apostles, and moreover one that carries a lesson taught to them by Christ. On the several occasions in this series when I have examined in detail the form of individual flowers – 'how they grow' – I have always been led to a realization of how wonderful is God's nature, but Christ's 'Yet I say unto you' is just as important. His lesson is, of course, that we should put total trust in God, for if he looks after 'the lilies of the field', how much more assiduously will he look after us.

Philip came from Bethsaida, a town on the shores of lake Galilee. Its actual site is the subject of dispute, but it was clearly not far from

Capernaum. It is thought that Philip may have been a follower of St John the Baptist before he became a disciple of Jesus. He persuaded Nathaniel to follow Jesus (John 1:43–51), and when the Greeks wanted to meet Jesus they approached Philip first (John 12:21ff.). He remarked before the feeding of the five thousand that there would not be enough food to go round (John 6:5–7). Clearly, his trust in the Lord was not yet of the order enjoined by Christ in the 'lilies of the field' texts. And he seems to have lacked recognition of Jesus' identity when he said to him during the 'last discourse', 'Show us the Father , and we shall be satisfied.' This elicited a gentle rebuke from Jesus: 'Have I been with you so long, and yet you do not know me, Philip? He who has seen me, has seen the Father; how can you say, "Show us the Father?"' (John 14: 8). And yet Philip was with the others at Pentecost (Acts 1:12–14) and is traditionally thought to have preached later in Phrygia and to have died and been buried at Hierapolis. His supposed relics were taken to Rome and put in the basilica of the Apostles. In art he is usually shown with a cross (he is thought to have been crucified), or with a loaf, in reference to his comment at the feeding of the five thousand. There is a screen painting of him at Salle church in Norfolk (where the Tallis Scholars made many of their recordings). Early manuscripts place St Philip's day on 1 May, indicating that James was added later. However, an ancient inscription in the Basilica of the Twelve Apostles records that it was originally dedicated to Philip *and* James.

James (the Less) was the son of Alphaeus and is often associated with the James whose mother stood by the cross and as the 'brother of the Lord' (cousin in modern parlance) who saw the risen Christ. He is also identified as the author of the Epistle of St James and, as already noted, is traditionally held to have been the first bishop of Jerusalem. Indeed, he seems to have stayed there until the end of his life: that is, if the tradition that he was condemned to death by the Sanhedrin in AD 62 is correct. If none of these associations is correct, then we know absolutely nothing about him.

In any case, as I appreciate the beauty of the wild flowers in my little woodland sanctuary, and consider God's care for them and for us, I remember that, like Philip and James, who were probably more used to examining fish than flowers, I am trying to follow our Lord's instructions.

Readings
Matthew 6:28–9: Consider the lilies of the field.
Luke 12:27: Solomon in all his glory was not arrayed like one of these.

Ephesians 4:11–13: Some Christ has appointed to be apostles.

Ephesians 2:19–22: You are no longer aliens in a foreign land.

2 Corinthians 5:19b–20: God has entrusted us with the news that God and humankind have been reconciled.

Acts 5:12a–14: Many remarkable things took place at the hands of the apostles.

1 Corinthians 15:1–8: The Lord appeared to James and then to the apostles.

Psalm 19: Their voice goes out through all the earth.

John 14:6–14: 'Have I been with you all this time, Philip and you still do not know me?'

Intercessions

Thanksgiving for the beauty of wild flowers and the lesson Christ drew from them.

For more trust in God.

That we may proclaim the Good News in our actions and in our manner of living.

For priests and people whose churches and institutions are under the patronage of SS Philip and James.

4 MAY
Feast (in England) of The Beatified Martyrs of England and Wales (died 1535–1679)

ROSE 'HERITAGE'

Characteristics and history

This English rose is from the main David Austin collection and was introduced in 1984. It is a repeat-flowering, well-formed, bushy shrub that grows to 4 feet × 4 feet. The medium-size cup-shaped flowers are a soft pink at the centre, fading to white at the edges. The David Austin catalogue describes the fragrance as having overtones of fruit, honey and carnation over a myrrh background. Some years ago David Austin had the brilliant idea of crossing some of the old garden roses with modern varieties, and his success has been prodigious. Even his catalogue is a rose-growers' dream, particularly for a literary and spiritual gardener. He is to be thanked not only for his exquisite roses, but also because he often names them after saints and characters from literature. (The catalogue, which has excellent photographs and close descriptions of each rose, is available from David Austin Roses Ltd, Bowling Green Lane, Albrighton, Wolverhampton WV7 3HB; email *retail@davidaustinroses.com*; website: www.davidaustinroses.com)

The beatified martyrs and the 'Heritage rose'

Thirteen of these martyrs were seminary priests; ten were Jesuits; three Benedictines; three Carthusians; one Brigettine; two Franciscans; one Austin Friar; four laymen; and three laywomen. They were executed for refusing to take the oath of supremacy, or simply for being priests, or for harbouring priests. A famous series of paintings in the English College in Rome includes, by papal permission, the martyrs of England from 1535 to 1583, who are accorded the same veneration as the proto-martyr St Alban (20 June, below), St Boniface (5 June, below); St Thomas of Canterbury (29 December in *Gardening with God*); and St Edmund (29 November and therefore not yet included in these volumes). The earth of England and Wales is soaked with the blood of her martyrs. They are our heritage and part of a shameful past that was riddled with intolerance, greed, appalling cruelty and religious faction, but they defended the faith we hold, and their blood is, as St Augustine famously said, the seed of the Church. Arguably the Catholic faith in England and Wales would be much weaker without their witness, and in this sense they are flower and fruit as well. They were canonized by Pope Paul VI on 25 October 1970.

Readings

2 Timothy 2:11–12: If we die with Christ, we shall live with him, and if we are faithful to the end, we shall reign with him.

2 Maccabees 7:1–2, 9–14: We are prepared to die rather than break the laws of our ancestors.

Revelation 12:10–12: In the face of death they would not cling to life.

Psalm 34: From all my terrors the Lord set me free.

Psalm 126: Those who sow in tears reap with shouts of joy.

2 Corinthians 6:4–10: Said to be dying, and here are we alive.

1 John 5:1–5: This is the victory over the world – our faith.

Matthew 10:17–22: You will be dragged before governors and kings for my sake.

Intercessions

Thanksgiving for our martyrs, and for the survival of our faith in England and Wales.

For an ecumenical spirit between the churches in these islands; for an end to intolerance, bigotry, cruelty and greed.

That we may bear our own trials, sorrows and pains with courage and endurance.

That we may stand up for our faith, amid the indifference, and even mockery or animosity from those around us.

For the priests and people who live and work in parishes and institutions dedicated to the Martyrs of England and Wales.

14 MAY
Feast of St Matthias, Apostle (first century)

PEACH *Prunus persica*

Cultivation and history

The botanical name means 'Persian plum' because *Persica*, from the Greek *persike*, means 'Persian'. The fruit is thought to have reached Europe from China by way of Iran and to have been grown in Spain for about two hundred years before arriving in Britain and having to cope with the vicissitudes of our climate. It was probably brought here by the Romans and then re-introduced in the thirteenth century. Lack of hardiness is not the problem in growing it here, and in fact a cold winter can be quite helpful. The problem is that, when the blossom opens in February, pollinating insects are scarce and there is still a danger of hard frosts at that crucial time. It also has to contend with our high winds and squally rain. If the peach survives all this, it must have a hot, sunny summer or its fruit will not ripen. (The related nectarine may look tougher but in fact is more delicate, and even when successful it does not yield as abundantly as the peach.) Gardeners in the south have the best chance of an edible crop if the tree is grown as a fan against a south- or south-west-facing wall. The peach is self-fertile so you only need one tree. 'Peregrine' and 'Duke of York' are the most frequently recommended varieties. It is possible to grow a peach in a large pot, taking it indoors from February until the cessation of frosts, or the tree can be grown against the wall of a lean-to greenhouse facing south-west, south, or south-east. There should be an annual spraying against peach-leaf curl, and the occasional hand pollination may be necessary. My own first 'Peregrine will be *in situ* in time for me to be able to report on its progress in the final book of this series.

St Matthias and the peach

The peach tree is chosen for St Matthias because the Church has dedicated it to him. The reason for this may have been that traditionally its fruit represents immortality, and one of the conditions of the candidacy of those who were suggested to replace Judas Iscariot was that they should have seen the risen Christ, as well having followed him from his Baptism in the Jordan to his Ascension into heaven. The field narrowed to two men with apparently the same qualifications, and so the other apostles drew lots and Matthias was elected. This has bothered some critics who would have preferred them to wait for the Holy Spirit to dictate the choice. In my humble view, this is rather precious. The Lord had presented them with two equally qualified candidates, and therefore the apostles could not be blamed if they thought that he would not mind which one was chosen. And also they could not know how soon the Holy Spirit *would* come.

Matthias is said to have preached first in Judaea but later, according to Greek tradition, in Cappadocia and near the Caspian Sea. He is also linked with Ethiopia. The fictitious *Acts of Andrew and Matthias in the City of the Cannibals* was very popular, but it confused St Matthias with St Matthew in some of its stories. This is also the case in the Anglo-Saxon poem *Andreas*, and there is often the same confusion in art. St Matthias's emblem is the axe or halberd with which he is thought to have been martyred. His supposed relics were taken from Jerusalem to Rome by the empress Helena, and some of these were moved to Trier in the eleventh century.

Readings

Acts 1:15–17, 20–6: The lot fell to Matthias and he was listed as one of the twelve apostles.
Psalm 113:1–8: The Lord makes him sit with the princes of his people.
John 15:16: You have not chosen me; I have chosen you. Go and bear fruit that will last.
John 9:17: I shall not call you servants anymore; I call you friends.

Intercessions

That we may seek to serve Christ above all things and obey his call wherever it may lead.

That we may constantly seek the truth.

Thanksgiving for the lives and mission of the twelve apostles.

For the priests and people of parishes and organizations under the patronage of St Matthias.

16 MAY
Feast (in Ireland) of St Brendan of Clonfert, Abbot
(died *c.* 580)

BIRD OF PARADISE *Strelitzia reginae*

Cultivation

This spectacular conservatory plant is an evergreen clump-forming perennial and is surprisingly easy to grow, provided it is given a temperature of 41–50°F. The only drawback is that new plants take up to six years to produce their first flowers. After that the blooms should appear each spring or summer and last for several weeks. The 6-inch orange and purple flowers are borne on 4-foot stems in skiff-shaped red-edged bracts, and are surrounded by large bluish-green leaves. The name 'Bird of Paradise' is given because the flowers resemble the heads of some exotic tropical bird. Feed and water freely in summer and water sparingly in winter.

St Brendan and the Bird of Paradise flower

Brendan was probably born near Tralee, fostered and educated by St Ita, and educated by St Erc, bishop of Kerry. He became a monk and founded several monasteries, the most important of which were Clonfert, Anna-down, Inishadroun and Ardfert. Like many another Celtic saint he was a great traveller, and he is believed to have visited St Columba (9 June, below) at Himba in Argyllshire. Other traditions are that he founded a monastery in Scotland, was abbot of Llancarvan in Wales and that he also went to Brittany with St Malo. From the ninth century onwards his cult has been strong in Ireland, Wales, Scotland and Brittany. This owed a great deal to the famous *Navigation of St Brendan*, a romance of the tenth or eleventh centuries. In it, the voyaging historical Abbot Brendan appears as a heroic adventurer who performs amazing feats before returning at last to die in Ireland. Written by Irish monks, at least in part, several centuries after Brendan's death, it seems to derive in content and style from Irish folklore and from early apocryphal Christian writings. Its popularity is witnessed by the survival of a hundred and sixteen medieval Latin manuscripts and the fact that it was translated into German, Italian, Flemish, Provençal and Norse, as well as into Middle English and French. In the nineteenth century Matthew Arnold (1822–88) wrote the tale in verse.

The *Navigation* is largely a fiction, but it has led me to choose 'Bird of Paradise' to celebrate St Brendan's feast day. It is basically the story of Brendan's quest, in the company of fourteen other monks, for the Island of Paradise in the Atlantic Ocean. His desire to leave Ireland in the tradition of Irish saints had been instilled by his mentor St Erc, and, after praying that God will provide an unknown country to visit, he is told by a holy man to search for 'The Land of Saints'. He sets sail from the Aran Islands. (There is probably a grain of truth here for many Irish missionary monks made their way from Ireland to the Hebrides, and round the northern-most part of Scotland to the Isles of Orkney, Shetland and the Faroes.) On the first stage of the journey he and his monks find an island with a holy man, and after going back to see him a year later they continue from that island until they find another, this time 'the paradise of Birds'. Here a bird, through its song, tells them that they must plan their future voyages around the liturgical year. They must punctuate their journeys as follows: Maundy Thursday with the holy man, Easter on the island; from Easter to Pentecost on the Island of Paradise with the birds; and from Christmas to Candlemas on the Island of Ailbe. The symbolism so far seems clear: each year of our lives is a voyage; our life is a voyage; and both should be punctuated as the bird indicated to St Brendan. The story continues with the monks eventually finding 'the Land of Promise', which is full of flowers and angels. Perhaps this section can be taken to represent the loveliness of our good intentions and our progress in the spiritual life. Brendan now goes to Britain and, after surviving great dangers, performing many miracles and founding many monasteries, he visits his sister Brig before he dies. He gives instructions for his body to be transported to Clonfert on a humble cart, so that it will go unnoticed and people will not quarrel over it. But although the body is unostentatiously accompanied by only one of his brother monks, it is buried with honour and reverence, but also with liturgy in honour of the Trinity. In this section of the story I read that the eventual success of our Christian lives is dependent on our fulfilment of the original good intentions, on spiritual formation and prayer, and on energetic and devoted service of others to the best of our means and ability. Finally St Brendan's instructions for his obsequies teach that our concern in arranging our own funerals should be that they should honour the Holy Trinity rather than ourselves.

Readings

1 Corinthians 7:29–31; 2:12: Our time is growing short. It is not the spirit of the world that we have received.

Colossians 3:1–17: Your life is hidden with Christ in God.

Psalm 21: He asked life of thee; thou gavest it to him, length of days for ever and ever.

Romans 12:1–28: The Christian life, a spiritual worship.

1 Corinthians 4:9–14: You are honourable, but we without honour.

Matthew 19:28–9: You who have left all things and followed me shall receive an hundredfold and shall possess life everlasting.

Luke 12:35–6; Matthew 24:42: See that you are dressed and ready for action, with you lamps lit: Stay awake because you do not know the day when your master is coming.

Intercessions

Thanksgiving for the life of St Brendan.

Thanksgiving for myths and legends surrounding the saints, which carry a spiritual symbolism that helps us prioritize our lives aright.

That we may follow the liturgy of the year with greater understanding and devotion.

That whatever good we do will be done for the glory of God.

For the priests and people of churches and institutions under the patronage of St Brendan.

126

19 MAY
SS Dunstan (909–88), Ethelwold (died *c*. 984) and Oswald (died 992), Bishops

ST DUNSTAN'S ROSE
BEAR'S BREECHES *Acanthus mollis*

Cultivation, characteristics and history

The St Dunstan's rose is a Kirshru rose and was introduced in 1991. It is a shrub of medium height, with vigorous foliage and bears clusters of fragrant, medium-sized lemon flowers. It is repeat-flowering.

Bear's Breeches is a statuesque long-lived plant with handsome leaves and tubular flowers borne on tall spikes above the foliage. These appear in July and August and are white or purple. The plant reaches a height of 3 feet and a spread of 2 to 3 feet. Plant singly or in groups from October to May in well-drained soil. It prefers alkaline dry soil in sun or light shade. Cut back almost to ground level after flowering but do not disturb the roots. If absolutely necessary, lift for division from October to March. The English name comes from the size and appearance of the leaves, which can be big, broad and hairy. *Acanthus* is the Latin form of the Greek *akanthos*, from *akanthea*, meaning thorn or prickle. It was introduced to Britain by the Romans and used for ornamental display, and is believed to have been re-introduced in 1548.

SS Dunstan, Ethelwold and Oswald, St Dunstan's Rose and Bear's Breeches

It is an amazing fact that by the early tenth century no monasteries for men had survived in England. I think of today's saints as a golden trio because in their restoration of English monasticism they relit the flames of faith, education and the arts. But each is golden in his own individual way: Dunstan, because of his skill as a metalworker, is patron of goldsmiths, jewellers and locksmiths; Oswald, of Danish descent, and therefore probably golden-haired, is reputed to have had a fine physique; and Ethelwold was a cook during his early life as a monk. All three receive a nod of respect every time I tend or gather my golden marjoram. However, I have chosen Bear's Breeches for them because in the language of flowers it signifies the arts. (This is probably because it was a favourite decoration in classical architecture, as on the capitals of Corinthian columns.) In the exercise of their authority as abbot–bishops, all three men contributed hugely to the arts. And it is appropriate that they should share a plant with St Benet Biscop (628–89), the teacher of Bede, who himself achieved so much in the same field (see *Gardening with God*, p. 292).

Dunstan was born at Baltonsborough in Somerset and began his religious life in a group of clerics at Glastonbury. His family was connected by marriage to the Wessex royal family, but Dunstan's erudition was so great that he was suspected of having attained it by witchcraft and was expelled from the court of King Athelstan. After his ordination by St Alphege (d. 951) he spent some time as a hermit, where he seems to have developed his talents in painting, embroidery and metalwork. In 939 King Edmund of Wessex gave Glastonbury to him and he was able to begin the creation of a truly Benedictine monastery there. Later he criticized the lax behaviour at the coronation of Edmund's successor, Edwy, and as a result was forced into exile in Ghent, where he experienced reformed monasticism according to the continental model. He was eventually recalled when King Edgar acceded to the throne and was made bishop of Worcester in 957, of London in 959 and archbishop of Canterbury in 960. Between them, and largely through monasticism, king and archbishop reformed the Church in England. Dunstan was personally responsible for the reform of several monasteries including Glastonbury, Bath and Westminster. One strong feature of this reform, which was supported and encouraged by Ethelwold and Oswald, was an emphasis on the work of the monastic scriptoria and craft workshops. This inspired some of Edgar's laws. Those of Andover, for instance, insisted that every priest should practise a handicraft. Edgar, whose personal life was a scandal, was not crowned until 973. The ceremony was largely drawn up by Dunstan and remains to this day the basis for the coronation of British monarchs. Dunstan's close association with royalty helped to secure his foundations against the jealousy of local landowners and the secular priesthood, who resented the restored prominence of the monks. Edward succeeded his father as king with Dunstan's help, but he was then murdered, and Ethelred, Edgar's half-brother, took the throne. In spite of a difficult relationship with the new king, Dunstan's work had resulted in the burgeoning of learning in the monasteries and in society at large, in marriage laws and in more faithful observance of the practice of fasting and abstinence. His reputation as a metalworker and artist is not without foundation. There are bells and organs attributed to him, and a set of tools at Mayfield convent in East Sussex is allegedly his. Manuscripts survive in the Bodleian library in Oxford that were probably written or owned by him. One, *The Glastonbury Book*, contains a painting of him kneeling before the cross. This could be his own work, as claimed by a thirteenth-century inscription beneath it: 'I, Dunstan, beg the merciful Christ to protect me, lest the storms of the underworld swallow me up.' Also attributed is a series of four drawings in the *Sherborne Pontifical*. These demonstrate Dunstan's christology, for they depict Christ crucified, as King, as the harbinger of the Gospel and finally as the Risen Lord.

Both Glastonbury and Canterbury claimed to have the bodily remains of St Dunstan, and the dispute was not settled in favour of the latter until 1508, when the tomb was opened at Canterbury. The turn of the millennium saw a revival of interest in him, and his tomb was again marked. In the view of this humble writer it is a pity that St Dunstan, and indeed SS Ethelwold and Oswald, have not been given at least a Memoria in the local calendar for England, so great was their joint contribution to our faith and culture.

Ethelwold was born in Winchester and, like Dunstan, was at the court of King Athelstan. Here they became friends and were ordained on the same day by St Alphege. Ethelwold joined Dunstan in his initial attempts to reform Glastonbury according to the Benedictine rule. Later he was given the derelict abbey at Abingdon and sent his disciple Osgar to study at Fleury in France. During Dunstan's exile under King Edwy, Ethelwold became the most important figure in the monastic reform and tutor to the future king Edgar. In 963 he was made bishop of Winchester, where a year later he replaced the cathedral canons with monks from Abingdon, thus founding the first monastic cathedral, a particularly English phenomenon. As a result the monastic reform gained ground and became associated with the monarchy, the king's main palace being but a stone's throw from the cathedral. Ethelwold restored several monasteries, including Milton in Dorset, and founded Peterborough in 966, Ely in 970 and Thorney, where he sometimes spent Lent living as a hermit, in 972. Ethelwold was apparently austere but dynamic in character, and one of the scribes who copied his work referred to him as *Boanerges* (son of thunder). He never returned to bed after Matins and ate meat only once every three months. He possessed considerable practical gifts. A cook at Glastonbury, as has already been noted, he later involved himself in the actual building work in new foundations. We know this because he is recorded as having fallen off a ladder and cracked his ribs while working at Abingdon. At Winchester he oversaw the building of the most powerful organ in England. This needed two monks to play it and had 400 pipes and 36 bellows. Bells and a candle sconce at Abingdon are also attributed to him. More importantly, a new style of illumination developed in Ethelwold's monasteries, apparently surpassing the products of many scriptoria in mainland Europe. Aelfric is the most famous product of Ethelwold's school of vernacular writing at Winchester. It produced accurate translations designed to meet the needs of the laity and the secular clergy. Ethelwold's Winchester also made a significant contribution to music in the form of the *Winchester Troper*, which contained the first English polyphony. As a result the cathedral enjoyed a rich and varied liturgy. However, the practical Ethelwold did not forget the earthly needs of Wintonians and built an aqueduct for them! He probably also wrote the *Regularis Concordia*, which was given out at a Congress in about 970. This was a statement of the reformed Benedictine observance as practised at Ghent, Fleury and Glastonbury and was sent to the thirty reformed monasteries in southern England. He also wrote a vernacular account of the reform and a version of the rule of St Benedict. By 971 the reformed monasteries provided about three-quarters of the episcopate. Ethelwold was an excellent advisor to the king and a kind father to his monks, but he also had a reputation for intransigence, a characteristic that must frequently have been necessary in the execution of his many varied and often difficult projects.

Oswald was the nephew of two archbishops, Oda of Canterbury and Oskytel of York. He was a canon of Winchester before becoming a monk. His training took place at Fleury, and he returned to England towards the end of the 950s. On Dunstan's recommendation he was made bishop of Worcester. Here he reformed the cathedral chapter much as Ethelwold had done at Winchester, building St Mary's Church, which developed finer liturgy than was current in the cathedral. This was so popular that it eventually became the cathedral. Later Oswald founded the monastery at Ramsey and filled it with most of the monks from Westbury-on-Trym, which he had founded earlier, and both Evesham and Pershore were founded from Ramsey. The scholarly Abbo of Fleury spent several years at Ramsey. He may have been the author of *The Life of Oswald*, a source that tells of his fine physique and wonderful singing voice. From it we know that he had an attractive and accessible personality and a great love of the poor. On the other hand he has been criticized for holding the see of York in plurality with that of Worcester and for failing to revive the monastery at Ripon, with the result that the monastic reform was mainly confined to the south and west of England. However, it must be said that some time after his death, St Oswald's monks *did* successfully venture north of the Humber. After the death of Edgar in 975 there was an anti-monastic backlash and some of Oswald's foundations were temporarily dispersed, but Ramsey survived this, and Oswald himself remained an influential figure until his death. In 991 he visited Ramsey for the last time and then spent the winter at his beloved Worcester. He began Lent of 992 with his usual practice of washing the feet of twelve poor men every day, and he died while completing this task and reciting the gradual psalms. In spite of his pluralism which was odd for a reformer, there is no doubt that his sanctity made a great impression on his contemporaries, and the example of his life and works was to inspire his successors especially Wulfstan (1008–95; see *Gardening with God*, p. 293), who translated his remains to a new shrine in about 1086.

Readings

Isaiah 6:1–8: Whom shall I send? Who will be our messenger?
Isaiah 61:1–3: The Lord has anointed me and sent me to bring good news to the poor.
Ezekiel 34:11–16: As a shepherd keeps all his flock in view so shall I keep my sheep in view.
Psalm 89(90): I will sing forever of your love, O Lord.
Psalm 96(97): O sing to the Lord, bless his name. Proclaim the wonders of the Lord among all the peoples.
Romans 12:3–13: Our gifts differ according to the grace given us.
1 Corinthians 4:1–3: Christ's servants are stewards entrusted with the mysteries of God.
2 Corinthians 3:1–6: He has given us the qualifications to be the administrators of this new covenant.
Ephesians 4:1–7, 11–13: In the work of service, building up the body of Christ.
1 Peter 5:1–4: Be the shepherds of the flock of God that is entrusted to you.
Mark 1:14–20: I will make you fishers of men.
Luke 5:1–11: If you say so, I will pay out the nets.

Intercessions

Thanksgiving for the life and work of SS Dunstan, Ethelwold, Oswald, Alphege, Aelfric and Wulstan, and for the work of scribes that enables us to know more about the lives and characters of the saints.

For artists, embroiderers, metalworkers, architects, engineers, builders, musicians, organ builders and teachers.

For determination, humility and courage.

For a greater love of learning and of the faith among our young people.

For the priests and people of parishes under the patronage of SS Dunstan, Ethelwold and Oswald, and for organizations and institutions that bear their names.

24 MAY
Solemnity (in Australia) of Our Lady Help of Christians

WOOD SORREL *Oxalis acetocella*

Cultivation, uses and lore

Oxalis is from the Greek *oxys,* meaning 'sharp' or 'acid', and is probably a reference to the flavour of the leaves. These contain oxalate, and as early as the fourteenth century their lemony tang was used to flavour salads and sauces. It is still widely cultivated for this purpose in our region of France where it is treated much like spinach and known as *pain de coucou* (cuckoo bread). Gerard said that this was because 'either the cuckoo feedeth thereon, or by reason when it springeth forth and flowereth, the cuckoo singeth most'. It also contains salts of lemon, another French name being *sel d'oseille,* and it can be used to remove ink stains from white material. It is very sharp and therefore needs to be used sparingly for food flavouring. The high content of oxalic acid can cause corrosion in the mouth and stomach if taken in large quantities, but a few leaves are perfectly harmless. It is one of the plants named 'shamrock' because of its three drooping, clover-like, leaflets. It is an elegant little plant with an interesting system of flower and seed production. In spring lilac-veined flowers appear on stalks up to 6 inches long. These droop at night or in rain, seemingly to protect pollen and, although they are popular with bees, they produce little seed. In summer white flowers appear on short stalks close to the ground where they seldom open but pollinate themselves and produce most of the seed for the following season.

Our Lady Help of Christians and Wood Sorrel

Wood Sorrel is chosen for today because in the language of flowers it represents maternal tenderness. This is perhaps because of the way the plant protects its seed, and this habit certainly makes it appropriate for this feast of Mary. Ever since Christ's words to his mother from the cross, that she should regard St John the Evangelist as her son, Catholics have respected and loved her as their mother, and turned to her for help and comfort.

Our Lady Help of Christians is patroness of the dioceses of Shrewsbury and Menevia, and her Mass was listed in the Supplement for Great Britain as a first-class Feast in the *St Andrew Daily Missal* of 1962. The title 'Help of Christians' was given to the Blessed Virgin by Pope St Pius V and added to the 'Litany of Loreto' after the victory of the Christians over the Turks at Lepanto in 1571. (The victory had been won at the very hour when on the pope's orders the Rosary was being recited throughout western Christendom.) Pope Pius VII established the Feast when he returned to Rome in 1815 after a period of imprisoned exile at Savona. It no longer appears in standard British missals, but in the local supplement of the breviary we find that Mary is Patroness of Australia, and today's celebration is kept as a Solemnity there. The choice was made in 1844 at the first provincial synod of Sydney. And so in Australia today Morning Prayer will conclude as follows: 'Loving Saviour, while hanging on the cross, you gave your mother Mary to be the mother of John; let us be known as her children by our way of living.' And on the eve of the Solemnity and at its close: 'Through the prayers of Mary, our help, protect our country, comfort the sorrowful, pardon sinners.' As I join in these prayers for Australia, and indeed offer them for England and for France, I remember that our relationship with Mary is a two-way one. And as John did we should take her into our own homes (John 19:26–7).

Readings
Genesis 3:9–15: I will make enemies of your offspring and the offspring of the woman.
Acts 1:14: The disciples were constantly at prayer together, with Mary the mother of Jesus.
Isaiah 9:1–6: The people that walked in darkness have seen a great light.
Isaiah 61:9–11: They are a race whom the Lord has blessed.
Micah 5:1–4: They will live secure.
Ephesians 1:3–6, 11–12: God chose us in Christ.
Matthew 2:13–15, 19–23: Take the child and his mother and escape into Egypt.
Luke 11:27–8: Happy the womb that bore you.

Luke 2:41–51: See how worried your father and I have been.
Luke 2:1–11: The mother of Jesus was there at the wedding at Cana.
John 19:25–7: This is your son; this is your mother.

Intercessions

For the people of Australia, and particularly for family and friends who live there.

That we may love Mary, our help, fight vigorously for the Faith on earth and come to praise the victory of Christ in heaven.

For the priests and people of parishes and institutions who have Our Lady Help of Christians as their patroness.

25 MAY
St Bede the Venerable, Doctor (673–735)

CANDLEBERRY *Myrica cerifera*; Bayberry; Wax Myrtle

Cultivation and uses

This hardy evergreen shrub is native to the coastal areas of North America from New Jersey to Florida and Texas. It is not always self-fertile, so you will need trees of both sexes in order to be sure of seeing the purplish-white wax-covered berries that appear along the branches between autumn and midwinter. It can reach a height of 10 feet and likes wet conditions and partial shade. (If you cannot provide these, try the deciduous *M. pennsylvanica*, which grows to about 8 feet and thrives in dry, acid soil.) Pruning is not necessary, so avoid cutting back unless essential. Candleberry contains tannins, resins, gums and bactericidal substances and is used externally for sore throats, ulcers, skin complaints, dandruff and hair loss. For feverish illnesses it is taken internally with either elder or mint, with pepper (*capsicm*) for blood circulation and with lavender for hair and scalp treatment. Bark, root and wax are used dried for decoctions, infusions, extracts and powders. Harvest berries when the wax is ripe, and root and bark in early winter or spring.

St Bede the Venerable and the candleberry

I have chosen the candleberry for St Bede because its name associates it with light, and because the berry wax provides aromatic tallow from which candles are made. As author of the *Ecclesiasical History of the English People*, which he completed in 731, Bede sheds light on our early Christian past. He had a special delight in learning and teaching and spread this through his writing. His emblem is a gold pitcher, with light from heaven indicated by silver rays emanating from the gold centre, on a blue field. He was born near the monastery at Wearmouth, was educated by St Benet Biscop, and was ordained in about 703. He was apparently musical, liked singing and was coherent, modest and detached. Dante referred to him in the *Paradiso*, and St Boniface said that at Bede's death 'the candle of the Church lit by the Holy Spirit had been extinguished'. St Cuthbert (*c*. 634–87) wrote that 'the English should thank God that he gave them so marvellous a man'. Cuthbert regarded Bede as a saint while he lived, and it is thanks to a letter of his to a fellow teacher named Cuthwin that we know in detail of Bede's behaviour and attitude during his last illness. Although mortally ailing he continued to sing the Offices, to teach and to work on a translation of St John's Gospel into English and on excerpts from the *Book of Cycles* by St Isidore. In regard to the latter, he considered it important that his students should be left with an accurate translation so that after his death their understanding of the text would not be faulty. On the Tuesday before Ascension Day, Bede's breathing became more laboured, but he taught all day and then spent the night in thanksgiving. On the following day he worked again with his students and then distributed to the priests of the monastery, as little gifts, the few possessions he had accumulated – pepper, handkerchiefs and incense. He asked for Masses and prayers in return and warned them that he would not survive much longer. They wept at this but rejoiced at something else he said : 'I have lived a long time and the Holy Judge has provided well for me during my whole life. The time of my release is near; indeed my soul longs to see Christ my king in all his beauty.' At about Vespers time on Bede's last day he was asked by his pupil Wilbur to complete the last sentence of the translation they had been working on. When this had been done, apparently in Bede's cell, he said to the boy: 'Take my head in your hands, for it pleases me very much to sit opposite my holy place where I used to pray, so that as I sit there I may call upon my Father.' And so, 'On the floor of his cell, singing: "Glory be to the Father and to the Son and to the Holy Spirit" and the rest, he breathed out his spirit from his body.'

St Bede the Venerable has the distinction of being the only English Doctor of the Church, but it was not until 1899 that Pope Leo XIII conferred this honour upon him. His remains are in the Galilee chapel in Durham Cathedral, where there is a burial slab. In the twentieth century Dean Allinton placed a memorial on the wall behind it, inscribed with some of Bede's own words from his commentary on the Book of Revelation: 'Christ is the morning star who when the night of this world is past, brings to his saints the promise of the light of life and opens everlasting day.'

Readings
Acts 13:26–33: God fulfilled the promise by raising Jesus from the dead.
Psalm 36(37): The just man's mouth utters wisdom.
Matthew 5:16: Your light must shine.
Matthew 5:13–16: You are the light of the world.

Intercessions
That the English may thank God for having sent them 'such a marvellous man'.

That with God's help and the prayers of St Bede we may approach our working life, and our death, as he did.

For the priests and people of parishes and institutions that have St Bede the Venerable as their patron.

26 MAY
St Philip Neri, Founder (1515–95)

BROMPTON STOCK *Matthiola incana*

Cultivation and history

This biennial has been called 'Brompton' Stock since the eighteenth century when it was bred by George London and Henry Wise in a nursery in Brompton Park, where the museums at South Kensington now stand, in other words just down the road from Brompton Oratory. It is a cross between our own native stock, *M. sinuata*, which has white flowers and favours coastal regions, and *M. incana*, which grows wild along coasts in south and west Europe, south and central Asia, and South Africa. *Matthiola* is named after a sixteenth-century botanist who wrote a celebrated life of Dioscorides, and *incana* means 'grey-leaved'. Brompton Stock produces crimson, pink, lavender, mauve or white, scented flowers from March to May on sturdy, branching stems. This sturdiness is possibly the origin of the name 'stock' for this word also means 'tree trunk'. Single or double varieties are available and the plants can reach a height of 2 feet and a spread of 6 to 9 inches. Sow in June and July in a cold frame or greenhouse, preferably in a sunny position in alkaline soil. In cooler areas keep the plants under glass over winter and plant out in spring. Stake in windy areas and deadhead faded flowers.

St Philip Neri and the Brompton Stock

I have chosen the Brompton Stock for St Philip because he is the sound trunk from which sprang his English legacy, famously residing at Brompton Oratory in London. This was developed by Fr Frederick William Faber, a convert from the Oxford Movement, from the London Oratory, which together with that of Birmingham, had been founded by Cardinal John Henry Newman, England's most eminent Oratorian. The performance of the 'oratorio' has come to be regarded as a very English musical activity, and it is perhaps surprising that it developed from the services of the early Oratorians, which made full use of musical and artistic resources (Palestrina was among St Philip's penitents), and the Brompton Oratory still maintains a high standard of liturgical music.

Philip was born in Florence. He lost his mother while he was still a child but was fortunate in having a good stepmother. He was educated at the famous Dominican convent of San Marco, where the frescoes of

Blessed Fra Angelico (*c*. 1400–55) must have made a deep impression. He worked for a while in the business of an uncle who planned to make him his heir, but Philip began to yearn for solitude and to realize that he was not destined for a life in commerce. When he was eighteen he left for Rome and, while tutoring his landlord's two sons, he began to live almost as a hermit, studying theology and philosophy and spending whole nights at prayer, often in the catacombs. There one night in 1544 he had a shattering 'vision' in which it seemed that a globe of fire entered his mouth and dilated his heart. The experience apparently left permanent physical effects, for at his autopsy his heart was discovered to be so enlarged that several of his ribs had broken to accommodate it. But at the time of the experience Philip felt that the globe of fire was the Holy Spirit filling him with a love that he was unable to endure. Perhaps this is what made him turn from study to the active apostolate, at first informally by engaging the young in conversation, encouraging them to turn aside from sin and to accompany him in the service of the sick and on visits to the churches of Rome. In 1548 he founded a confraternity to look after the many pilgrims who visited Rome and later to care for poor convalescents. He was ordained in 1551 and at first lived in community with a group of secular priests at San Girolamo della Carità. Here he showed extraordinary skill and power as a confessor, and was always to regard the confessional as a means to conversion of life in his penitents, and therefore as the foundation of an incorrupt society in both Church and State. St Ignatius of Loyola (see below, p. 218), who met and befriended him, held the same view, as did the entire group who had founded the Society of Jesus about twenty years earlier. At one time, inspired by St Francis Xavier (see *Gardening with God*, pp. 169–71), Philip thought of becoming a missionary. He was discouraged from this by a Cistercian who told him that Rome was to be his mission field, and this probably explains why he is sometimes called 'the second Apostle of Rome'. His confraternity was the basis of the eventual Congregation of the Oratory, and was so called because Philip and his disciples used an oratory built over the nave of San Girolamo church for public services, which were announced by the ringing of a small bell. At first five priests shared a community life with St Philip, and were obedient to him as superior even though they were not bound to do so by vows, nor was the renunciation of property a condition for membership. The congregation was approved in 1575, by which time their leader had attracted a huge personal following. He still lived at San Girolamo, where he received cardinals and paupers. He experienced spiritual ecstasy and there are stories than when he was saying Mass the server sometimes felt free to absent himself for two hours until the saint had regained normal consciousness. In 1593 he resigned as superior and, through his influence, a conflict between France and Rome was averted by the absolution of Henry IV of Navarre, who had temporarily embraced Protestantism. On 25 May 1595 Philip celebrated Mass and heard confessions as usual. He died early the following morning. He is noted for his charitable works, love of his neighbour and evangelical simplicity, but perhaps above all for his extraordinarily attractive personality and for his joy in the service of God. Today's second Office reading from St Augustine's *Sermon 171* is entitled 'Rejoice in the Lord always'. He set this example of happiness. And yet who knows how much constant discomfort, if not pain, he must have suffered from the time of his 'vision' as a young man. One of his maxims was: 'It is easier to guide cheerful persons in the spiritual life than melancholy ones.' One has the feeling that no one could have been melancholy in his presence for long. Perhaps that was his secret.

Readings

Revelation 21:5–7: Water from the well of life to anybody who is thirsty.
Psalm 14(15): The just man, Lord, shall dwell on your holy mountain.
Matthew 5:6: Hunger and thirst for what is right.
Matthew 13:44–6: He sells everything he owns and buys the field.

Intercessions

Thanksgiving for the lives of St Philip Neri, Cardinal Newman and Father Faber, and for the work of the Oratory in London and Birmingham.

Thanksgiving for our sense of humour, and the ability to be cheerful in the face of difficulty.

That we may follow the example of St Philip and be joyful in our Christian lives, so that by our example we may draw others to joy in Christ.

For the priests and people of parishes who have St Philip Neri as their patron.

27 MAY
St Augustine of Canterbury, Bishop (died *c.* 604)

CANTERBURY BELL *Campanula*; Bellflower

Cultivation and history

Campanula is the Latin diminutive of *campana* for 'bell', and is an allusion to the flower's form. Our native *C. trachelium* (nettle-leaved bell-flower) is called Canterbury bell because the shape of the flower resembles the small bells used by medieval pilgrims to Canterbury to decorate their horses, ponies and donkeys. Perhaps they gathered the flowers as they approached the end of their journey as trophies or souvenirs, because they grew in abundance in the woods near the city. It is difficult to know whether the plant was named from its location or from its popularity with the pilgrims. At any rate many of today's garden *campanulas* were introduced from Italy in the sixteenth century. These cultivated varieties have wider bells and can be pink or white, as well as the usual blue of *C. trachelium*. The latter was also called throatwort and was used as a gargle, the botanical name possibly coming from this practice.

There are now so many types, sizes and shapes of Canterbury bell available that it is impossible to recommend a variety. Personally I would choose a garden variety of *C. trachelium*. These have mid-blue to purple-blue flowers, widely spaced on upright stems that appear in mid to late summer. The plants will reach a height of up to 3 feet depending on variety. Grow in well-drained soil with some sun. They do not object to dry shade and will naturalize well in a woodland garden. Propagate by seed or division in autumn or spring.

St Augustine and the Canterbury bell

Both the imported Italian Canterbury bells and the native ones are appropriate for St Augustine. He himself was a most important Italian import, but the native flower would have bloomed in Kent during his time and he would very probably have been familiar with it. Augustine was famously sent to England by Pope Gregory the Great, who having seen some Anglo-Saxons for sale in the Forum slave market, was moved to plan the evangelization of their country. And so as a result: 'The light of holy faith was poured out upon the race of the Angles.' The race of the Angles, yes, but here I remind myself to correct the impression I was given at primary school that St Augustine was the first to bring Christianity to our islands. (This was a strange emphasis from a north of England school.) After all, St Alban had been martyred in about 265, many Celtic saints predate Augustine and there was already an established episcopacy in other parts of Britain when he landed with his band of monks at Ebbsfleet, Thanet, in 597 (the probable year of the death of Columba of Iona). British Christianity, however, had been weakened by successive invasions of Jutes and Angles, and paganism had regained a hold in many parts. Moreover, although Bertha the wife of King Ethelbert was Christian, she and her chaplain appear to have made no effort to convert him and, when Augustine appealed to the native bishops for help in evangelization, this was not forthcoming. Perhaps they had enough to deal with and were insular and suspicious of the Roman arrivals. Also they had had long enough to develop their own spirituality, forms of liturgy and methods of calculating Easter. This last was to be a sticking point at the later Synod of Whitby, and it would be many years after that before the native Celtic Church would accede completely to the practice of the universalizing Roman one.

Before he set out from Rome, Augustine, who was already prior of a community there, had been made abbot over the group of monks who were to be his companions on the English mission. When they reached Provence, there seems to have been a dispute as to whether to continue, and there are grounds for thinking that Augustine felt he did not have enough control over the party or, indeed, enough authority to strike the right note upon arrival in England. In the event, the pope consecrated him bishop and the journey continued. Another halt was made at Angers in northern France, where the tradition is that yet again some of the mission wanted to turn back. All this notwithstanding, a party of about forty monks and Frankish priests (as interpreters) eventually arrived in Kent.

It is clear from letters that passed between Pope Gregory and Augustine that the latter was guided in his policy by the former. A feature of the strategy was to concentrate on a small area, establishing a sound base for future missions, rather than spreading the net too wide at the outset and risking confusion and failure. After the conversion of Ethelbert this aspect of the mission was successful with the foundation of a cathedral and abbey in Canterbury, which became known as a centre of 'Gregorian' chant as developed in Gregory's Rome. Augustine was also responsible for the creation of sees at Rochester and London. A plan to found a see at York did not come to fruition until over a century after

Augustine's short episcopacy which lasted only for the ten years preceding his death. Much had been achieved, but much was left to do, by successors who mostly proved equal to the task. A good testimonial comes from Pope Gregory himself, who wrote of Augustine in a letter to King Ethelbert that he 'has been trained under monastic Rule, has a complete knowledge of holy scripture, and, by the grace of God, is a man of holy life ... listen to his advice ....'

The evangelization of the Angles was not Augustine's idea; and he gives the impression of being the hired man fulfilling the vision of a master who could not be on the spot himself because he was the pope. He therefore must have been a man of humility, obedience, determination and faith. It is claimed in some quarters that, since the association between Augustine and Gregory, pope and archbishop of Canterbury have never been as closely united in their intentions and beliefs. And so St Augustine has become a symbol of hope for ecumenism. As today closes I can only pray that the people of God may yet again become one flock, under the guidance and care of one shepherd.

Readings
1 Thessalonians 2:2–8: We were eager to hand over the Good News.
Psalm 95(96): Proclaim the wonders of the Lord among all the peoples.
Philippians 3:17, 4:9: Put into practice the lessons I taught you.
1 Corinthians 1:10: In the name of Jesus, agree among yourselves.
John 10:14: I know my sheep and my sheep know me.
Matthew 9:35–7: The harvest is rich but the labourers are few.

Intercessions
Thanksgiving for the part played by St Augustine in the conversion of the people of England to Christianity.

For priests and people in parishes and institutions under the patronage of St Augustine of Canterbury.

31 MAY
Feast of the Visitation of the Blessed Virgin Mary

IRIS

Cultivation, history and uses

Irises fall into two main categories, the rhizomatous and the bulbous. Into the first category are the bearded iris, also known as flag, or German iris. This flowers in virtually every colour and is best planted in June or early July in fan-shaped holes about 4 inches deep. *Iris florentina* belongs to this group, although some regard it as a hybrid. Called *florentina* because it grew in abundance near Florence, it is well known as orris root and widely used as a fixative in pot-pourris, its violet scent intensifying as the rhizome gets older. It was employed in perfumery in ancient Egypt, Greece and Rome, and in modern herbalism the rhizome is used internally for coughs, catarrh and diarrhoea and externally for deep wounds. Roots are lifted in early autumn and dried for use in decoctions and powders.

In the second category comes the *reticulata* type of iris. This flowers between December and March and is normally hardy and suitable for the rockery or border edging. Also in the second group are the Dutch, Spanish and English irises. These are excellent for cutting and for providing a colourful display in midsummer. They should be planted in September.
Note: Do not use iris as a remedy without medical supervision, even for animals. The sap may cause vomiting, colic and loss of consciousness.

History of the Feast of the Visitation

Although it celebrates a gospel account, the Feast did not become universal until the fourteenth century, when Pope Urban VI established it on 2 July as a continuation of the former octave of the Birthday of St John the Baptist, which certainly had things the wrong way round! The date of the feast is now more logical, separated from St John's birthday by almost a month to symbolize the three months that Mary is said to have stayed with Elizabeth (Luke 1:56). And, had the Visitation not replaced the Queenship of Mary (which has now been moved to 22 August under the adjusted title of 'Our Lady Mother and Queen'), we would have no Marian feast in May. This would have been odd since May is traditionally regarded as one of Mary's special months (the other being October). Around 1868, according to *The Catholic Dictionary* (*op. cit*, 1928) an Italian Father of Charity, Doctor Gentili, introduced the celebration of May devotions among the English. This was probably a result of the pope, Pius IX, having introduced the granting of a plenary indulgence to those who practised devotion to Mary during May, provided they went to Confession and Communion. This is certain to have appealed to English Catholics, whose country had been known as 'the dowry of Mary' since as least 1399. In that year Archbishop Arundel of Canterbury published a mandate that included the words, 'But we, as the humble servants of [Mary's] inheritance, and liegemen of her especial dower – as we are approved by common parlance – ought to excel all others in the fervour of our praises and devotion to her.' Father Mark Elvins (in his *Catholic Trivia*, HarperCollins Religious, 1992) is persuasive in his theory that the term goes back slightly further, and that the young Richard II, in thanksgiving for the ending of the Peasants' Revolt, had solemnly consecrated his kingdom to Mary after his successful meeting with Watt Tyler and his rebels, on the Saturday after Corpus Christi in the year 1381.

The Visitation and the iris

The ancient Egyptians considered the iris as a symbol of eloquence, and they placed the flower on the brow of the Sphinx and on their kings' sceptres, the three leaves representing faith, wisdom and courage. In the mysteries of the Annunciation and the Visitation, Mary demonstrates all four attributes: wisdom in her reaction to Gabriel, faith and courage in her acceptance of his message, and eloquence in her *Magnificat* (see *Gardening with God*, 22 December, p. 102).

In Christian art the flower came to represent the Queen of Heaven and her Immaculate Conception, calling to mind that Mary could not be Queen of Heaven unless she had been immaculately conceived, nor could she have become Christ's mother without that conception.

Purple *Iris reticulata*: In the work of the early Flemish artists there is rivalry between the lily and the iris for the name 'flower of the holy Virgin'. But perhaps the iris has the edge because its sword-shaped leaves gave it the added symbolism of the sword that was to pierce Mary's heart (Luke 2:35). There is a medieval monastic legend that echoes this: at the death of Jesus, all nature grieved and a dead silence fell upon the earth. Only the plants still whispered, and the iris said, 'Dark violet will forever be the mourning colour of my flowers.'

Iris 'Rosario': The Visitation is a joyful mystery of the Rosary, and indeed in parts of Italy the roots of the Bearded iris were used to make rosary beads (de Cleene and Lejeune, *op. cit.*).

144

Iris 'Early Light' and 'Shepherd's Delight': The iris is named after one of the Greek messengers of the gods who travelled along the rainbow between heaven and earth in order to deliver the commands of the gods to the people. Her veil contained the colours of the rainbow, and she came to be thought of as the personification of the rainbow itself. Indeed the iris blooms in almost all the colours of the spectrum. Later Iris was believed to bring the souls of women and children to the land of everlasting peace, taking the latter group into her lap. In this personification and action she was regarded as the connection between heaven and earth. This mythology is clearly the reason why the iris has come to signify a message, and usually a good one, in the language of flowers. And it easy to see how these attributes of the iris were Christianized, as they applied so clearly to Mary in her role as messenger to Elizabeth at the Visitation, and to her role as mother of us all. We continually ask her to pray for us 'now and at the hour of our death'.

Above all I think of the Visitation as full of joy, the joy of Mary, the joy of Elizabeth and of the unborn John within her womb. But it is an occasion of our joy too, because Mary is bringing Christ to us. The mystery of the Visitation foreshadows the coming of Jesus into our lives and the union of our souls with him. As Maisie Ward puts it: 'Our Lord in this Mystery has not only taken a human nature from Mary but has left Himself helpless, powerless in the darkness of her womb to be taken where she wills. Even so, it is the beginning of a divine economy of grace whereby God saves mankind by giving *Himself* into the power of mankind. The Curé d'Ars, marvelling over the Blessed Sacrament, said: "I bear Him to the right and He stays to the right; I bear Him to the left, and He stays to the left"' (*The Splendour of the Rosary*, Sheed & Ward, 1948).

A meditation on the *Magnificat* is an appropriate way to end Mary's month, but at any time it proves an inexhaustible well for meditation. For instance, to magnify and to rejoice in God is the beginning of realization of our own nothingness; Mary would be called blessed by all generations because of her humility, and only to the humble can God entrust his gifts; and later our Lord blessed those who hunger and thirst after justice. Here the *Magnificat* points the way to a solution for our social problems and to true Christian living.

At some point today I will be bound to read 'May Magnificat' by Gerard Manley Hopkins (1844-89) again, but I should wish to end it with Caryl Houselander's prayer:

Breath of Heaven,
Carry us on the impulse
Of Christ's love,
as easily as thistledown
is carried on the wind;
that in the Advent season of our souls,
while He is formed in us,
in secret and in silence –
the Creator
in the hands of his creatures,
as the Host
in the hands of the priest –
we may carry Him forth
to wherever he wishes to be,
as Mary carried Him over the hills
on his errand of love,
to the house of Elizabeth.

Readings
Song of Songs 2:8–14; 8:6–7: The coming of the Beloved.
Zephaniah 3:14–18: Shout for joy, daughter of Zion.
Isaiah 2:2–6: Great in your midst is the Holy One of Israel.
Luke 1:39–56: And why is this granted me, that the mother of my Lord should come to me?

Intercessions
For those being treated with *Iris florentina*.

For the people of Florence and all who work in the perfume and aromatherapy industries.

Thanksgiving for the life and work of Father Gentili.

For greater articulacy in the expression of our beliefs.

Thanksgiving for the lives and works of Gerard Manley Hopkins, Caryl Houselander and Maisie Ward.

For the Order of the Visitation.

For an increase in faith, wisdom and courage.

Thanksgiving for the work of the early Flemish painters.

That Our Lady and St Elizabeth may pray for us, and that we may pray the *Hail Mary* and the *Magnificat* with ever-increasing understanding and devotion.

Thanksgiving for our joy on the feast of the Visitation; for Mary's acquiescence; which led to Christ's being incarnate in our own lives.

For the priests and people of parishes who hold the Visitation of the Blessed Virgin Mary as their Feast of Title.

THE IMMACULATE HEART OF MARY
Saturday after the Most Sacred Heart of Jesus

BLEEDING HEART *Dicentra spectabilis; Coeur de Marie*

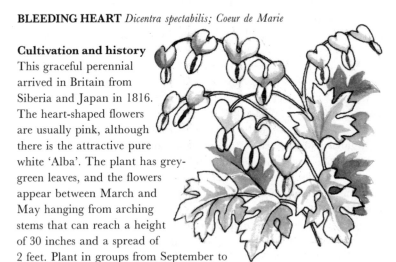

Cultivation and history
This graceful perennial arrived in Britain from Siberia and Japan in 1816. The heart-shaped flowers are usually pink, although there is the attractive pure white 'Alba'. The plant has grey-green leaves, and the flowers appear between March and May hanging from arching stems that can reach a height of 30 inches and a spread of 2 feet. Plant in groups from September to March, in well-drained soil previously enriched with garden compost, leaf-mould or peat. Bleeding heart appreciates light shade and shelter and is excellent as ground cover under trees and shrubs. Mulch in late spring. The plants die back naturally after flowering. Leave undisturbed for as long as possible. Division, between October and March, must be gentle and careful as the roots are fleshy and brittle.

History of devotion to the Immaculate Heart of Mary
This devotion was first proposed by St John Eudes (1601–80). Born in Normandy, he was educated by the Jesuits at Caen. He later joined the Oratory but left to found his own congregation. This was to be hampered by the vicissitudes of state and church politics, but in the end, his inspiration, commitment and toil won through – for which, as someone devoted to the Sacred Heart of Jesus and to the Immaculate

147

Heart of his mother, I thank God. Through him we have a devotion based on the same principles as that of the Sacred Heart of Jesus. And so, as devotion to that Heart leads to *worship* of the Person of the Word, so devotion to the Immaculate Heart of Mary leads to *veneration* of the person of the mother of Jesus. In each case, the natural heart is taken as a symbol of love and of the inner life. In the case of Mary this divine motherhood makes her mother's heart a special focus for reverence, though of course this is in no way comparable to the infinitely greater attributes of the Heart of Jesus.

The Congregation of Rites twice declined to sanction the devotion, first in 1669 and again in 1726, but Pius IV permitted local celebration in 1799, and this was extended further by Pius IX in 1855. About 1835 the Archconfraternity of the Immaculate Heart, at the church of Notre Dame des Victoires in Paris did a great deal to spread popularity of the devotion. The greatest impetus came about in 1917 with the appearances of the Blessed Virgin to three young children at Fatima in Portugal. She asked that her immaculate heart be honoured by repentance and penance for the outrages that a Godless world continued to heap upon her Son. Then in October 1942, when the world thought that war would never end, Pope Pius XII consecrated it to the Immaculate Heart of Mary, urging prayer through the Rosary, Holy Communion and small acts of self-denial in daily life. Holy Communion in reparation for sin was to become the devotion of 'First Saturdays', in the same way that the 'First Fridays' had become the result of devotion to the Sacred Heart of Jesus. The feast of the Immaculate Heart of Mary was originally fixed on 22 August, the octave of the Assumption, but now – in the general post of Marian celebrations – ranks only as an optional memoria. I must admit to surprise that Pope John Paul II, who is well known to be devoted to the heart of Mary, has not restored the intention of his predecessor, who instituted the feast for the whole Church so as to obtain by the intercession of Mary, 'peace among nations, freedom for the Church, the conversion of sinners, the love of purity and the practice of virtue' (Decree of Pope Pius XII, 4 May 1944). As humanity lurches into the twenty-first century in all its arrogance, warmongering, cruelty, gratuitous violence, intolerance, destructiveness, confusion and wrong-doing of every kind, it seems that never was Pope Pius's prayer more vitally necessary than it is now.

The Immaculate Heart of Mary and the flowers of *Coeur de Marie*
We are taught that an unfailing test of the spiritual validity of any devotion, Marian or otherwise, is whether or not it leads us to Christ. So let us see:

Clearly the English name for *dicentra* came from the colour and habit of the flowers, which droop sadly like drops of blood from the length of the arching stems. I prefer the French name because it encompasses the totality of Mary's heart, and not just the sorrows it experienced. *Dicentra* is from Greek *dis*, 'twice', and *kentron,* 'a spur'. The flowers of *Coeur de Marie* have two spurs, just as the heart has two ventricles, and to me these represent Mary's joys *and* sorrows and the whole flower her glories.

Sometimes I wish I could combine the pre-conciliar liturgy with the reformed one, and today is a case in point. For instance, the new Mass has changed the Collect, in which we remembered, before God, the Virgin who prepared a dwelling worthy of the Holy Spirit and asked God that in his mercy 'we who celebrate the festival of Mary's Immaculate Heart, may be able to live according to his own Heart'. And I miss the Gradual verses from Psalm 13:5b–6 and 45:17: 'My heart shall rejoice in thy salvation. I will sing to the Lord because he has dealt bountifully with me; *r.* I will cause your name to be celebrated in all generations; therefore the peoples will praise you for ever and ever.' Here one felt that one's own joy was being *joined* to that of Mary and the response had a twofold meaning. Mary herself will be the cause of God's name being celebrated forever, but also it echoes her words in the *Magnificat* 'All generations shall call me blessed'.

On the other hand the former Gospel (John 19:25–7; now assigned to Mary Help of Christians), while it comforts us in the love of Mary our mother, does not have the wide-ranging significance of the present one: 'Mary stored up all these things in her heart' (Luke 2:41–51). St Laurence Giustiniani (1381–1455) expounds this Gospel text in today's second Office reading. He concludes that we should not merely turn to Mary for help and maternal comfort, but that we should imitate her example of obedience and humility. Whether we are in action or contemplation we should be motivated by the love of Christ alone, as she was, so that our purification is of the Spirit and offered not in a man-made temple 'but in the temple of the heart, where Christ the Lord is pleased to enter'. And so indeed, Mary *does* lead us, through devotion to her immaculate heart, to Christ her son, and the *Coeur de Marie* in my garden ensures that I do not forget the fact.

Readings

Chronicles 15:3–4, 15–16: They brought the ark of God in and put it inside the tent that David had pitched for it.

Zechariah 2:14–17: Sing, rejoice daughter of Sion, for I am coming to dwell in the midst of you.

1 Samuel 2:4–8: My heart exults in the Lord my saviour.

Judith 14:18–20; 15:9: You are the highest honour of our race.

Romans 5:12, 17–19: However great the number of sins, grace was even greater.

Romans 8:25–30: The ones God chose specially.

Luke 2:15–19: She treasured all these things and pondered them in her heart.

Luke 2:27–35: A sword shall pierce your soul.

Intercessions

Thanksgiving for the life and work of SS Laurence Giustiniani and John Eudes and for the Popes who encouraged devotion to the Immaculate Heart of Mary.

For the Holy Father, John Paul II; For peace in the world and for an end to violence and cruelty.

That we may turn to the Immaculate Heart of Mary not just for her maternal love but for an example of how we should conduct our active and spiritual lives, and that consecrated to her we may become more fitting temples for her son Jesus Christ.

For priests and people whose parishes are under the patronage of the Immaculate Heart of Mary.

1 JUNE
St Justin Martyr (c. 100–c. 165)

NOBLE LIVERWORT *Hepatica nobilis*

Cultivation and uses

This small perennial occurs throughout northern temperate regions and is native to European woodlands. Attractive in the rockery and in pots, it is semi-evergreen with a thick rhizome. The leaves are silky and hairy, and often have purple undersides. The flowers, which appear in early spring, are blue, purple, pink or white, and the plant grows to a height of about 3 inches and a spread of 5 inches. *H. nobilis 'Rubra Plena'* has double pink flowers but is not as vigorous as the species and needs more care. It favours deep, moist, rich alkaline soil in shade and does not like being moved. It is not employed much in modern herbalism but can be used to make a digestive or mild tonic for the liver. In the past it was used occasionally for minor injuries and ringworm. Plants are cut from late spring to midsummer and dried for use in infusions, extracts and tinctures.

St Justin Martyr and the Noble Liverwort

Justin was born in Samaria, a pagan of Greek origin. He became a philosopher and in about AD 130 converted to Christianity. He proposed the relationship between philosophers and Christ as being like that between the incomplete and the complete, or between the imperfect and the perfect. In about 165 he was beheaded, with six others, one of them a woman. He came to be regarded as the first Christian philosopher and the father of apologetics. The *Saint Andrew Daily Missal* calls him important for having described how Mass was celebrated and Baptism administered during his time. But his writings were mainly apostolic in their aim, and he was confident that conversions would come through articulate, well-presented exposition of the faith. In the language of flowers, noble liverwort signifies confidence, and I have chosen it for St Justin not because of his confidence in the potential success of his writing, which sadly proved unfounded, but because of today's second Office reading from *The Acts of the Martyrdom of St Justin and his companions*. Here we read that, in the face of martyrdom under Marcus Aurelius, he displayed an altogether more important confidence, saying to those who condemned him: 'We have prayed that we may suffer for the sake of our Lord Jesus Christ and in this way be saved. This will give us confidence and assure our salvation when we come to the judgment seat of our Lord and Saviour, who presides over a universal court more formidable than yours'.

Readings

Acts 20:21, 24: I have testified to the faith.
Romans 1:16: I am not ashamed of this Gospel.
1 Corinthians 1:18–25: God wanted to save those who have faith through the foolishness of the message we preach.
Psalm 33(34):2–9: From all my terrors the Lord set me free.
2 Corinthians 1:3–4:God comforts us in all our sorrows.
John 17:11–19 Jesus prays for his disciples.

Intercessions

For philosophers.

For confidence in the performance of the duties of our earthy vocations and, although we may not face martyrdom, for that other confidence shown by St Justin in Christ's promise of eternal life.

For priests and people in parishes under the patronage of St Justin Martyr.

3 JUNE
St Charles Lwanga and Companions, Martyrs
(died 1885–7)

FIRETHORN *Pyracantha*

Cultivation and history

Firethorn is an almost direct translation of the Latin name, in its turn derived from the Greek *pyr*, 'fire', and *acantha*, 'thorn', alluding to the glowing fruit and the thorny branches of this shrub. It was introduced to Kew Gardens from western China in 1899 by a Lieutenant Jones. Nowadays it is often grown against walls, although it will stand free. It is quick growing and will need to be cut back frequently if space is at a premium. Its thorns make gloves a necessity when pruning in late winter or early spring. Firethorn is tough and will thrive in an exposed or shady site. Any reasonable soil will suffice. The berries, which appear from early autumn until midwinter, can be yellow, orange or red, and the choice takes on a horrible relevance today. There is the variety 'Orange Glow' and, for yellow, *Soleil d'Or*. These grow to between 6 and 12 feet. For red berries there is the dwarf 'Red cushion' growing to only 3 feet, the significance of the name of this particular variety being particularly and terribly apt in view of the reed mats used in the martyrs' execution (see below).

The Ugandan Martyrs and Firethorn

These young men and boys, all under twenty-five, were killed in a most appalling way. Joseph Mkasa had reproached the ruler Mwanga for debauchery and for murdering the Anglican missionary bishop James Hannington; he was beheaded before the main massacre. Charles Lwanga was in charge of the royal pages and had baptized five of them, including

Kizito, aged thirteen, whom he had earlier saved from Mwanga's alleged pederasty. Most of these martyrs died by being burned alive on a pyre, their suffering being prolonged and made even more excruciating by the fact that their bodies had been wrapped in reed mats beforehand. Mwanga was fanatically opposed to Christianity, and his persecution also claimed the lives of Matthias Murumba, a judge, and Andrew Kagwa, a catechist. Twenty-four Anglican and Protestant Christians are also recorded as having died for their faith. Charles Lwanga and his companions are venerated in the calendar as the protomartyrs of Black Africa, but as Pope Paul VI pointed out in his homily at their canonization in 1964, Christian martyrdom is not new in Africa. He recalled the martyrs of Scillitan, Carthage, Utica, Egypt and of the Vandal persecution, as well as the fact that SS Felicity and Perpetua were African, as were Cyprian and the great Augustine of Hippo. And, although he mourned the circumstances of the deaths of the Ugandan martyrs as a terrible tragedy, he saw their deaths, and the deaths of 'those others of the Anglican communion who died for the sake of Christ', as part of the birth pangs of a new age for Africa itself, believing that 'in the new society, there can be an awareness of the higher things of which the human spirit is capable and an effort to provide better conditions for social life' (from today's second Office reading). The responsory hints at the helplessness one feels at the fate of these young men: 'God looks on, his angels look on, Christ, too, looks on as we struggle and strive in the contest of faith.' I hope I can be forgiven for suspecting that the compilers of this Office were at a loss to know what to include in it, but they were right to include the passage from 2 Maccabees, which records a particularly bloodthirsty period in the history of the people of God, in the Mass.

Pope Paul's hopes had already been fulfilled in a local sense, for the massacre of the Ugandan martyrs led to an increase in conversions. Catholic and Protestant shrines were set up at Namugongo, the site of the main massacre. Both were to become popular places of pilgrimage on the martyrs' Feast day. Namugongo had formerly been a place of pagan ritual sacrifice, and the Christian shrines symbolized the rebirth of which Pope Paul was to speak. He was the first pope to go to Africa, and he made a pilgrimage to Namugongo during the course of his travels there.

I close today by thinking and praying hard about something said by one of the martyrs, Bruno Serunkuma: 'A well that has many sources never runs dry. When we are gone, others will come after us.'

Readings
2 Maccabees 7:1–2, 9–14: We are prepared to die.
Psalm 123(4): Our life, like a bird, has escaped from the snare of the fowler.
Matthew 5:1–12: Happy the pure in heart, they shall see God; happy those who are persecuted in the cause of right; happy are you when abused and persecuted on my account; your reward will be great in heaven.

Intercessions
For the well-being of Africa and her peoples.
Thanksgiving for the Martyrs and Pastors of Africa.
That we may face whatever combat may come to us with pure hearts and unshakeable faith and courage.
For the priests and people of churches that have the Ugandan Martyrs as their patrons.

5 JUNE
St Boniface, Bishop and Martyr (*c.* 673–754)

PATIO ROSE 'ST BONIFACE'

Cultivation and history
This rose was introduced by Kordes in 1980 and was awarded a Certificate of Merit by the Royal National Rose Society in 1981. The flowers, which are moderately scented, are orange-vermilion and a typical hybrid tea shape, produced in clusters on low-growing bushes.

St Boniface and the rose 'St Boniface'
Winfrith (later Boniface) was born in Devon, possibly at Crediton, of free land-owning parents. He was educated first at Exeter and then at Nursling in Hampshire, where his brilliance eventually led to his being made head of the school. As a monk of Nursling, he developed a reputation as an excellent schoolmaster, producing the first Latin Grammar to be written in England. He was ordained at the age of thirty, and his profound biblical knowledge then allowed him to preach as well as teach. He seemed set for a successful if quietly secure career in his homeland, but at the age of forty-one he went to Friesland (now northern Holland) to assist St Willibrord (658–739), who ten years previously had,

with St Wilfrid (633–709), attempted to evangelize the area. This first mission was largely unsuccessful, and opposition from the local ruler, Radbod, forced Winfrith to return to Nursling, where the monks elected him abbot. This failed to keep him at home, and he went to Rome to ask Pope Gregory II for an official instruction to evangelize Germany. This was granted and Boniface (as he has since been known) set out for Bavaria and Hesse. On the way he received news that, following the death of Radbod, conditions in Friesland had improved, and he again went to the aid of Willibrord in Utrecht. He stayed there for about three years and then went to Hesse, where he preached so successfully that the pope consecrated him bishop with jurisdiction over Germany. It was during this time that the famous incident took place of his splitting the Donar oak, a tree sacred to the pagans, in Geismar. Boniface is reported to have hacked this down with four mighty strokes and then used the wood to build a church dedicated to St Peter. The astonishment of the locals that he had not been struck dead on the spot led to the conversion of many of them, and thus began the triumph of Christianity in Germany. After this success in Hesse, Boniface pushed on to Thuringia (in the east of Germany) where he restored existing churches and rooted out corruption. This caused friction with Frankish clergy, who wanted to carry out the task single-handed, but in 732 Pope Gregory III consecrated Boniface as archbishop with authority to appoint subordinate bishops of the Rhine. In spite of this the Frankish lack of cooperation in his mission prevented Boniface from establishing his see at Cologne, and he had continually to call for help from England. The response was generous, and many of his followers from there were installed in his newly founded bishoprics in Hesse, Bavaria and later Franconia. Several of the missionaries who came from England helped Boniface in the founding of abbeys and convents, which became centres of learning and were a source of spiritual food to his many converts. Amoneburg and Fritzlar in Hesse were among these founda-tions, and in 744 came the most famous of all, at Fulda. In 754 Boniface set out again for a third missionary campaign in Friesland, winding up his affairs in Hesse and leaving Fulda in the care of his friend and relative, Lull of Malmesbury (710–68). He took a burial shroud with him, and this has led to the suspicion that he may have anticipated martyrdom, or even that he invited it. However, as he was by then almost eighty years of age, it does not seem a particularly surprising item of luggage. However, on the Wednesday of Pentecost week in that same year he was awaiting a host of converts, whom he was about to confirm, when he and his party were set upon and massacred by a horde of pagans. The book that he was reading just before he died, apparently stained with his blood, survives at Fulda, where he is buried.

St Boniface is widely venerated in Germany and Holland, but has never been much regarded in England, and yet he had a lasting and deep influence on the history of Europe, in a politically formative as well as religious sense. He sparked a rebirth of the old Roman Empire in newly Christian guise in northern Europe and, by bringing together the papacy, the Frankish kings and the German emperors, he paved the way for Charlemagne and for a reorientation of the papacy towards western Europe and away from Constantinople. He was therefore influential in the creation of medieval Christian Europe in all its glories, faults and contradictions. For this reason he has been called 'founder of the West'. It is highly unlikely that he could have foreseen or even intended all this. His motivation was all for Christ. Clearly, he was a man of great courage, loyalty, intellect, determination and organizational skills. And his personal correspondence often shows him as affectionate and kind. He deserves to be better appreciated in England. It is always pleasing to find a rose named after a saint and, although, like its namesake, this patio rose is perhaps not widely known or appreciated, it is most apt for St Boniface. Excellent as ground cover, it is a reminder that St Boniface himself covered a wide area and brought a plentiful harvest to Christ in the shape of an entire nation.

The second Office reading today is from one of St Boniface's most famous letters (No. 78). I find it really helpful when a saint's proper reading contains his or her own words. Here, as in every case where this is so, St Boniface comes alive. He is not a stone cipher from the past, an inaccessible, impossibly virtuous icon, but a real person, who experienced doubts and the temptation to give up in the face of problems. In this reading he remembers others like himself who fought paganism, including Athanasius in Alexandria. But he admits to having been filled with dread and trembling when he considered their example: 'The darkness of my sins almost overwhelmed me. I should have been only too glad to give up the government of the Church which I had accepted.' He then, however, goes on to say that this course of action proved impossible because he could find no such example in any of the Fathers or in sacred scripture. He can find only texts that inspire trust in and reliance on God: 'What we cannot bear on our own, let us bear with the help of the one who is all-powerful and who said: "My yoke is easy, and my burden light." ' The reading ends with some of the most famous and stirring words of St Boniface, and they will be with me as I go about my work today: 'Let us stand firm in battle on the day of the Lord, because days of distress and anguish have come upon us. Let us die, if God wills, for the sacred laws of our fathers, so that we may be worthy to share an eternal inheritance with them. Let us not be dumb watchdogs or silent spectators; let us not be hirelings that flee at the approach of the wolf. Let us be watchful shepherds, guarding the flock of Christ, preaching to great and small alike, to rich and poor, all that God has decreed to men of all degrees and ages, in so far as God gives us the power.'

Readings

1 Thessalonians 2:6: We desired nothing better than to offer you our own lives, as well as God's gospel.
Galatians 4:19: I am in travail over you afresh until I can see Christ's image formed in you.
Acts 26:19–23: Christ was to proclaim that light now shone for our people and for the pagans.
Psalm 116: Go out to the whole world: proclaim the Good News.
John 10:11–16: The good shepherd is one who lays down his life for his sheep.

Intercessions

For the people of Devon and the people of Germany.

For monks, missionaries, preachers and teachers.

Thanksgiving for the life and work of St Boniface, and that he may be more widely known as an example of Christian strength, energy, determination, courage and love of Christ's flock.

For the priests and people of parishes and institutions under the patronage of St Boniface.

9 JUNE
(1) St Ephraem, Deacon and Doctor (*c*. 306–73)

ROSE 'METANOIA'

Cultivation and characteristics

It is always my intention that my readers should have access to the plants featured in my books. Sadly, this has been thwarted in the case of the rose

'Metanoia', as the Royal National Rose Society tell me that it is not available in the United Kingdom. I have one in my French garden, but I am unable to find details of its history and I wrote to the Society for help. All they could find in foreign listings is that it produces pink flowers in clusters. This does not do it justice at all. 'Metanoia' is in fact a robust climber with luxuriant medium-green foliage. Its fragrant flowers are prolific and a vibrant coral-pink as buds, opening to medium-sized blooms of a lighter, more delicate shade. It is healthy and resistant to blackspot and is now growing happily against one of the pillars of my 'Way of the Cross'. (I bought it from a French mail order supplier at least ten years ago and I believe this firm now exports to Britain, so perhaps its inclusion here will not be in vain: Willemse France, 59984 Tourcoing Cédex, France. www.willemse.fr.)

St Ephraim and rose 'Metanoia'

Ephraem is the only Syrian ever to have been made a Doctor of the Church. Deacon he certainly was, but it is not known for certain whether he was ever ordained priest. He was however, a prolific preacher, poet and musician, whose writings occur with some frequency in the Breviary. Rose 'Metanoia' is chosen for him because the 'Prayer of St Ephraem' is recited three times by Orthodox monks at the Offices of Lent. During this recitation, they bow their heads to the ground in an obeisance known as *metanoia*, which in this context means 'conversion of life'.

Ephraem was born in Nisibia, Mesopotamia. He was baptized at the age of eighteen and seems to have become a protégé of his bishop, whom he probably accompanied to the Council of Nicaea. He eventually became head of the cathedral school until the Christians left after a siege by the Persians. He went to live in a cave and led an ascetic life, but he was not eremitic and continued to preach in nearby Edessa. Most of his work dates from this period. St Jerome was impressed by the power of his treatise on the Holy Spirit, and St Basil is alleged to have asked upon meeting him, 'Are you Ephraem, who follows the way of salvation so well?' His self-effacing character is shown in his answer: 'I am Ephraem, who walks unworthily in the way of salvation.' Besides his written achievement he managed to organize the supply of food and money during a famine, the task being given him because no one else could be trusted to do it fairly. After this he returned to his cave above Edessa and died not long afterwards.

St Ephraem became known as 'the harp of the Holy Spirit', and this may be due to his hymn writing as well as to his treatise on the Holy

Spirit. Noël Coward once mused that the potency of cheap music is a strange phenomenon. In his fight against heresy Ephraem harnessed this power in the service of the gospel. The Bardesanes were a Gnostic sect that was gaining ground by setting their teachings to popular tunes. Ephraem played them at their own game and circulated his own words to the same tunes. These 'hymns' were sung in church by a choir of women that he had trained, and because of their popularity they were probably whistled and sung in the streets of fourth-century Edessa. It is indeed strange to realize that this particular root of the history of hymns flourished in the soil of heresy and 'pop' music.

The concept of *metanoia* as 'conversion of life' will be familiar to those with Benedictine spirituality and training. Today's second Office reading is an extract from one of St Ephraem's sermons and, although he does not actually use the phrase that has proved to be his legacy, he provides some insight into what it meant to *him*. The sermon prays to Christ for the grace we need to attain *metanoia*. And I think we will miss his point if we read him as merely playing with metaphors. I am sure he means that if we attain 'conversion of manners', we will perceive and value spiritual things as more truly real and important than material or corporal ones. Light for instance, will mean not merely the light of the sun but also the light and life of the resurrection. The sun gives us our mortal days, but Christ himself is our eternal day. In our reception of Holy Communion we will apprehend a great beauty that Christ's 'will arouses in our mortal bodies', and we will 'crucify our will to give birth to the spiritual life'. The sacraments are a mirror in which we may recognize the resurrection; we will see the natural order as an image of the Spirit, and St Ephraem asks that we may 'live in it as truly spiritual men'. The mortal nature in our bodies is a source of corruption, and so St Ephraem asks of Christ: 'Let the outpouring of the spirit of your love wipe away the effects from our hearts.'

Readings

Sirach 47:8, 9–10: With his whole heart he sang hymns of praise; he appointed musicians to sing sweet music to the harp, that men should praise the Lord and the sanctuary resound from morn to night.
Sirach 39:1–10: He is wise through his study of the word of God; his understanding will not be blotted out, his memory will not disappear.
Sirach 15:5–6: The Lord found words for him.
Psalm 7: Your words are spirit Lord, and they are truth.

1 Corinthians 2:10–16: We are those who have the mind of Christ.
2 Timothy 1:13–14; 2:1–3: Keep this precious thing with the help of the Holy Spirit.
Matthew 23:8–12: You must not allow yourselves to be called Rabbi since you have only one Master, the Christ.
Matthew 5:13–16: You are the light of the world.

Intercessions
Thanksgiving for the life, work and writings of St Ephraem.

For the Orthodox churches and for their study centre in Cambridge.
For Orthodox monks and nuns.

Thanksgiving for the writers and composers of church music and for the choirs who perform their work.

That we may manage the resources of the world with greater wisdom, justice and efficiency.

For priests and people whose parishes are under the patronage of St Ephraem.

(2) ST COLUMBA (COLUMCILLE), ABBOT (DIED 597)

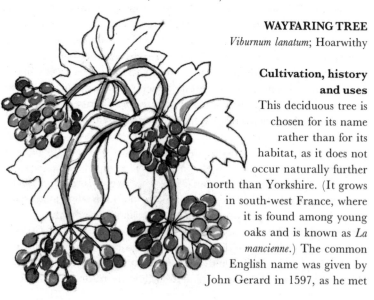

WAYFARING TREE
Viburnum lanatum; Hoarwithy

Cultivation, history and uses
This deciduous tree is chosen for its name rather than for its habitat, as it does not occur naturally further north than Yorkshire. (It grows in south-west France, where it is found among young oaks and is known as *La mancienne*.) The common English name was given by John Gerard in 1597, as he met

it so often in hedgerows beside the drovers' roads over the chalk downs between Wessex and London. *Lanatum* refers to the woolly undersides of the leaves, which reduce water loss when the tree is growing on dry soil. *Hoar* and *withy* are both of Anglo-Saxon derivation, the former meaning 'greyish-white', also a reference to the woolly-backed leaves; and the latter meaning 'a tough pliant stem', also used in reference to the willow or osier. The stems of the wayfaring tree are as flexible and strong as the willow and were frequently used before the advent of string and for making drovers' switches. The black berries were formerly used to make ink, and the wood from the ground stems, which is very hard, to make pipe mouthpieces. The white, flattish flower heads, which appear in May and June, are similar to elderflower but more dense. The berries, which are palatable to birds but not to humans, start red and turn black in maturity. The tree can reach 20 feet but is often smaller. *L. 'Aureum'* is a rare and spectacular garden cultivar that is worth a search. It grows to 5 feet only, and its leaves appear golden yellow in sun and lime green in shade. Otherwise it behaves much as the species. As a general rule *viburnum* prefers a chalky soil and appreciates sun or light shade. It is not normally necessary to prune, but cut back damaged branches after flowering.

St Columba and the wayfaring tree

The wayfaring tree is chosen for St Columba because, after his ordination and in the tradition of Celtic saints, he travelled widely in his native Ireland, preaching and founding monasteries. Later, from Iona, he traversed difficult terrain in order to reach and convert the nothern Picts from their Druidic religion. Also the tree represents, for me, the countless pilgrims who have visited Iona over the centuries and those who go there still to find the 'unfeigned love and peace' of which St Columba was later to speak. His last blessing on Iona prophesied that they would come there: 'This place, however small and mean, will have bestowed on it no small but great honour by the kings and peoples of Ireland, and also by the rulers of even barbarous and foreign nations with their subject tribes. And the saints of other churches too will give it great reverence.'

Columba was born of royal stock in Donegal. He left Ireland in 561 and sailed by coracle to Iona. Here he remained till his death, preaching in the Highlands and Western Isles of Scotland. Most of his foundations are in these islands, and perhaps he should be seen as the apostle of the Irish in Scotland rather than as the apostle to all Scotland. He did occasionally return to Ireland, but only for important occasions. In about 580 he took part in the Assembly of Druim-Cetha, which decided that the Irish of Scotland should supply a fleet but not an army for their native land. The same assembly debated the social status of the Order of Bards. Columba, who was a bard himself, saved them from extinction and therefore assured an educated presence among the Irish laity. There are no surviving examples of his poems in the vernacular, although there are three in Latin. His skill as a scribe is demonstrated in a Psalter kept in the Irish Academy. It is the oldest example of the Irish majuscule form.

The major source of our knowledge of St Columba is a biography by Adomnán, a later abbot of Iona. Although not distinguished as history, this work portrays St Columba as having a powerful presence, both physically and spiritually. It tells that he combined his scholastic and poetic gifts with those of a wise counsellor and teacher, training his monks, building monasteries and guiding local laity. The occasional harshness of his earlier years mellowed with age. The second Office reading proper to his feast is an extract from Adomnán's Life of St Columba. Here we read that he was 'loving to everyone, his holy face was always cheerful, and in his innermost heart he was happy with the joy of the Holy Spirit'.

Whereas St Brendan seems to have been an intrepid seafarer and did not mind (if the *Navigation* is anything to go by) where and how far he travelled, there seems to be, at least in the pre-conciliar liturgy of St Columba, a tinge of sadness. The old introit poignantly expresses the plaintive, yet firm faith of the exile in his God: 'If I take the wings of the morning and dwell in the uttermost parts of the sea, even there thy hand shall lead me, and thy right hand shall hold me' (Ps. 139:9–11). There is a tradition that St Columba never really got over the pain of being separated from Ireland. This is probably rooted in the fact that he may have left Ireland not necessarily to preach the gospel in another land, but because of unpleasantness caused by his having copied a book he had borrowed, and further that he had been held responsible for a battle between his own clan and the followers of King Diarmid. His supposed sadness on leaving Ireland is recalled in 'St Colm-Cille and the Cairn of Farewell', a poem by John Irvine (1903–64). It tells the legend of how St Columba first landed in Scotland on the Isle of Oronsay but climbed a hill and found he could still see his native land on the horizon. He took to his boat and settled on Iona, having assured himself that Ireland could not be seen from it. A cairn was raised where he first landed and is still known as the Cairn of Farewell. Another poem, 'St Columba', by Lionel Johnson (1867–1917) hints at St Columba's pain in exile, but speaks of the joy he now has with God in heaven:

> No more for him thy fierce winds blow,
> Iona of the angry sea!
> Gone, the white glories of thy snow,
> And white spray flying over thee!
>
> Now, far from the grey sea, and far
> From the sea-worn rocks and the sea-birds' cries
> Columba hails the morning star
> That shines in never-nightèd skies.
>
> High in the perfect land of Morn,
> He listens to the chaunting air:
> The Land where music is not born,
> For music is eternal there.
>
> There, bent before the burning Throne,
> He lauds the lover of the Gael:
> Sweet Christ! Whom Patick's children own:
> Glory be thine from Inisfail!

If Columba did suffer from homesickness that would only have been natural, but a deep spiritual contentment is conveyed in Adomnán's description of his death. Just before the night Office of Mattins he appears to have given his last command to his community, saying: 'I commend to you, my children, these last words of mine, that you keep among you unfeigned love with peace.' After this the bell rang for the Office and Columba went alone to the church. When his attendant Diormuit and the rest of the community arrived they found him dying before the altar. From there, helped by Diormuit, he managed to raise his hand above them, 'and immediately after he had so expressed his holy blessing he breathed his last'.

Readings
Genesis 12:1: Go from your country and your kindred to the land I will show you.

Colossians 1:24–9: I became the servant of the Church.

Psalm 16: You will show me the path of life.

Luke 10:2: Pray the Lord of the harvest to send out labourers into his harvest.

Matthew 28:19–20: Go, make disciples of all the nations.

Mark 10:17–30: Sell everything you own and follow me.

Matthew 9:35–8; 10:1–16: He had compassion on them because they were like sheep without a shepherd; I send you as sheep in the midst of wolves, therefore be wise as serpents and simple as doves.

Intercessions

Thanksgiving for the life and work of St Columba.

For exiles, refugees and asylum seekers.

For the peoples of Ireland and Scotland.

For pilgrims to Iona, and for all who welcome them there.

That we may seek Columba's 'unfeigned love and peace'.

For priests and people whose parishes and institutions are under the patronage of St Columba.

11 JUNE
St Barnabas, Apostle (first century)

ALBA ROSE 'MAXIMA'; GALLICA ROSE 'APOTHECARY'; SWEET WOODRUFF *Asperula odoratum*

Cultivation, characteristics, history and uses

The Albas have been in cultivation since the time of the ancient Greeks. Their fragrant white flowers are often tinged with delicate pink, and their foliage is an attractive grey-green. 'Maxima' is alleged by some to date from 1400, although Peter Beales dates it in the sixteenth century (*Classic Roses, Peter Beales Collection, 2003–4*). It is a vigorous double variety and grows up to 6 feet. The strongly fragrant flower is white with a creamy centre, and it bears good hips in autumn. The Gallica rose (meaning 'of France') is also known as the Provins or Provence rose, and was the garden rose of the Middle Ages and Renaissance. *R. gallica* var. *officinalis* is a neat upright, showy bush that grows to about 3ft x 3ft. This is the Apothecary rose, so named because it was valued for its alleged medicinal properties. The flowers have a strong fragrance and are semi-double. They are a light crimson and appear all over the bush in June.

Woodruff belongs to Our Lady's bedstraw family. The stems are hairless and tinged with crimson, and the leaves are prickly edged. Woodruff flowers are white and the fruits have hooked black-tipped spines. The plant is rhizomatous, perennial and creeping. It flowers during early summer and can reach a height of 20 inches with an indefinite spread, thus making it a good ground-cover plant in a shady woodland garden. It is found throughout Europe, in northern and western Asia, and in North Africa. It is aromatic only when dried and therefore useful in pot-pourris. It also has sedative, diuretic and tonic properties, is good for the liver, and reduces spasm and blood clotting. In the Alsace region of France it is soaked in wine to make a tonic called 'Maitrank'. *Asperula* is the diminutive of Latin *asper* and is a reference to the rough stems of the species. It is hardy but appreciates moist, well-drained, neutral to alkaline soil in shade. Sow ripe seed in summer and divide in spring or autumn. Cut the flowering plants and dry for infusions, liquid extracts and pot-pourris.

St Barnabas, the 'Maxima' and 'Apothecary' roses, and sweet woodruff

During the celebrations on St Barnabas's day long ago young clerks used to bedeck themselves with roses, and the practice is reflected in the saint's official emblem. This is a shield shape and is divided into three rows; the top one has three silver Tudor roses on a red field, the middle row two red roses on a silver field and the bottom row a single silver rose on a red field. The 'Tudor rose' is an amalgam of the *Alba*, thought to have been the original white rose of the York household, and the *Gallica*, which was the red rose of the house of Lancaster. It came into being as an emblem of unity under the Tudors, after the end of the Wars of the Roses, and is still the emblem of England today. In Germany and other parts of Europe it was the custom to decorate churches and houses with 'Barnaby garlands' of roses and sweet woodruff. In the language of flowers woodruff means 'of modest value'. However, we should not regard St Barnabas himself in that light, even though he is given only a memoria instead of the feast one might expect for an apostle. This is possibly because he was not one of the original twelve.

Barnabas was a Cypriot Jew, originally named Joseph but renamed Barnabas by the apostles, who must have valued him from the beginning, as the name Barnabas means 'son of encouragement, or consolation'. In any case, we know that 'he was a good man, full of the Holy Spirit and of faith' (Acts 11:23), and those who cavill at the apparently chance election of St Matthias cannot criticize the choice of St Barnabas, who *was* most definitely singled out by the Holy Spirit: 'Set apart for me Barnabas and Saul for the work to which I have called them' (Acts 13:2b). Indeed we know far less about the work of St Matthias than we do about the contribution of Barnabas to the development of the early Church. This is clearly traced, from Acts 4:36–7, when he sells a field he owns and gives the proceeds to the apostles, to Acts 15:39, when he and Paul part company and Barnabas goes to Cyprus with John Mark. In between, it seems that at the beginning Barnabas is the leader over Paul in taking the gospel to the Gentiles. Together, and in the face of opposition and danger, they make many converts in Antioch, Cyprus, another Antioch in Asia Minor, Pamphylia, Iconium and Lystra. At Antioch again (in northern Palestine) a dispute arises as to whether salvation is dependent on circumcision. At the resulting council of Jerusalem they are accorded respect when they tell of 'the signs and wonders that God had done through them among the Gentiles' (15:12b), and the council eventually agrees that circumcision is not necessary to the salvation of Gentile converts. Barnabas is therefore a contributor to this important development in the complexion of the early Church. The parting of Paul and Barnabas in Acts 15 seems to have been caused by disagreement over 'John called Mark'. They were planning to revisit all the places where they had already met with some success. Barnabas wanted to take Mark, but Paul objected on grounds of the latter's 'desertion' when he had returned to Jerusalem from Pamphylia on their first visit there. Barnabas on the other hand, has faith in Mark and takes him with him to Cyprus. From this point, Acts follows the journeys of Paul, we lose track of the biblical Barnabas, and tradition takes over. He is supposed to have met a martyr's death by stoning and, although he was buried at Salamis, his remains were later taken to Constantinople to be housed in a specially built shrine.

Readings
Acts 11:21–6; 13:1–34: Barnabas was a good man, full of the Holy Spirit and of faith.
Psalm 98: The Lord has shown his salvation to the nations.
John 15:16: I have chosen you out of the world, that you should bring forth fruit that will remain.
Matthew 10:7–13 You received without charge, give without charge.

Intercessions

For sufferers from liver complaints.

Thanksgiving for the courage and faith of St Barnabas and all the apostles.

For the priests and people of parishes under the patronage of St Barnabas.

13 JUNE
St Antony of Padua, Priest and Doctor (1195–1231)

WATER LILY *Nymphaea alba*; Lady of the Lake; Swan among the Flowers
ROSE 'NOBLE ANTONY'

Cultivation, characteristics and lore

The botanical name of the water lily is from the Greek *nymphaia*, 'water nymph'. The European *N. alba* has symbolized purity of heart since Elizabethan times, and for apothecaries it was the source of oils used in the treatment of skin blemishes, sunburn and baldness. Its fleshy underwater stems grow as deep as 6 feet below the surface of natural ponds and slow-moving rivers. A domestic pond must be at least a foot deep for it to grow successfully, and a fountain is out of the question in the same water feature because it needs still water. The flowers, which are borne on stems of up to 9 feet long, open towards midday and close as evening approaches, sinking partly below the water surface. Plant in mid-spring in special aquatic compost in submersible mesh baskets lined with hessian or newspaper. Ordinary garden compost is not suitable as it is too rich and its nutrients escape into the water and encourage algae. Ordinary fabric is not suitable as basket lining because it will not decompose. When established plants need dividing they produce so many leaves that some will stand proud of the surface and flowering will be inhibited. They appreciate a feed of aquatic fertilizer at the time of division. The pond should be deep enough not to freeze solid in winter, normally at least a foot. The best way to ensure a continual supply of essential air is to float a small rubber ball on the surface and remove it every morning after ice has formed. As winter approaches, bring moveable water features indoors or into a conservatory or greenhouse, or store the rhizomes in cool, moist sand once they have died down. Re-pot after overwintering. Dwarf water lilies are popular in small ponds. They do not produce rhizomes but are self-sowing. *N.*

tetragonia alba is an example. It has pure white flowers and small green leaves, is low-growing and needs a water depth of 4 to 12 inches. It is slow-growing and needs several years of undisturbed development.

The rose 'Noble Antony' is suggested in the absence of a pond. This bush rose, from David Austin's main collection, was introduced in 1995. It has dark foliage and flowers of deep magenta-crimson. It is an unusual shape, having outer petals that turn back to form a domed bloom. It is ideal for small gardens and has a beautifully rich old rose fragrance that recently won it a prize at the Glasgow trials. It grows to 3 × 2½ feet.

St Antony of Padua and the water lily

St Antony is remembered for his inspired preaching, humility and kindness. He is usually depicted with a Madonna lily to symbolize his purity, but the water lily seems equally apt because in the language of flowers it represents eloquence as well as purity of heart. He was born into a noble Portuguese family and educated at Lisbon cathedral. He joined the Augustinians at the age of fifteen but, distracted by constantly visiting friends, was granted permission to move to the priory at Coimbra, where he spent eight years in prayer and in the acquisition of a profound scriptural knowledge. Later, he was inspired to missionary fervour by the Franciscans who had been martyred in North Africa, and he left the Augustinians to become a Franciscan himself. He went briefly to Morocco, but illness resulted in his being sent home. His ship was blown off course and landed in Sicily, where he met other Franciscans and went with them to a general chapter of their Order. There he met St Francis, who, impressed by Antony's humility, sent him to a hermitage. His learning was not discovered until a preacher was needed at an ordination ceremony. His sermon was so impressive that he was sent to preach in Lombardy, attracting so many people that the churches could not hold the crowds. In 1222 St Francis made him the first lector of theology in his order, a teaching post that took Antony first to Bologna and then to France, where he worked in Montpellier, Toulouse, Puy and Limoges in the fight against the Albigensians and earned the sobriquet 'hammer of heretics'. He returned to Italy on the death of Francis in 1227 and spent the remainder of his life in or near Padua. His effect on the town was extraordinary and resulted in a reduction in crime and usury and therefore in the number of debtors in the jails. He is also reputed to have healed feuds of the 'Montagu and Capulet' type. But his constitution was delicate, and he died at the age of thirty-six. His canonization just a year later was confirmation of the people's firm belief that a saint had worked among them. He was made a Doctor of the Church in 1946. Earlier he had been named patron of the poor, and collections for their relief became known as 'St Antony's Bread'. His fame as a finder of lost objects seems to have originated in the story that a novice had taken one of Antony's books. As the alleged result of his prayers for its return, the novice brought the book back after experiencing a warning vision ordering him to do so.

The second Office reading today is from the sermons of St Antony and is titled 'Language comes alive when it speaks by deeds'. It reads very much as an address to trainee preachers, and we find an extremely forthright and no-nonsense lecturer here. This is refreshingly counter to the impression given by the sugary piety of the prayer cards of one's youth. 'A person filled with the Holy Spirit', says St Antony, 'speaks several languages.' These are languages such as humility, poverty, obedience and patience and are his way of witnessing to Christ. A preacher must practise what he preaches: 'Enough of talking; let actions speak. We are bloated with words and empty of deeds.' And then he warns that a preacher must speak under the inspiration of the Holy Spirit and not 'as his own human spirit suggests'. And he is careful to warn his listeners to beware of false prophets, who claim to be inspired by the Spirit and yet are not. The reading ends with an exhortation to pray for the grace of the Holy Spirit so that we may 'fulfil the day of Pentecost ... let us ask for a keen sense of contrition, and for fiery tongues to profess the true faith, so that inspired and enlightened by the splendours of the saints, we may be found worthy to behold the Blessed Trinity, the one God.'

Readings
Hosea 14:6; Psalm 92:13; Sirach 24:4: The righteous flourish like the palm tree; they flourish in the courts of our God. He will be praised by all God's people.
Isaiah 61:1–3: The Lord has sent me to bring good news to the poor.
Psalm 89:24: My truth and my love shall be with him.
Luke 10:1–9: Carry no purse, no haversack.

Intercessions
For sufferers from skin complaints; for chemists.

For the people of Italy and France; for the well-being of Augustinians and Franciscans, and for God's blessing upon their Orders.

For all who preach the Word of God.

That we may show our love of the poor through action rather than empty words.

That we may study the scriptures in the light of the Holy Spirit.

For greater humility and purity of heart.

For priests and people whose parishes and institutions are under the patronage of St Antony of Padua.

20 JUNE
St Alban, Martyr (died *c*. 287)

ROSE 'ST ALBAN'

Cultivation and characteristics
This is another beautiful English rose, introduced by David Austin in 2003. It has a lovely round bud that develops into a shallow cup with many petals. The colour is a rich yellow at first, tending to a softer tone as the blooms mature. The shrub arches and grows to 4 × 3½ feet, or about 8 feet as a climber. The foliage is luxuriant and disease-resistant, and the scent of the flowers, according to the David Austin catalogue, calls to mind the smell of a flower shop. The rose was named in honour of the Royal National Rose Society, founded in 1876 as the first society of its kind. Their office is in St Albans, and I hope they will not mind my borrowing their rose for St Alban himself. If you buy the rose, 5 per cent of the proceeds will go to the Society, which is presently in need of all the support it can raise. (The reasonably priced annual publication *Find that Rose* lists all the roses currently available in the United Kingdom, and can be ordered from The Royal National Rose Society, The Gardens of the Rose, Chiswell Green, St Albans, Hertfordshire, AL2 3NR; email *mail@rnrs.org*.)

St Alban and the rose 'St Alban'
St Alban is venerated as the protomartyr of England and links his country, as no other saint does, with the age of the early Fathers. Our knowledge of him comes chiefly from the writings of the Welsh abbot Gildas (*c*. 500–*c*. 570) and from Book 1, Chapter 7, of Bede's *Ecclesiastical History*, and part of the latter provides the day's second Office reading. Alban's martyrdom took place, according to Bede, on 22 June, near the city of Verulamium (now St Albans), which grew up around his burial site. The breviary gives the year as about 287, which would place Alban as having suffered under the persecution of Decius (*c* .254), although others have suggested that it

could have happened under Diocletian (*c.* 305) or Septimius Severus (*c.* 209). His story, according to Gildas and Bede, is as follows: Alban gives protection to a Christian priest and is converted and baptized by him. When his mentor is in danger of arrest, Alban gives him the chance to escape and, having donned the priest's cloak, is captured in his place. His subterfuge is discovered, and he is threatened with the torture and beheading that would have been the priest's fate, unless he renounces his Christianity. This he refuses to do, and he is condemned to immediate execution. The appointed executioner refuses to carry out his duties and is straightaway killed, together with Alban, by another man, whose eyes drop out as the martyr's head falls to the ground.

Cures of the sick were reported at the site of Alban's burial, and in 429 St Germanus of Auxerre (d. 446) visited it and removed dust for his reliquaries, leaving relics of the apostles and earlier martyrs in exchange. As a result of his influence St Alban's fame spread throughout England and parts of France, and the *Vita S. Germani* by Constantius of Lyon (*c.* 480) helped to ensure that his cult survived the withdrawal of the Romans from Britain. The first shrine survived at least until the time of Bede. A new shrine was built later as a result of the growing importance of St Albans Abbey, which developed a high standard of artistic work and became England's wealthiest abbey. Part of this shrine can still be seen. Unsurprisingly, St Alban is a candidate to replace St George as patron of England.

Readings

Wisdom 3:1–5: The souls of the virtuous are in the hands of God and there shall be no torment come near them; great will be their blessing.

2 Timothy 8–13; 3:10–12: Anyone who tries to live in devotion to Christ is certain to be attacked.

John 12:24–6: If a grain of wheat dies, it yields a rich harvest.

Intercessions

For the work of the Royal National Rose Society.

Thanksgiving for the life and witness of St Alban.

For the souls of those who recently suffered death by beheading in Iraq, and for their families.

That the nations may fight judiciously to rid the world of barbarism.

For the priests and people of St Albans Abbey, and the many pilgrims who visit the shrine there.

For priests and people whose parishes have St Alban as their patron.

21 JUNE
St Aloysius Gonzaga, Religious (1568–91)

HOLY THISTLE *Cnicus (Carduus) benedictus*; Blessed Thistle

Cultivation, history and uses

This spiny annual grows to a height of about 2½ feet and can spread for a foot. *Carduus* is from Latin for 'thistle', as is *Cnicus,* itself derived from the Greek *knekos.* The plant thrives in well-drained soil and sun. It is a native of the Mediterranean region and probably came to be called holy (or blessed) because it was popularly cultivated in monastery herb gardens for use as a cure-all in the infirmaries. Nowadays it is grown mostly in central Europe for the pharmaceutical industry, which makes use of its antiseptic and antibiotic properties. In modern herbalism it is prescribed internally in the treatment of anorexia, depression, poor appetite and indigestion, and to stop bleeding, lower fever and increase lactation. Externally, liquid extracts are applied to ulcers and wounds. Sow seed in spring, harvest whole plants when flowering, and dry for infusions, liquid extracts and tablets.

Note: *Overuse causes vomiting. The plant is legally restricted in some countries.*

St Aloysius Gonzaga and the Holy Thistle

Aloysius was born into the nobility and had been baptized in the womb because his life was in danger. He made a vow of chastity at the age of nine, and later, while he was a page at the court of Francesco de 'Medici in Florence, he contracted kidney disease and thus had time to develop his precocious piety. When he was sixteen he gave his inheritance to his younger brother and joined the Jesuits. Obedience curbed his desire for excessive austerity, but his weak health prevented him from being the perfect novice. During his last years, before his early death, he was directed by St Robert Bellarmine (1542–1621), who, while encouraging him in his single-minded devotion to God and his neighbour, also managed to rid him of some of his apparent priggishness, particularly in regard to human affection.

I have chosen the Holy Thistle for St Aloysius because it shares several characteristics with him. Its leaves are extremely prickly and require careful handling. Aloysius's approach to his religious life was also extreme, so much so that even in the fervid atmosphere of the Counter-Reformation, his superiors counselled a less rigorous practice. The Holy

Thistle has one taproot, and Aloysius was nothing if not single-minded. The plant produces a single yellow flower, which seems to reflect this saint's singular personality and iron will to 'go it alone'. The flower is attractive in a bold, rather rough way; and St Aloysius, in all his aspects (which do not meet with general popularity today), did without doubt achieve holiness in his *own* extreme and singular way. His behaviour can perhaps be seen as a reaction against the politics of Church and State in his time, and he was indeed a flower of faith and commitment, growing among the injurious leaves of a corrupt and worldly environment. The Holy Thistle was used to treat plague victims. Aloysius nursed victims of the plague and died of it himself, so he may well have been familiar with the plant, which also traditionally symbolizes austerity and independence, both of which marked his life and character. (He shares the Holy Thistle with SS Robert of Molesmes, Alberic and Stephen Harding, the twelfth-century Cistercian reformers, who were also austere and independent in very different ways. See *Gardening with God*, p. 294.)

The *Saint Andrew Daily Missal* is glowing in its praise of the 'radiant purity' and 'perfect innocence' of St Aloysius, whereas the new Missal and Breviary give only the bald facts of his life in terms that strike an unenthusiastic chord. Even during his life there was dispute among the Jesuits as to the wisdom of his austerities. Nevertheless, he was canonized only thirty years after his death. In 1729 Pope Benedict XIII proclaimed him patron and model of youth, a fact that does not appear in the modern Missal or Breviary. It is almost as if the Church is slightly embarrassed about him in that rôle, particularly in an age when voluntary self-denial and discipline are widely out of fashion with adults and young people alike.

I never sow Holy Thistle in my garden; I do not need to. At least one springs up each year and, although I do not harvest it, I leave it out of respect for this saint, who in the letter to his mother which is his proper Office reading, shows an undeniable sincerity in his meeting death at the age of twenty-three as 'a joyful gift from God'.

Readings

1 John 5:1–5: This is the victory over the world – our faith.
Psalm 16:1–11: The Lord is my chosen portion and cup.
Matthew 22:34–46: Love the Lord your God, and your neighbour as yourself.

Intercessions

For those who work in the pharmaceutical industry, and for those who are being treated with Holy Thistle.

For young victims of corruption.

That a healthy balance may be found in the bringing up of young people.

For an end to corruption in our society, in both State and Church.

For a single-minded faith, for independence, and for less self-indulgence.

That having fought the good fight, we may face death without fear and with confidence and serenity.

For the priests and people, and the young, whose parishes and institutions are under the patronage of St Aloysius Gonzaga.

22 JUNE
Feast (in England) of SS John Fisher, Bishop and Martyr (1469–1535) and Thomas More, Martyr (1477–1535)

ROSE 'PRIDE OF ENGLAND'

Cultivation and characteristics

This Harencore hybrid tea rose is reasonably strongly scented, with medium red blooms and is chosen for its name. There is also the rose *Pomifera*, its apple-scented leaves evoking the orchards of Kent, for St John Fisher, and the Rosemary rose for St Thomas, who famously had a rosemary bush in his Chelsea garden.

SS John Fisher and Thomas More and the rose 'Pride of England'

John Fisher was born at Beverley in Yorkshire, the son of a draper. He was educated at Cambridge from the age of fourteen and became a distinguished scholar. He was ordained in 1491 and in 1501 was appointed chaplain to King Henry VII's mother, Lady Margaret Beaufort. Together they reformed and re-endowed Cambridge University, where he reintroduced Greek and Hebrew into the curriculum, learning them himself in his middle age. He invited Erasmus to lecture there and developed a reputation as a preacher, giving the panegyric at the funerals of both the king and Lady Margaret. In 1504 he was made chancellor of Cambridge and bishop of Rochester, refusing wealthier sees because of lack of ambition. He was a scrupulous shepherd of his flock and built up a fine library. Doctrinally, he strongly upheld the Real Presence and the Eucharistic Sacrifice; he wrote four large volumes against the teaching of Martin Luther. Henry VIII spoke of him as the most distinguished prelate of any land, and Charles V said he was an example of learning and holiness that all bishops should emulate. In his capacity as chaplain to Henry's first queen, Catherine of Aragon, he acted as one of her counsellors in the nullity suit of 1529, brought by the king because he wanted to marry Anne Boleyn. John Fisher showed clearly that Henry's marriage to Catherine could not be legally dissolved, and probably from then on he was a doomed man.

At the Bishops' Convocation of 1531 he objected to the King's taking the title 'Head of the Church of England' and inserted 'so far as the law of Christ allows'. Three years later he was condemned to perpetual imprisonment and confiscation of his property. He was alleged to have supported Elizabeth Barton, the nun of Kent, whose visions had predicted punishment for Henry if he did not renounce Anne Boleyn. Clemency was applied because of his poor health, but he continued to oppose the king and refused to take the Oath of Succession in 1534. He was arrested and imprisoned in the Tower of London, where he wrote a treatise on prayer for his sister who was a Dominican nun.

Later he was deprived of office and his see left vacant. Pope Paul III made him a cardinal and sent him the cardinal's hat, at which Henry famously quipped that soon the bishop would not have a head on which to wear it. John Fisher is supposed to have been visited by a spy who managed to elicit a statement of his true opinion, with the result that, at a travesty of a trial, he was condemned to die as a traitor. He was sixty-six when he met martyrdom but looked eighty. He was weak from illness and the austerities of imprisonment and, although he was carried in a chair most of the way to the scaffold, he managed to walk the last few steps. Before execution he referred to John 17:3–4: 'I glorified thee on earth, having accomplished the work which thou gavest me to do; and now Father, glorify thou me in thy own presence with the glory which I had with thee before the world was made'. Then after pardoning the executioner and declaring that he died for the faith of Christ, he asked for the people's prayers and recited the *Te Deum* and a psalm. His body was buried at All Hallows in Berkshire without rite or shroud. His head, which was displayed on London Bridge for a fortnight, was afterwards thrown into the Thames.

St John Fisher was in the habit of keeping a skull on his desk, which must have been a constant reminder that his opposition to the king could only lead to eventual death on Tower Hill. He must have known it was merely a question of time. He has been somewhat overshadowed by St Thomas More, but his integrity, courage, scholarship and devotion to his flock deserve to be more widely recognized and appreciated.

Thomas More was the son of a lawyer, Sir John More. At thirteen he joined the household of John Morton, the archbishop of Canterbury, who sent him to Oxford. However, after two years More's father called him home, fearing that his son was coming under too much humanistic influence. He entered Lincoln's Inn in 1496 and was called to the Bar in 1501. In 1505 he married Jane Colt, having spent four years in residence at the London Charterhouse, where he had considered either joining the Franciscans or becoming a secular priest. From these years, and for the rest of his life, he is reputed to have worn a hair shirt, to have used the discipline and to have recited daily *The Little Office of Our Lady*. Notwithstanding these austerities, his marriage was happy, and Jane bore him three daughters and a son. By the time she died in 1511 her husband had made friends with and been influenced by Erasmus in the course of their joint efforts to reconcile Christian doctrine with classical thinking. Possibly through his classic work *Utopia* ('no place'), Thomas More came to the notice of Henry VIII, who promoted him to a series of public offices, culminating eventually in that of Lord Chancellor in 1529. After Jane's death he was married to Alice Middleton, a capable widow senior to himself in age, who was to prove a caring mother to his children.

In 1524 the household moved to Chelsea, and the king developed the habit of making informal visits, arriving by barge. On one such occasion he consulted Thomas about his marriage to Catherine of Aragon. Forced to express an opinion, he made it clear that he could see no grounds for its invalidity. This did not prevent the king from choosing him as Lord Chancellor, but the 'king's matter' hung over their friendship. Eventually, when asked to acknowledge Henry as head of the Church of England, More at first refused but finally agreed with the addition of Fisher's proviso, 'so far as the law of Christ allows'. But as the king's intentions became clear, the chancellor saw his position as impossible and resigned. Thomas further sealed his fate by refusing to attend the coronation of Anne Boleyn and then refusing to sign the Act of Succession. The latter refusal had been declared treasonable, and on 13 April 1534 he was committed to the Tower of London, where he stayed for the remaining fifteen months of his life. In 1535 the Act of Supremacy came into force, giving the king the title 'only supreme head of the Church in England'. Thomas More was tried for treason in Westminster Hall on 1 July that same year. Physically weak from imprisonment, he produced a strongly reasoned defence, based not on stubborn will but on long years of study. Perhaps in an attempt to find a loophole, he had searched the ancient Fathers and could not find a single one who agreed that a secular ruler could be head of a Christian State. A temporal monarch could not take upon himself the spiritual supremacy that Christ had given to St Peter. Therefore, More reasoned, both scripture and tradition supported his refusal to take the oath required by the Act of Supremacy. Nevertheless, he was condemned to death and was executed on Tower Hill on 6 July, famously remarking on the scaffold that he died for the faith of the Holy Catholic Church and was 'the king's good servant, but God's first'. His body was buried in Saint Peter ad Vincula inside the Tower, and his head was exhibited on Tower Bridge and then buried in the Roper vault at St Dunstan, Canterbury.

St Thomas More has been criticized for setting his conscience above the well-being of his family, who, even though they had taken the oath themselves, were reduced to penury as a result of his actions. But as a judge he had been renowned for fairness and incorruptibility, so his attitude should not have been a surprise to anyone. In any case his family's love for him, although put to the ultimate test, remained unshaken to the end, as did his for them. *Utopia* had perhaps been a witty and erudite humanist conceit, but in his later works, written in the Tower, St Thomas shows greater depth, his *Dialogue against Tribulation* and *Treatise on the Passion of Christ* forming his spiritual legacy. He was a complex man, and this, together with his eminence as a writer, the portraits of him by his friend Hans Holbein, and his greater accessibility as a humorous and caring family man, is probably why he has attracted so many biographers. The more traditionally 'saintly' John Fisher remains under his shadow. Both men knew well where their opposition to the king could lead. St John had his skull, and St Thomas once prophetically remarked of the king, in safer days, that even then, 'If my head would win him a castle in France it should not fail to go.'

Today's second Office reading is from a letter of St Thomas written from prison to his daughter, entitled 'With good hope I shall commit myself wholly to God'. The extract shows humility, utter trust in God and resignation to his will: 'Nothing can come but that which God wills. And I make myself very sure that whatever that be, seem it never so bad in sight, it shall in deed be best.' These words are surely ones that St John Fisher would have endorsed. He and St Thomas were not canonized until 1935, and their joint feast is now in the universal calendar on the anniversary of his death as he was the first to be martyred.

Readings

2 Maccabees 6:18–31: I am glad to suffer because of the awe that he inspires in me.
Psalm 31: Into your hands I commend my spirit.
John 10:23–8: None shall pluck them out of my hand.
Matthew 24:13: You will be hated by all the nations on account of my name.

Intercessions

For the people of Chelsea and Rochester.

Thanksgiving for the lives and witness of SS John Fisher and Thomas More.

For an increase in humility, faith and trust and for the courage to stand up for our convictions.

For the priests and people of parishes and institutions who are under the patronage of these English martyrs.

24 JUNE
Solemnity of the Birthday of St John the Baptist

ST JOHN'S WORT *Hypericum perforatum*; Rose of Sharon; Midsummer flower; Scaredevil

Cultivation, uses and lore

This perennial is native to woods and hedgerows in Europe and temperate Asia. It is upright in habit and has woody stems nearer the ground. The yellow, five-petalled flowers appear in summer, and the plant reaches a height of up to 2 feet, spreading for 18 inches. A red pigment called hypericin oozes like blood from the crushed flowers. St John's wort is probably the best known of herbal treatments for depression, but it also has anti-inflammatory properties, promotes healing and is antiseptic and analgesic. In modern herbalism it is used to treat burns and injuries involving nerve damage. It is a hardy crop and favours a dry to well-drained soil in sun or light shade. Sow seed in spring or divide in autumn or spring. Cut the plants as they begin to flower and use fresh or dried in creams, infusions and tinctures. *Note: This plant can cause skin irritation in bright sunlight. In some countries, including the USA, it is subject to legal restrictions.*

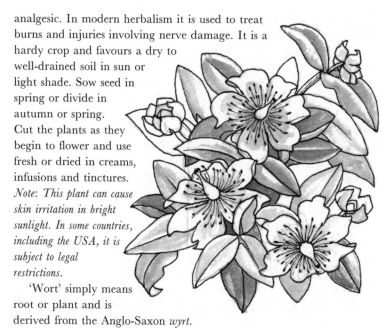

'Wort' simply means root or plant and is derived from the Anglo-Saxon *wyrt*.

Hypericum is possibly from the Greek *hyper*, meaning 'above', and *eikon*, meaning 'picture'. In Northern Europe it was the pagan practice to place flowers above religious pictures to deter evil spirits. *Hypericum* was considered to be particularly effective (hence the English folk name 'Scaredevil'), but other plants such as vervain, bracken and sundew were also valued for the purpose. Throughout Europe fires were burned on the eve of the Midsummer solstice, also to obtain protection from evil powers. The whole summer solstice celebration was later Christianized into the Solemnity we keep today. (St Augustine, for instance, was advised by St Gregory not to tear down pagan temples or change days of celebration, but rather to use them in the promotion of Christian worship and feasts.) The St John's fires came to represent St John as a light to the people, and the belief came about that the devil, in revenge against all these plants and fires that were meant to keep him away, had pierced the leaves of *hypericum* with a needle. This is the *perforatum* of the plant's botanical name. Later, herbalists would follow the doctrine of signatures and believe that these holes show that the plant will help internal or external lacerations, and that the red juice that oozes like blood when the plant is crushed will be good to close up wounds. In the Christian age, as far back as the Crusades, the Knights of St John of Jerusalem used this herb to heal wounds inflicted in battle. Whether they used it because they knew its powers, or because it was already named for their patron or whether their use of it resulted in its being so named, are all moot points. However, the devil's 'holes' are in fact glandular dots, which can be seen when the plant is held up to the light. Many old customs and superstitions that have their roots in pagan and early Christian practice are still prevalent in country districts. In many parts of '*France profonde*', *les herbes de Saint-Jean* are still collected on the eve of 24 June, and in my own village there is an annual bonfire with fireworks on the Saturday nearest to the feast of St John the Baptist's birthday. St John's wort is an obvious choice for today's Solemnity, even though it is connected with him only by name, and by its quasi-Christian lore and history.

St John the Baptist

John's birthday is calculated from the Gospels as being six months before that of Christ. This led to the belief that he received special grace in the womb, and therefore never committed sin. This is thought to be why the Church celebrates his earthly birth as well as his heavenly one (29 August), the latter being the date that normally dictates a saint's commemoration. John is set apart from all of them in his multi-faceted role as prophet, pastor of his own disciples and martyr. Moreover, because of his eremitic life before he began his public ministry of prophecy and baptism, he is also venerated as the prototypical monk. And in his role of preparing the Jews for the coming of Christ, he prefigures the priest, who brings Christ into our own souls in Communion. We reflect on all these roles on 29 August, but today in the proper Office reading St Augustine helps us to meditate on his birth. In an extremely cogent extract from his *Sermon 29*, the great Doctor illuminates its mystery thus: first he compares John's birth with that of Christ. Elizabeth was old and barren; Mary was a young virgin. Zachariah was struck dumb for not believing the angel's announcement that he would have a son; Mary accepted the angel's message in faith and obedience, and shortly afterwards gives voice to her *Magnificat*. Then St Augustine examines St John the Baptist as 'the frontier between the Old and the New Testaments'. Christ himself spoke of John in these terms and said that the old law was valid only until John's appearance. The age of his parents symbolizes his role of prophet; and his salutation of Christ from within Elizabeth's womb symbolizes his role as forerunner of Christ, his mission thus being made clear before he was born. We next consider the symbolism of Zachariah's dumbness. St Augustine sees it as a hidden prophecy 'kept secret and, as it were, pent up before Christ could be proclaimed by his son John. His voice returns after John is born, at the very moment of his naming'. St Augustine further likens Zachariah's restored speech to the rending of the veil of the temple when Christ died on the cross. John described himself as the 'voice crying in the wilderness'. John was a 'voice' for a specific time in history, 'but Christ, who in the beginning was the Word, is the Word in eternity'.

Readings
Acts 13:23–5: John said, 'What do you suppose that I am?'
Jeremiah 1:4–19: Before I formed you in the womb, I knew you; I am putting my words into your mouth.
Psalm 71: From my mother's womb you have been my help.
Isaiah 49:1–6: I will make you the light of the nations.
Acts 13:22–6: Jesus, whose coming was heralded by John.
Luke 1:15–17: She is to bear you a son and you must name him John.
Luke 1: 57–80: You, little child, shall be called a prophet of God.

Intercessions
That there may be less recourse to superstition.

Thanksgiving for the multi-faceted significance and role of St John the Baptist.

For greater repentance for sin.

For all who will be baptized today.

For the priests and people whose parishes and institutions are under the patronage of St John the Baptist.

28 JUNE
St Irenaeus, Bishop and Martyr (*c.* 130–200)

ROSE 'LYON'

History and characteristics
This classic shrub rose has flowers of a coral pink/yellow and red blend. It is fully double and has a good fragrance, growing to 3 feet by 3 feet. It was introduced in 1907.

St Irenaeus and rose 'Lyon'

Irenaeus is thought to have been a Greek, born into a Christian family in Asia Minor, possibly in Smyrna, since he is known to have met and listened to St Polycarp, who in his turn had known St John the Evangelist. He probably reached Lyon in Gaul by way of the trading route from the east, for the city had by his time become a great commercial centre. In the interests of peace he agreed to go to Rome with a letter from the bishop of Lyon in defence of a sect with whom he himself had little sympathy. (The name Irenaeus means 'peace', and he was again faithful to it in 190 when he made peace between Pope Victor II and a group called the Quartodecimans, who celebrated Easter on the day of the Jewish Passover, rather than on the following Sunday. Irenaeus persuaded the pope that this was not a sufficiently important matter on which to risk schism.) While he was away from Lyon in the 170s a sudden persecution arose and the bishop was killed. On his return in 177 Irenaeus was appointed to succeed him. He seems to have been a successful bishop and caring towards his flock, taking the trouble to learn the vernacular, the better to communicate with them. However, it is as a theologian that he is chiefly remembered, and moreover the one responsible for the refutation of Gnosticism that largely ensured its defeat. As we have seen, St Ephraem still had to combat it two hundred years later, and it has never been totally eradicated. Nevertheless it was thanks to St Irenaeus that orthodox Christianity triumphed over it. Gnosticism was and is an entirely different religion, not merely a heretical form of Christianity. It has taken many forms but usually enshrines the belief that the Supreme God is totally aloof from the world and that its creation was the botched job of some lesser deity, often identified with the God of the Old Testament. It thus denies the possibility of the Incarnation. Salvation comes not through Christ but from knowledge (*gnosis*; hence 'Gnostic') and is achieved in an esoteric, 'magic', way in the learning of secret passwords or through a more philosophical achievement of existential self-knowledge, whereas in orthodoxy Christ himself is our salvation. Irenaeus's arguments against Gnosticism – which he did include among heresies – are contained in his *Against Heresies* (an extract from which forms the second Office reading today). He described the different Gnostic systems in detail (thereby providing much of our information about them). However, some of their beliefs were so ludicrous as to allow him to write, 'Merely to describe such doctrines is to refute them.' Then he challenged Gnostic claims to have secret knowledge, which had come to them through one or other of the apostles. Irenaeus pointed out that the apostles had been charged by Christ to preach the Good News to all, and that their teaching had throughout the history of the young Church been openly given in public. He lists the leaders of all the churches beginning with those who had been appointed by the apostles themselves. His point is that apostolic Christianity is far more likely to be found in churches whose teaching has been open and continuous and who agree with one another, rather that among the Gnostics, whose claims to apostolic tradition were unverifiable because of their secrecy and in any case were often mutually contradictory. It was especially because the Gnostics did not accept the New Testament that Irenaeus had to appeal largely to the apostolic tradition of orthodoxy up to his time. For us, the gospel is unassailable and tradition supports it; for Irenaeus to refute the Gnostics, he had to turn the argument round.

St Irenaeus is venerated as a martyr, but we have no reliable details of his death in Lyon in the year 200. He was buried in the crypt of Saint-Jean, now Saint-Irenée, where his shrine remained until it was destroyed by the Calvinists in 1562.

Readings
Sirach 6:35: Stand in the company of the elders. Who is wise? Attach yourself to such a one.
Sirach 24:32–4: I will make instruction shine forth like the dawn.
Malachi 2:6; Psalm 88:22: The instruction he gave was true; my hand shall be ready to help him.
2 Timothy 2:22–6: The Lord's servant must be kind and gentle when he corrects people.
Psalm 37. The law of his God is in his heart, his steps shall be saved from stumbling.
John 17:20–6: Father, may they be one in us, as you are in me and I am in you.

Intercessions
Thanksgiving for the contribution of St Irenaeus in his refutation of Gnosticism and exposition of orthodoxy.
That, guided by the Holy Spirit, we may not fall prey to false doctrines.
For the people of Lyon.
For priests and people who have St Irenaeus as their patron.

29 JUNE
Solemnity of SS Peter and Paul, Apostles and Martyrs
(died *c.* 64)

LOVE-LIES-BLEEDING *Amaranthus*

Cultivation, uses and lore
This annual originates from Africa
and Java and was once extremely
popular as a cottage-garden
flower. It was valued for its
long, drooping, crimson tassels,
which can be up to 16 inches
long. In autumn the stems, too,
turn crimson. The plant can reach
a height of 4 feet and a spread of
18 inches, but it does not normally
need to be staked. It appreciates a
sunny spot in any reasonable garden
soil. Do not deadhead if you wish to
appreciate a fine display. The plant
was used in Ethiopia to treat
tapeworms, and Gerard mentions
its efficacy as a blood coagulant.
Culpeper endorses this, adding that
it is particularly useful if blood is flowing,
'either at the nose or wound'. It is still used in
this way by some modern herbalists in the form of a decoction from the
flowers.

The botanical name is from the Greek *amarantos*, 'unfading', because
the flowers retain their colour for a long time. In classical times the
Amaranthus was especially used in pagan burial rites, and the Greek
theologian Clement of Alexandria (150–214) warned against its use. He
said that an *amarante* (everlasting crown) was the one referred to by St
Peter as being reserved for those who obeyed God. Nevertheless it became
Christianized as symbolic of eternal life. Milton knew this and refers in
Paradise Lost to 'Immortal Amaranth'. In the nineteenth century at
Toulouse a golden amaranth was awarded to the author of the most
beautiful poem to Our Lady.

I have already mentioned, in Part 1, the roses 'Paul's Scarlet' and 'St Piers' and for St Peter I could also have chosen the cowslip or primrose, since both of these are sometimes called St Peter's keys or wort. This has its origin in the legend that St Peter once dropped the keys of heaven to earth and they sprang up as either one of these flowers. Rushes would also have been appropriate, since there is an old English tradition of rush-bearing at Petertide, to the extent that in the south-east Midlands, the Sunday nearest to 29 June was known as Hay Sunday. It is difficult to find a rush-bearing these days, although as recently as 1998 at Warcop near Brough in Cumbria, the rule was that if 29 June fell on a Sunday, a rush-bearing procession would take place the day beforehand. Girls would carry a floral cross and boys a cross of rushes tied with red ribbons. Hay strewing may also still be found at Wingrave near Aylesbury and at St Giles Church, Farnborough. At Folkestone in Kent there is a blessing of the fishermen, boats and sea, obviously because of St Peter's literal and metaphorical connection with matters piscean and maritime.

SS Peter and Paul and Love-lies-bleeding

St Peter has always figured more prominently in the liturgy of today's Solemnity and, as St Paul is spoken of at length on 25 January and during the period leading up to Lent (see *Gardening with God*, pp. 230–2), I have concentrated today mainly on St Peter. However, as far as the choice of plant is concerned, I wanted something appropriate to St Paul as well. Love-lies-bleeding is chosen because both Apostles died for their belief in Christ and his promise of eternal life and also out of their love for him and his flock. The plant sometimes symbolizes undying friendship and this too makes it appropriate.

Today seems an excellent time to reconsider why St Peter is regarded as the leading apostle. Most of the answer is of course to be found in the New Testament. Originally called Simon, he was like Philip a native of Bethsaida. His brother Andrew introduced him to Jesus, who gave him the name Cephas (Peter), which famously means rock. (The French name Pierre is also the word for 'stone', and in our area a traditional feature of internal decoration is *pierre apparente*, that is exposed stone, so my kitchen walls are a constant reminder of St Peter.) Whether Christ went on to say the famous words that he would found his church on the rock of Peter, that he would give to him the keys of the kingdom of heaven and, with the other apostles, the power to bind or loose sin, or whether these clauses were later additions, is a matter for scholars. Nevertheless they have stuck in common lore, and St Peter has always come first in any list of the apostles and is accepted even by non-believers as the legendary keeper of 'the pearly gates' of heaven. Moreover, the 'binding and loosing' text is the foundation for the sacrament of Reconciliation. St Peter was a man of humble origins, beginning as an ordinary married fisherman, not without weakness, as demonstrated by his threefold denial of Christ after his arrest. However, Peter had been among the three disciples privileged to witness the Transfiguration, the raising of the daughter of Jairus and the Agony in the Garden. St Peter was the first apostle to whom Christ appeared after the resurrection. He then, having forgiven the earlier betrayal, gave him the mission to feed the lambs and the sheep of his flock.

In the early chapters of Acts we learn that he presided over the election of Matthias as successor to Judas, preached with authority at Pentecost, was the first apostle to work a miracle, justified the teaching of the apostles to the sanhedrin and admitted Gentiles into the church in the person of Cornelius. Later he took part in the council at Jerusalem (see the entry for St Barnabas, June 11th).

The early tradition that St Peter had a long apostolate in Rome and was martyred there is not based on the New Testament, but it is consistent with it, since in 1 Peter (which is generally agreed to be by him, whereas 2 Peter is not) he refers to 'Babylon', which is usually identified with Rome, and it is believed that Paul's preaching there had been delayed because it was not his practice to preach where other apostles were at work. Furthermore, St Peter's presence in Rome is supported by Clement of Rome, the fourth pope (d. c. 100), Ignatius of Antioch (d. c. 107), and Irenaeus (see above), who knew St Polycarp, who in his turn knew St John the Evangelist. The same sources imply that Peter founded the episcopal succession and suffered martyrdom. Traditionally this took place under Nero. Origen (c. 185–c. 254) seems to be the source of the belief that St Peter was crucified head down, because he felt unworthy to die in the same way as Christ. Recent excavations of the supposed tomb of St Peter have proved only that the tomb is probably his. The remains within it have not been so proved, but they would fit with the tradition that St Peter was a short and stocky man with a square jaw. It is also quite significant that Rome is the only place ever to have claimed to be the place of his death. In many other cases, several places claim the saint's body or relics.

St Peter's contribution to the New Testament is, as already mentioned, enshrined in 1 Peter, and scholars normally agree that he was a great influence on St Mark, and that the latter's Gospel represents his teaching. 2 Peter and other works not in the New Testament, but which bear his name, all date from after his death. They do, however, witness to his huge importance in the early Church. In spite of his later power, he remains accessible because of the ordinariness of his beginnings and the human weakness of some of his reactions as recorded in the Gospels.

Today's second Office reading is from St Augustine's *Sermon 295* and concentrates on the fact that Peter and Paul are the two martyrs who connect us most closely to Christ. They 'saw what they proclaimed', and their fame has 'reached the ends of the earth'. At the conclusion of the extract we are reminded of the tradition that Peter was martyred first. Paul followed. But, more importantly, the passage ends with the exhortation, 'Let us love their faith, their life, their trials, their passion, their profession, and their teaching.'

Readings
Romans 1:1–7: Paul, servant of Christ Jesus, apostle by God's call.
Acts 1:11–20: God chose me whilst I was still in my mother's womb.
Acts 3:1–10: Peter cures the cripple in the name of Jesus.
Acts 12:1–11: Peter's miraculous release from prison.
Acts 15:7–9: God chose me from among you to preach the Good News to the Gentiles.
Galatians 1:15–2:10: Discussion between Peter and Paul.
1 Peter 4:13–14: Be glad to have a share in the sufferings of Christ.
2 Timothy 4:6–18: All there is to come now is the crown of righteousness.
John 21:15–19: Feed my lambs, feed my sheep.
Matthew 16:13–19: You are Peter.

Intercessions
For the peoples of Africa and Java.

Thanksgiving for the works of John Gerard, Nicholas Culpeper and John Milton.

For the people of Warcop, Wingrave and Farnborough.

For the Holy Father, Pope John Paul II.

For all who live and work in the Vatican City State.

Thanksgiving for the New Testament scriptures, and for the writings of the early Fathers, which enable us to 'see' and know St Peter and to trace our faith back to its earliest days.

That we may follow St Augustine in his love for St Peter and St Paul.

For priests and people who live and work under the patronage of St Peter.

3 JULY
Feast of St Thomas, Apostle (first century)

SNAPDRAGON *Antirrhinum*; Calves' Snout

Cultivation

This is another popular cottage-garden annual, whose flower spikes bloom from July until the first frosts. It will reach a height of up to 4 feet and spread for 2 feet, and is available in a great variety of colours. Sow from February to March in a minimum temperature of 61°F and plant out when frosts are over. Snapdragons enjoy a sunny position in any well-turned soil, but dig in rotted compost for really good results. Pinch out the centres to encourage bushy form, remove faded spikes to prolong flowering and stake in windy areas.

St Thomas and the snapdragon

The botanical name is from the Greek *anti*, 'counterfeiting', and rhis, 'nose' or 'snout', alluding to the flower, which vaguely resembles a dragon's snout. The 'mouth' can be made to open by gently pinching the corolla. St Thomas could be said to have been open-mouthed when Christ appeared after the resurrection. The other morning, walking to school (in late September), I spotted some mauve-pink snapdragons, escapees from local gardens, growing wild on waste ground, and, unable to resist touching the velvet petals, I was forcibly reminded of Christ's instruction to St Thomas to put his fingers into his wounds. Traditionally the snapdragon means 'No', but Gerard wrote, 'They report (saith Dioscorides) that the herbe being hanged about one, preserveth a man from being bewitched, and that it maketh a man gracious in the sight of the people.' Thomas said 'No' but then more than graciously accepted the truth of the risen Christ, uttering the words I was taught long ago to say in my heart at Communion, 'My Lord, and my God'.

After Pentecost the most persistent tradition about St Thomas is that he evangelized in India and was eventually martyred there with a spear and buried at Mylapore near Madras. An ancient cross marks the spot where he was supposedly buried before the translation of his relics to

Edessa in 394. Another tradition has it that he is still buried in India at a place now called San Tomé. The Indian tradition was well accepted in the ninth century, and King Alfred sent alms to India because of him. The tradition was strong throughout the medieval period, as is witnessed by the mystery play cycles. In art St Thomas is sometimes represented with a builder's T-square because he is supposed to have built a palace for an Indian prince. For this reason he is patron of architects, while on account of his initial spiritual blindness he has often been associated with the care of the physically blind and invoked on their behalf, as exemplified in St Thomas's Hospital in London.

At times it is much easier to believe in the garden than it is to keep faith. A fellow-Christian once told me that I am too sure of my faith. Little did my accuser know! But indeed, it may be thought strange that I am approaching the end of a third book and have hardly dealt with doubt at all, except perhaps in relation to 'the problem of pain' and the apparent divine unfairness. One good reason for the omission is that the books are meant to affirm and encourage faith, and not to pick it apart destructively. There is also perhaps a deeper-seated reason, and I will be brutally honest and admit that doubt scares me stiff! In a way it is more terrifying than the 'Dark Night of the Soul' during which, although God hides himself, we still continue to believe, some of us for extremely long periods. Dame Felicitas Corrigan revealed that Dame Scholastica Hegbin spent thirty years of religious life in spiritual aridity. This is truly awesome. How did she survive it without going crazy? And yet one only has to read her poems, which are far from dark and doom-laden, to realize that she was eminently sane and full of faith (see Felicitas Corrigan OSB, *Benedictine Tapestry*, Darton, Longman & Todd, 1991). But the frightening 'What if?' questions that assail me (and I think most ordinary Christians at one time or another) have to be faced. I must make it plain however, that I set out from the premise that doubt cannot really be conquered by reason, but can only be 'faithed' away by grace. The first question usually shapes itself as 'What if I have denied myself, when I could have been having a better time, indeed the only time I *will* have?' This I find is the most easily dealt with, even in non-religious terms. Self-indulgence leads to self-destruction, harms those who love us and adversely affects the society around us, and is therefore of itself intrinsically bad. The second question: 'What if faith is all humbug and a mere invention of mankind in case there is something after death, and because we cannot bear the thought of oblivion?' Answer: This 'insurance policy' approach is in itself a weak form of faith, and therefore is capable of being deepened and strengthened. The third question is perhaps the most difficult: 'What if I have wasted my life, following a man who claimed to be God, but who, however holy, is in fact no such thing?' Here the Christian flees (sometimes in a state of panic) to the Gospels, and often to the passages that involve today's saint, St Thomas, the twin. Here we find one of Christ's most comforting sayings, and one with which we immediately identify: 'Blessed are they who have not seen and yet have believed.' St Thomas represents us, both in his incredulity and in his faith. But, as St Gregory points out in today's second Office reading, there is far more to it than that, as indeed there is to Thomas's role in the incident of his initial disbelief in the resurrection. It is a reading that I always turn to when assailed by doubt, and I recommend it wholeheartedly to others in the same plight.

St Gregory believes that Thomas was missing from the first appearance of the risen Christ, not by accident but by God's intent. He characterizes Thomas's touching of Christ's wounds as curative of not only his but also our disbelief. 'His scepticism was more advantageous to us than the faith of the disciples who already believed.' If he had not doubted, where should we turn for comfort? In his touching of Christ's wounds, our faith is made whole, for the doubting Thomas thus became a witness to the reality of the resurrection. When Thomas cried out 'My Lord and my God', he was recognizing the reality of Jesus as God even though as a mortal man he could not see God. Quoting St Paul, St Gregory affirms that 'faith provides the proof for those things that cannot be seen'. Moving to all human beings, St Gregory brings us to realize afresh that Christ already knew us and prophesied us. He knew that even though we would not be able to see him in the flesh, yet we would know him in our souls. And so at the end of today, at any time I can, and particularly in times of doubt, I pray for grace and for a strengthening of faith, and indeed that prayer often features in the Intercessions of this series. It is something for which I believe we should pray unceasingly, and for which, when granted, we should offer continual thanksgiving, while at the same time never taking it for granted.

Note: *The Catholic Herald* (14 January, 2005) reported that the people of Chennai (India) firmly believe that their newly restored Cathedral of Santhome had been spared destruction by the Tsunami through the intervention of the apostle after whom it is named. Survivors were still sheltering in it when the paper went to press.

Readings

Ephesians 2:12–22: You are part of a building that has the apostles for its foundations.

Ephesians 2:19–22: You are no longer aliens in a foreign land.

Ephesians 4:11–13: Some Christ has appointed to be apostles.

1 John 1:1–3: We have seen with our eyes and touched with our hands the Word who is life.

John 20:29: Happy are those who have not seen and yet have believed.

John 20:24–9: My Lord and my God.

Intercessions

For architects and for the blind.

For the peoples of India.

For all who doubt or who are suffering from spiritual aridity.

Thanksgiving for the lives and work of Dames Felicitas Corrigan and Scholastica Hegbin; thanksgiving for the writings of St Gregory; thanksgiving for the life and witness of St Thomas, for his doubt and faith, both of which contain important lessons for us.

For parishes and institutions that have St Thomas the Apostle as their patron.

11 JULY
St Benedict of Nursia, Abbot (c. 480–547)

CHASTE TREE *Vitex agnus-castus*; Monk's pepper

Cultivation, history and uses

This hardy deciduous tree can reach up to 15 feet in height but can be controlled to shrub size. Its leaves are small, elongated, aromatic and dark green, and its lilac-blue flowers are borne on long, erect spikes in the autumn. These are followed by small, round fruits containing aromatic seeds. The tree will grow well in full sun on light, well-drained, acidic soil and is usually best against a wall. Sow seed in spring, layer in summer, or take cuttings in early autumn. Cut back the previous year's growth in spring. Seed may be ground and used as a pepper substitute. The stems can be woven in basketwork and the fruits used fresh or dried to make decoctions and powders for the external treatment of haemorrhoids, migraine and eye problems. The name monk's pepper originates in the

191

fact that the ground seed was used in monasteries as a condiment to curb libido (much as in the 1960s a seminarian friend of mine swore that 'they' were putting bromide in the tea!). Indeed the dried fruits of the chaste tree do have hormonal constituents that affect the pituitary gland and they are used in modern herbalism to relieve menopausal symptoms. It seems likely that St Benedict may not have been familiar with monk's pepper, and in any case he is famously known to have rolled in nettle patches or bramble bushes in order to control the urges of 'the old Adam'. Had he known about the tree, he would have been advised to warn his brothers that overuse of 'monk's pepper' causes formication (derived from Latin for ant), a nerve disorder that produces a sensation of ants crawling under the skin, a condition no less tiresome than the one the monk's pepper is meant to quell!

St Benedict and the chaste tree

As many a monk or nun will tell you, chastity is not necessarily the most difficult vow to keep, but, once it is achieved, the other vows and demands of the rule will be the more easily kept (see Appendix 1 in *Gardening with God*, pp. 290ff). *Vitex* is Latin for tree, but the word *casta*, when used in a religious context, means 'holy' and in ordinary usage 'clean' or 'pure'. So the species name can mean 'Holy Lamb', which encompasses the result of keeping all the vows and is, of course, symbolic of Christ, the model of holiness for everyone. This is why I have chosen it for St Benedict.

Pope St Gregory (the same who helps us in times of doubt) also provides, in his *Dialogues*, the only source of our knowledge about St Benedict's life, but since he claims to have learned the details from abbots of Subiaco and Monte Cassino, there is every reason to believe that they are correct. Benedict was born in the Sabine Hills to the east of Rome (the modern province of Nurcia) and was eventually sent, accompanied by his nurse, to study in Rome. Disillusioned by the moral laxity he found there, he left before completing his studies, to become a hermit. His intention was disturbed intermittently by different groups of followers who alternately asked him to be their leader and guide and then, when he complied, turned against him, one set even making an attempt on his life by poison. Finally, having been persuaded to leave his cave at Subiaco, he organized his numerous followers into groups of ten, but the parish priest of the area resented their presence, and in about 525 Benedict left for Monte Cassino, near Naples. Here, in the monastery that grew up around him, he finished his famous Rule. Benedict did not invent the concept of a monastic Rule, basing his own on those of Cassian (*c.* 360–*c.* 433) and Basil (329–79) and probably also on the anonymous *Rule of the Master*, but producing a monastic guide that was original in its lack of harsh physical austerity, combined with spiritual rigour. Today's second Office reading gives us a hint of these qualities: 'Let them show honour to one another; let them bear patiently their infirmities whether of body or character; let them vie with one another in mutual obedience; let no one follow what he judges advantageous to himself but rather for another; let them love the brotherhood in all chastity; let them fear God in love; let them love their abbot with sincere and humble charity; let them prefer nothing whatever to Christ, and may he lead us all alike to everlasting life.' Benedict was not a priest, and it is very unlikely that he set out to found a religious Order. He does not mention himself once in the Rule, but a clue to his character can perhaps be found in his description of the ideal abbot, who, he said, should be wise, discreet, flexible, learned in God's law and a spiritual father to his monks. *The Rule of St Benedict* was to have tremendous influence not only on monastic life but on Western culture as a whole. Its dissemination throughout Europe was definitely assisted by SS Willibrord and Boniface, the latter inspiring imperial decrees in 743, 754 and 757 that made it obligatory for all monasteries. Until the Cluniac reforms of the tenth century it appears to have been little known in Italy outside Monte Cassino and, in England, the earliest sure evidence of his Rule is of the same century. Today, apart from its continued observance in Benedictine monasteries throughout the world, its accessibility and common sense make it adaptable to the apostolate of several active congregations, to the spiritual life of the laity and even to the management of businesses.

Benedict's sister Scholastica (see *Gardening with God*, 10 February, pp. 256–8) predeceased him and was buried at Monte Cassino. At his own death he was buried with her, and the tomb has survived the centuries, including bombardment during the Second World War. The day of St Benedict's death is alleged to have been 21 March, but since 1969 his feast has been celebrated today so that it may always fall outside Lent, and thus be universally observed.

Benedictine monasteries were centres not only of hospitality but of learning in several fields other than scripture and theology. Botanists, herbalists and gardeners owe much of their knowledge of plants and their ancient use and properties to St Benedict's monastery at Monte Cassino. About the year 1000 ancient classical and Arabic documents were brought there for the monks to translate, copy and distribute. One of these was originally in Latin (*c.* 400) by Apuleius Platonicus and was eventually translated into Anglo-Saxon. It did not survive, but a herbarium made about 1050 combines the work of Apuleius and Dioscorides, author of the influential *De Materia Medica*. This herbarium is in the British Library in London. There are other late eleventh-century copies in the Bodleian Library at Oxford. All show clearly that a tremendous amount of information was being discovered and disseminated at the time. And the well-spring for all of it was Monte Cassino and other monasteries from where foundations spread across Europe to Britain. Monks and nuns (as witness Hildegard of Bingen, 1098–1179) were at the centre of learning about herbal treatment of all kinds of diseases and of knowledge of the cultivation and harvesting of plants. Information about growing crops and keeping livestock, particularly sheep, was exchanged. And so it is impossible to overestimate the contribution of Benedictines and Cistercians to our present knowledge. Each book of this series is dedicated to Our Lady under one of her titles, in memory of my own loved ones, but I have dedicated the series as a whole to Our Lady, Seat of Wisdom, in gratitude to St Benedict and his sons and daughters down the ages.

Readings
Proverbs 2:1–9: Apply your heart to truth.
Matthew 19:27–9: You who have followed me will be repaid a hundred times over.

Intercessions
For the grace of self-control.
    Thanksgiving for Benedictines and Cistercians.
    For their well-being and success of their work.
    For priests and people whose parishes are under the patronage of St Benedict.

15 JULY
St Bonaventure, Bishop and Doctor (c.1211–74)

TREE OF HEAVEN *Ailanthus altissima*

Cultivation, history and uses

This ornamental, hardy and deciduous tree appreciates fertile, well-drained soil in sun or partial shade. Its foliage is similar to that of the ash. Encourage large leaves by cutting back in spring. Male and female flowers are borne on separate trees, the females producing large clusters of dark red, winged fruits in autumn. The tree can reach a height of 80 feet and spread for 50 feet, but fortunately for the gardener it submits without permanent damage to annual hard pruning, the new branches producing bigger and even healthier leaves. It spreads rapidly because of its abundant suckers that often spring up at some considerable distance from the parent. In Britain it thrives best in the south, but it can survive without a great deal of moisture. It is a lovely tree and tolerates life in a polluted atmosphere. In 1751 the seed was sent from China to Peter Collinson (1694–1768), who gave it to James Gordon (*c.* 1708–80) for experimentation in his nursery. The Tree of Heaven was recently discovered to have anti-malarial properties. Only the bark is used in modern herbalism and that infrequently. It is so bitter that it is emetic. *Ailanthus* is the Latinized version of the native Moluccan name *ai lanto*, meaning 'sky tree'. According to the people of its native Indonesia its height results from its reaching towards paradise, and it is known also as 'tree of the gods'. The English name originally belonged to *A. moluccana*, but was transferred to *A. altissima* when it reached Britain.

St Bonaventure and the Tree of Heaven

Giovanni de Fidanza was born into a noble family near Orvieto in northern Italy. He entered the Franciscans, taking the name Bonaventure, which makes one think of the blessings of Advent, so an appropriate name for a man who would be so important to his Order and to the Church at large. He rose quickly to prominence, eventually becoming, in obedience to the pope, cardinal–bishop of Albano. He had refused the see of York, having visited England in his capacity as minister general, an office he had held since 1257. He was influential in the shaping of his Order and its emphasis, handling with skill the two opposed factions within it when he assumed the leadership. The 'spirituals' held that 'poverty' should be supreme in their lives, whereas the 'conventuals', mainly as a result of the huge numbers of friars, believed that buildings and books had become a necessity, which they had not been in the time of their founder. Bonaventure was originally attracted to the Franciscans because St Francis had been a model of the unlearned simplicity of the first apostles. Bonaventure himself, however, became a doctor of theology and believed that as the Church had produced her learned Doctors, so also should the Franciscans be able to reach the highest academic levels, otherwise they would be unable to influence the educated and therefore formative sector of society, and if they did not accept office in the Church they would have no chance of fighting abuses within it.

In character, according to contemporaries, Bonaventure was gentle, courteous, accessible and compassionate. This last is borne out by his placing his predecessor, John of Parma, who was suspected of heresy, in retirement, rather than imprisoning him. His own simplicity and frugality of life was the best demonstration of how the Order could develop according to its current situation without compromising the ideals of St Francis. (There is an attractive story that, when the papal messengers arrived bringing news that he was to be made a cardinal, he was washing the dishes, and asked them to wait until the chore was completed.) Theologically, rather than encompassing new patterns of thought deriving from Aristotle, he remained basically a Neoplatonist, and his theory of enlightened perception is a clear example of this. With St Augustine, he believed that concepts such as justice and beauty cannot be learned through observation or through hearing or reading about them. We only perceive such things through 'the true light that gives light to every man' (John 1:9). One thinks also of Psalm 36:9: 'In your light, we see light'. In his *Disputed Questions concerning Christ's Knowledge*, chapter 4, St Bonaventure writes: 'Nothing can be understood unless God himself, by his eternal truth, immediately enlightens him who understands …. God is to be called our teacher because our intellect attains to him as the light of our minds and the principle by which we know every truth.'

Some critics have valued St Bonaventure more for his mystical writings than his theology, and indeed if he had done nothing else but write of the triple way to union with God, he would still have laid the foundation for almost all mystical writing ever since. Using St Francis's reception of the stigmata on Mount Alverna as a sign of his union with the suffering Christ, Bonaventure expounds the three stages through which that union is achieved: the first is active purification from sin, bringing 'the calm of peace'; the second, the way of illumination, bringing 'the splendour of the truth'; and finally, the union with God, which produces 'the sweetness of love'. Apart from his great spiritual classic, *The Soul's Journey into God*, Bonaventure also wrote *The Tree of Life*, a series of meditations based mainly on the Gospels. As does *The Soul's Journey*, this work too withstands the pollution of our modern age and his tree is well worth climbing as a way of praying the scriptures. (It is also perhaps a simpler approach to St Bonaventure than his more famous work.) His style is economical, yet each of his passages points in many directions, much as leafy twigs do from the basic branch. The drawing of the 'Tree of Life' at the front of the work shows it to be of similar shape to the Tree of Heaven, with numerous large leaves. Its form is depicted as follows: the 'Closest Branches', that is those nearest the ground, deal with the origin of Jesus, his prefigurement in the Old Testament and his life on earth; the middle section of the tree bears the 'Painful Branches', those dealing with the passion and death of Jesus, depicted in the diagram hanging from the central trunk; the top section of the tree bears the 'Lofty Branches: Jesus glorified'. The Holy Spirit is shown above the head of Jesus in the form of a dove, and the subject of the work's last meditations accompanying these stages and 'branches' is 'Prayer for the Gifts of the Holy Spirit'.

Bonaventure died at the Council of Lyon (1274), having preached at the Mass of thanksgiving for its successful outcome of temporary reunion with the Eastern Church. He was canonized in 1482 and made a Doctor of the Church in 1588. In an allusion to the experience of St Francis on Mount Alverna, he is often referred to as the 'Seraphic Doctor', or as the 'second founder' in acknowledgement of his influential contribution to the Franciscan Order.

Readings

1 John 3:24; Sirach 1:9–10: The gift of his Spirit is our proof that he dwells within us; God created wisdom in the Holy Spirit.

Ephesians 3:14–19: To know the love of Christ, which is beyond all knowledge.

Matthew 23:8–12: You have only one teacher, the Christ.

Intercessions

For sufferers from malaria.

For the peoples of Indonesia; China, Italy and York.

Thanksgiving for the life and work of St Bonaventure and for the Franciscan Order; for the well-being of its living members.

That we may be given grace to value learning, justice and beauty.

16 JULY
Our Lady of Mount Carmel

THE TEREBINTH TREE *Pistacia terebinthus*; Cyprus turpentine

Cultivation and uses

The terebinth is native to Mediterranean regions and is thought to have been introduced to Britain in 1621 by John Tradescant the Elder (*c*.1570–1638). It is a deciduous tree or shrub that can reach a height of 28 feet and a spread of 20 feet. Its aromatic leaves are red in youth, turning to a dark green in maturity. The flowers are small and greenish and are followed by purple-brown fruits. Turpentine from *P. terebinthus* and from *T. lentiscus* (mastic) were two of the ingredients in Egyptian incense. Theophrastus (first century BC) mentions terebinth as a source of turpentine. *Terebinthos* is Greek for 'turpentine', and *pistacia* is from Greek *pistake* for 'pistachio tree'. (Pistachio nuts come from another member of the genus, *P. vera*.) Modern aromatherapy uses the essence of terebinth, which is made by distilling the raw turpentine. It is antiseptic and expectorant, relaxes spasms, controls bleeding, promotes healing, and is effective against some external parasites. It is applied externally in cases of arthritis, gout, sciatica, scabies, and lice. It is a tender crop and needs well-drained to dry soil in sun with a constant minimum temperature of 50F. Propagate by seed in spring, or by semi-ripe cuttings in summer. Trim in spring to control size. Resin is obtained by incisions in the bark, made from midsummer to mid-autumn.

Our Lady of Mount Carmel and the terebinth tree

In the middle of the twelfth century a Crusader named Berthold, having vowed before a battle to enter the religious life if his side met with victory, became a monk in Calabria. As the result of an alleged vision of Elijah, he left Italy for Mount Carmel (*c.*1156). There, near the summit, he found the ruins of an ancient monastery on the site venerated as the cave of Elijah himself. According to John Phocas, an eyewitness in 1185, Berthold, by then a priest, assembled a community of about ten brothers, 'who with him at present inhabit the holy place'. It is thought that these men had already been living there as hermits and joined Berthold, later accepting the rule drawn up for them by Albert, patriarch of Jerusalem (died 1214). It is not beyond the bounds of possibility that these 'Carmelites' came at the end of a long line of holy men who had lived on the mountain without interruption since the days of Elijah. This possibility became the Carmelites' own view of the origin of their Order; this was challenged in the seventeenth century, Rome imposing silence on the dispute in 1698.

'The wilderness and the dry land shall be glad, the desert shall rejoice and blossom; like the crocus it shall blossom abundantly .... The glory of Lebanon shall be given to it, the majesty of Carmel and Sharon' (Isa. 35:1–2). Mount Carmel is indeed majestic and was a rich source of timber in biblical times. The ridge of the mount stretches out to the Mediterranean and it was from this summit that Elijah's servant saw the rain cloud that ended the drought (1 Kings 18:44). Inland there are still streams, willows and blackberries. In spring it is astonishingly green, dotted with the colour of annual rock-roses and crocuses, and of course with the new red leaves of the terebinth, set in stunning contrast against the green of the oaks. But by 1238 the Carmel group had found life increasingly difficult because of the spread of Islam and had settled on Cyprus. Here too, they would have found the terebinth tree. Later, Carmelites spread into mainland Europe. They held their first chapter at Aylesford in Kent in 1245 and elected St Simon Stock (died 1265) as general. Our Lady is said to have appeared to him and shown him the brown scapular, promising that whoever wore it would go straight to heaven after death. I confess to a belief that Our Lady of Mount Carmel had been looking after her sons for a long time before this. Not a great deal is known about the early life of St Simon, but he is traditionally thought to have visited the Holy Land, and it was perhaps there that he became a Carmelite. If so, he would certainly have known the beauty of Carmel and have been familiar with the terebinth tree. By the time of his election as general, the Order was no longer eremitic but cenobitic (living in common), and in 1247 Pope Innocent IV had confirmed them as 'Friars of Our Lady of Mount Carmel'. At the dissolution of the monasteries in the mid-sixteenth century, they were flourishing in fifty-two houses in England, and 'in no other country in Europe did the glory of their institute shine out with greater lustre' (*A Catholic Dictionary, op. cit.*). The later distinction of the Order belongs mostly to Spain, but that is another story for other days (St John of the Cross, 13 December; St Teresa of Avila, 15 October). The feast of Our Lady of Mount Carmel was instituted for the Carmelites in 1332 and extended universally by Pope Benedict XIII in 1726, but now ranks only as an Optional Memoria.

The second Office reading is from Sermon 1 *On the Nativity* by Pope St Leo the Great (died 461). Entitled 'Mary conceived in her soul before she conceived in her body', it leads, as any sound reflection on Mary will do, to a meditation on her Son. There is also a reading from the Sermons of St John Chrystostom (*c.* 350–407), given as an optional reading for Saturday memoria of the blessed Virgin, which I like to read today. This too, leads to Christ and is entitled 'Adam and Christ, Eve and Mary'. St John notes that a virgin, a tree and a death were responsible for our defeat. 'The virgin was Eve; the tree was the tree of knowledge of good and evil, and the death was Adam's penalty. But in the Incarnation these symbols of the Fall become the symbols of victory. In place of Eve, there is Mary, in place of the tree in the Garden of Eden is the tree of the cross, in place of the death of Adam is the death of Christ. The first tree was responsible for Adam being overcome, but on the tree of the cross Christ vanquished sin. The first tree was responsible for hell, the second one calls back even those who had already gone there. The first tree hid man already spoiled and naked, the second shows a stripped victor raised on high for all to see. The earlier death condemned those born after it, the second death gives life again to those who were born before it.' St John then goes on to marvel that the victory was won without any sweat or toil on our part: 'Our feet did not stand in the front line of battle; we suffered no wounds'. He rejoices in amazement, and the reading closes in the full confidence of faith in the victory of Christ over death through his cross: 'The cross is the Father's will, the glory of the Only-begotten, the Spirit's exultation, the beauty of the angels, the guardian of the Church. Paul glories in the cross; it is the rampart of the saints, it is the light of the whole world.'

Readings

Sirach 24:8–31: Like Terebinth I spread out my branches and they are glorious and graceful.

Luke 11:27–8: Blessed are they who hear the word of God and keep it.

Matthew 12:46–50: Anyone who does the will of my Father is my brother, sister and mother.

Intercessions

For those being treated with terebinth essence.

Thanksgiving for the beauty of spring and summer.

Thanksgiving for the prayers, life and witness of Carmelites both living and dead.

For the well-being of each Carmelite; for the Friars at Aylesford and for the Carmelite Order, worldwide.

Thanksgiving for the prophecies of Elijah and Isaiah.

For the priests and people of parishes and organizations under the patronage of Our Lady of Mount Carmel.

22 JULY
St Mary Magdalene (first century)

ROSE 'MARY MAGDALENE'
PRAYER PLANT *Maranta leuconceura kerchoviana*

Cultivation, characteristics and history

The rose 'Mary Magdalene' is an English rose with an old rose character. The blooms are soft apricot pink, and the petals are delicate and silky, surrounding a central 'eye'. It has matt green leaves and a lovely tea-rose scent with a hint of myrrh. This rose was actually named for the church of St Mary Magdalene at Albrighton,

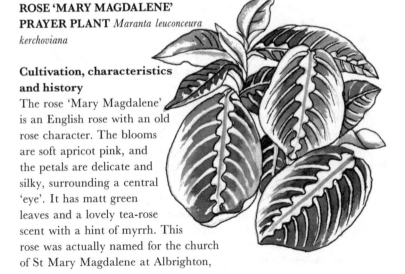

whose parishioners, I feel sure, will not mind it being dedicated here to their patroness. It was introduced by David Austin in 1998 and grows to a compact 3 feet by 3 feet.

Maranta is a house plant, grown for its distinctive foliage. It needs protection from the direct rays of the sun, high air humidity, warmth in winter, and seclusion from draughts. Keep the compost moist, using tepid soft water, and reduce watering in winter. Divide when re-potting, once every two years, and then cover with polythene and keep warm until new plants are established. Mist the leaves regularly. If possible surround the pots with damp peat. The common name 'Prayer Plant' is given for its habit of folding its leaves in a prayerful position at night, but in fact the ten dark blotches on its leaves could draw attention to the separate clauses of the Lord's Prayer, or those of the Easter Sequence, or to the ten 'Hail Marys' of the first glorious mystery of the rosary.

St Mary Magdalene, rose 'Mary Magdalene', and the Prayer Plant

The only woman we know definitely as Mary Magdalene is the one from whom Christ cast out seven devils (Luke 8:1–3); the one who stood by the cross (Matt. 27:61a, Mark 15:40a, Luke 23:55, John 19:25b); the one who went with others to the tomb of our Lord to anoint his body (Luke 24:1–12); and the one to whom he appeared on Easter morning, who then took the news to the male apostles (John 20:1–18). The latter role has resulted in her occasionally being referred to as 'apostle to the apostles'. As we know, they did not believe her at first. Legally, they did not have to, since women were not allowed to bear witness in the courts of the time. After the close of the Gospels the tradition surrounding Mary is unverifiable and in parts highly dubious. In the Eastern Church she is believed to have gone to Ephesus with the Blessed Virgin and St John the Evangelist and to have been buried there on her death. The English St Willibald (died 786) saw her supposed tomb there. In the West, the tradition arose that, with her brother Lazarus and sister Martha, she travelled to France and evangelized Provence. She is supposed to have lived as a hermit in a cave near Sainte-Baume. The name means 'holy balm' and one wonders whether it had the name before her supposed arrival or was given it subsequently because of her association with the woman who was a sinner and who anointed Christ with costly ointment (Luke 7:37). The legend claims that, before dying, Mary Magdalene was miraculously transported to the nearby Saint-Maximin, to receive the last rites at the hands of St Maximinus, reputedly the first bishop of Aix-en-Provence. Not surprisingly, in spite of the fact that the legend is almost universally rejected, it has maintained popularity in France and pilgrimages are still made to Sainte-Baume and Saint-Maximin. The English too seem to have subscribed to the legend, at least until the medieval period, since there is a Middle English *Play of Mary*, which places her in both the Holy Land and Provence.

In the East Mary Magdalene has always been kept separate from the repentant woman who anointed Jesus in the house of Simon the leper, as well as from Mary, the sister of Martha, who sat at Christ's feet while Martha prepared supper on one of his visits to their house in Bethany, thus becoming a symbol of the contemplative life. (And Christ's answer to Martha, that Mary had chosen the better part, has famously become the scriptural argument for the superiority of that life over the active apostolate.) In the West, however, St Jerome (c.341–420) and St Gregory (c.540–604) held that the three figures were one and the same person. Later, St Bernard of Clairvaux (1090–1153) reverted to the Eastern position that the women were three separate individuals, and the Western Church now officially takes the same view. One of the main arguments against their being one person is the fact that Mary Magdalene is mentioned by name when she appears in the Gospels – and so would have been had the two episodes involved her. Another is that her name shows that she came from Magdala and not Bethany. Nevertheless, I doubt that any of this will alter the perception of her, by many Christians and non-Christians alike, as the repentant prostitute, who was the sister of Martha, and who saw Christ on Easter morning.

If you prefer to think of the three women as one, then spikenard, and rue, the 'Herb of Grace', which also signifies purification, would be appropriate choices for today (see *Thorn, Fire and Lily*, pp. 122, 99). Heliotrope, signifying devotion, would also suit her as one person or as three. However, I tend to the belief that what really matters about them is not whether they were one or three, but what they symbolize and can teach us about the Christian life. All the incidents in which they appear show women as deeply reverent and compassionate toward Jesus. They were loyal and had no concern about what others thought of their devotion to him. They did not desert him in times of danger and crisis, as the men sometimes did. And so I feel that the woman in the house of Simon the leper represents the first impetuous joy and rush of love for Christ experienced at conversion, but in ignorance of the depths and heights of his importance (one could say that this is a symbol of Baptism at whatever stage in life it is received); Martha's sister represents the contemplative prayer life at his feet (which can be seen as part of our formal undertaking in Confirmation), which should underpin all our active works throughout the journey of life. Mary Magdalene's going to the tomb is symbolic of consistent, persistent loyalty to Christ, which leads to the final reward of his recognizing us and we in turn truly seeing and recognizing him. Mary reaches a symbolic heaven at this point, and so perhaps we do not need to know what happened to her afterwards, except that she was given the privilege of being the first to carry the Good News to others (and here we may see a symbol of Holy Communion and of our taking Christ out into the world). So much for not being able to bear witness in a human court! Thus, 'the Marys' show us the pattern and the progress of our spiritual and sacramental lives, that is our relationship with Jesus. In the second Office reading today St Gregory, in his *Homily 25*, dwells on the nature of Mary Magdalene's love for Jesus, and indeed it is that love which is constant, whether we see it as in one woman or in three. He points out that the more she sought him, the more she loved him. And his last remark applies to all the Marys, and indeed to all of us: 'Outwardly it was he who was the object of her search, but inwardly it was he who was teaching her to search for him.'

Readings

Song of Songs 3:1–5; 8:6–7: I found him whom my heart loves.
1 Corinthians 5:14–17: We once knew Christ in the flesh, that is not how we know him now.
Psalm 63: For you my soul is thirsting, O Lord, my God.
Luke 10:38–42: Mary has chosen the better part; it is not to be taken from her.
John 20:1–18: Jesus said to her, 'Mary!' She knew him then and said to him, 'Rabboni.'

Intercessions

Thanksgiving for the 'three Marys'.
    Thanksgiving for the Sacraments.
    For grace to be loyal, persistent, consistent, compassionate and brave in our following of Christ.
    For grace to love him, that he may recognize us and call us by name and that we may finally see and know him in heaven.
    For the Oxford and Cambridge colleges that bear the name of St Mary

Magdalene, and for priests and people whose parishes and institutions are also under her patronage.

23 JULY
St Bridget of Sweden, Foundress (1303–73)

ROSE 'THE PILGRIM'

Characteristics and history
This David Austin English rose was introduced in 1991. Its pure yellow and delicate flowers are quite large and evenly shaped, with many small petals forming a flat bloom. The petal texture is soft and the fragrance is balanced between tea rose and myrrh. It is an extremely healthy, versatile rose, growing as a shrub to 4 feet × 4 feet, but it can also be trained to reach 8 feet as one of the best climbers.

St Bridget and rose 'Pilgrim'
Bridget was the daughter of a Swedish provincial governor. She married Ulf Gudmarrson when she was about fourteen and bore him eight children, one of whom was to become St Catherine of Sweden. By 1335, when she was summoned to the court of King Magnus II to be lady in waiting to Queen Blanche, she had already begun to have visions and was in the habit of visiting the sick. She enjoyed the respect of her royal employers but apparently had no effect on their own lives. In 1340 Bridget's youngest son died and she went with her husband on a pilgrimage to Santiago de Compostela. Widowed shortly after their return, she went in 1343 to the Cistercian monastery where her husband had died and lived there as a penitent for three years. Her visions increased in frequency and power, to such an extent that she feared they were of diabolic origin. But Christ then assured her that she was to be his bride and that he would communicate messages through her. In 1346 she founded the joint monastery for men and women at Vadstena, and so was born the Order of the Most Holy Saviour (the Brigettines). The Rule and all the details of the monastery's organization (including the fact that there were to be sixty nuns and twenty-five monks) were to be according to instructions St Bridget had received in her visions. The monks and nuns were to live in separate enclosures but share the same church; poverty was to be paramount, but all the members could have as many books for study as they wished.

In 1350 St Bridget went to Rome to obtain approval for her new Order. She was given a house there by a cardinal and wrote her *Sermo Angelicus*, so called because she claimed that it had been dictated from revelations of an angel. She never returned to Sweden but spent the next twenty-four years of her life, until her death, on pilgrimages and – again in obedience to her visions – in usually abortive attempts to influence the affairs of the Church and of various secular States. One of her main concerns was that the papacy should return from Avignon to Rome. Pope Urban V did temporarily return in 1367 and while in Rome approved the Brigittine Rule. Bridget prophesied his imminent death and told him that he should not go back to Avignon. He ignored her and died in Avignon a few months afterwards. His successor Gregory XI took no notice of this and remained in France. In 1371, as the result of instruction in a vision, St Bridget made a pilgrimage to the Holy Land with two of her sons and her daughter Catherine. While there she experienced several visions at the sites of the nativity and passion of Christ, although the details occasionally departed from the Gospel version of events. Her son Charles died at Naples on the return journey, and in 1373 she arrived in Rome ill and exhausted and died that same year. Her body was taken back to Vadstena. St Bridget was canonized eighteen years later, not because of her visions, but as the foundress of her Order and for her charitable works. She is, of course, patron of Sweden.

St Bridget's visions had been recorded in Latin by her confessors from her dictation, and by 1415 they had been translated into English and were to have considerable influence on fifteenth-century piety. Henry V of England, who had a great devotion to her, built Syon Abbey in Isleworth, to the west of London, but it was destroyed at the dissolution of the monasteries. The only English Brigettines now reside at a monastery at South Brent in Devon, and there are about thirty other houses in Europe, North America and India. To date, these are all-female institutions: the idea of the double monastery is virtually extinct, despite an attempt to revive it in England during the twentieth century. (There is in fact a small double monastery of Benedictine Anglican monks and nuns at Burford Priory near Oxford. As Syon was closed at the dawn of the Reformation, so Burford, thought to have been an Augustinian foundation, was secularized in 1538, becoming a religious house again with the arrival of nuns from Wantage in 1949.)

The proper Office reading for St Bridget is an extract from prayers attributed to her. Entitled 'A Prayer to Christ our Saviour', it is a hymn of blessing, honour, joy, praise and thanksgiving to Christ, offered in separate paragraphs, each one marking a stage of his passion and death, clearly based on the Stations of the Cross. It therefore gives helpful starting points for meditation during that devotion, and certainly, although its language may be somewhat florid for the modern taste, St Bridget clearly bore that love for Christ on which St Gregory reflects during the celebration of St Mary Magdalene's day.

Readings

Galatians 2:19–20: I live now not with my own life but with the life of Christ who lives in me.
Psalm 34:2–11: I will bless the Lord at all times.
John 15:9–15: Remain in my love.
John 15:1–8: Whoever remains in me, with me in him, bears fruit in plenty.

Intercessions

Thanksgiving for the work of rose breeders.
    For members of the Brigittine Order throughout the world.
    Thanksgiving for the life and work of St Bridget.
    For the people of Sweden.
    For Burford Priory.
    For the work of retreat houses and those who staff them.
    For pilgrims in body and spirit, and for pilgrimage centres, particularly in the Holy Land and at Santiago de Compostela.

25 JULY
Feast of St James The Greater, Apostle (died *c*. 44)

CORNCOCKLE *Agrostemma githago*

Cultivation and history

Many are the farmers of yesteryear who would wonder why anyone should deliberately grow corncockle. Before the days of selective weedkillers it was one of the most troublesome annual weeds in cornfields because its seeds became mixed with corn and lowered the quality, and therefore the value, of flour. In French it is *nielle des blés*, *nielle* being a disease of wheat – the name surely indicating how much it was hated by

French farmers. The flowers are reddish-purple with five undivided petals, borne singly on stems that can reach 40 inches. These appear from June to August. The plant is now rare, but, if you are creating a meadow garden, seed can be obtained in wild-flower mixtures from specialist outlets. It is of course not the only meadow/cornfield plant that was in danger of extinction until organizations such as the HDRA (Henry Doubleday Research Association) got to work. In meadows the once-common spiked speedwell, blue and chequered fritillary, and the delightful pink meadow saffron are almost impossible to find; as are pheasant's eye (bright red); field cow-wheat (purple and yellow), and woad (yellow) in cornfields. The variety of colour they represent has almost disappeared. I do not think that the renewed interest in these 'lilies of the field' springs from mere nostalgia for a Hardyesque past and is simply a fashionable fad. In many quarters I believe it has more to do with the fact that we have begun to wake up, hopefully not too late, and to realize that we do not want these delightful creations of the Lord to disappear from our landscape. And so, disregarded, even detested, as they were in even in the time of Thomas Hardy, and having done our best to exterminate them, we are now encouraging the 'weeds' of our forebears into our gardens. We are an odd lot. An old definition of a weed is that it is a plant that insists on growing where it is not wanted, and so, if we now want them in our gardens, then there they are weeds no longer and can now be appreciated in all their glory.

The botanical *agrostemma* is a composite of the Greek *agro*, 'field', and *stemma*, 'crown'. In Yorkshire to 'cockle' means to overbalance, or not to sit straight on a flat surface, and perhaps this is the origin of the name corncockle. The plant affected the harvest and unbalanced its value. Cockle is also a shell of course, so perhaps the English name means 'field shell', from the perceived shape of the flowers. And that brings me to St James, whose emblem is another kind of shell, the ancient scallop shell of pilgrims, and particularly of those to his shrine at Santiago de Compostela in north-western Spain.

St James and the corncockle

This shell connection, however, is not the only reason why I have chosen the corncockle for today. Santiago de Compostela means 'St James of the field of stars' and comes from a legend that a shepherd was guided to discover his bones by stars shining on a particular spot. Bones were indeed found at some point, but there is no sound proof that they were those of St James, somehow translated from Jerusalem, where he died. This legend is, however, more believable than the other claim that he actually went to Spain and preached the gospel there. Nevertheless I would like to offer him an English field of stars, one that is full of the wild flowers mentioned above, the corncockle standing for them all. This vista of a meadow of 'lilies of the field' could also be in France, because they are native to its south-western region. Also I cannot forget that my French home is on one of the main pilgrim routes to Santiago, and our local parish church is dedicated to St James for that reason. The corncockle and the others would have been familiar to pilgrims over the centuries as they passed on foot through the towns and villages of France towards the border with Spain. (Many abbeys and convents provided hospitality to the pilgrims, and special hospices sprang up. A house of the latter type was known as a *Maisondieu*, and my own name derives from the word.)

All the information that we have about the apostle James is to be found in the New Testament, in the following texts:

Mark 1:19–30: James, a fisherman, the son of Zebedee and the brother of John, is called by Jesus and leaves everything to follow him.

Mark 1:29–31: He is present at the healing of Peter's mother-in-law.

Mark 5:35–43; Luke 8:49–56: He witnesses the raising of Jairus's daughter.

Matthew 17:1–8; Mark 9:2–8; Luke 9:28–36: He is present at the Transfiguration.

Matthew 26:36–46; Mark 14:32–42: Christ asks him to keep watch in the Garden of Gethsemane.

Luke 9: 51–6: He and his brother are nicknamed 'Boanerges' (Sons of Thunder) by Jesus, because of their hot temper and will to revenge on disbelievers.

Matthew 20:20–4; Mark 10:35–40: He and his brother, through their ambitious mother, ask Jesus if they may sit on either side of him in the kingdom of heaven.

Acts 12:1–2: As a victim of the persecution begun by Herod Agrippa, St James is the first apostle to be martyred.

The proper Office reading for St James is from *Homily 65: On St Matthew's Gospel* by St John Chrysostom. Entitled 'Partners in the Passion of Christ', it is a meditation on Matthew 20:20–4 (see above). Christ's admonition of the brothers is gentle but full of deeply significant teaching. He shows them that their request is unspiritual by comparing what they ask with what they should be asking: When Jesus asks them, 'Are you able to drink the cup that I am to drink?' he clearly refers to his own imminent passion and death, but in their uncomprehending zeal, James and John rush into an affirmative answer. Jesus then tells them that they will indeed do so, meaning of course that they will, through suffering, become worthy of reward, but certainly not of the worldly kind they now desire. Their desire will by then have become totally spiritual. Jesus does not bludgeon them with the cruel detail of what is to befall him – and, indeed, one of them. He knows they are not ready. On hearing his response to James and John, the other disciples are 'indignant' because they too do not understand the meaning or nature of the privilege of sharing 'his cup'. Arguably, it is not until after Pentecost that they all do, for in Acts, John, who is not to be martyred, always gives precedence to Peter in preaching and proclaiming miracles, all desire for supremacy having gone. And later he will be marked out by his love for Christ and for his flock, constantly enjoining them to love one another. As for James, St John Chrysostom suggests that his spiritual development was so speedy as to make him worthy of being the earliest apostle to be martyred. John in a long life, and James in a relatively short one, came a great distance from their spiritually immature question in Matthew 20. And of James, Chrysostom concludes:

'From the beginning he was moved with great zeal. He gave up all earthly interests and attained such an inexpressible degree of excellence that he was killed immediately.'

And so in a way St James the Greater, 'the son of thunder', did truly become (as the Santiago de Compostela cult was later to characterize him) the gentle pilgrim with his scallop shell, wide-brimmed hat, staff, cloak and water bottle. And in that guise I will spend today with him:

> Give me my scallop-shell of quiet,
> My staff of faith to walk upon,
> My scrip of joy, immortal diet,
> My bottle of salvation,
> My gown of glory, hope's true gage,
> And thus I'll make my pilgrimage.
> (Sir Walter Raleigh: *The Passionate*
> *Man's Pilgrimage*, 1604)

Readings

Ephesians 4:11–13: Some Christ has appointed to be apostles.
2 Corinthians 4:7–15: We carry with us in our body the death of Jesus.
Psalm 126: Those who are sowing in tears will sing when they reap.
Psalm 19:5: Their sound has gone forth into all the earth.
Matthew 20:20–8: You shall drink my cup.

Intercessions

For less anger and will to revenge.

That we may grow in spiritual maturity, and be worthy of heavenly reward.

For greater tolerance and less jealousy.

Thanksgiving for the life of St James.

Thanksgiving for the gentleness of Christ in dealing with our ignorance and incomprehension.

Thanksgiving for the writings of Sir Walter Raleigh and St John Chrysostom.

For the shrine at Santiago de Compostela, all who make pilgrimage to it; and all who extend hospitality there.

For priests and people whose parishes and institutions are under the patronage of St James.

211

26 JULY
SS Joachim and Anne, Parents of The Blessed Virgin

CLEMATIS 'HAPPY MARRIAGE' Virgin's Bower

Description

This pink and white-striped clematis would probably have to be ordered from the French mail order firm Bakker, at www.bakker.fr. However, if it cannot be obtained, a Nelly Moser will evoke the same symbolism. (For the uses and lore of Clematis, see *Gardening with God*, 22 December, pp. 100–1.)

SS Joachim and Anne and clematis 'Happy Marriage'

There are delightful legends of St Anne worrying about the hardness of her daughter's bed, going into the countryside to look for something to make it softer and coming back with bedstraw or thyme, depending on which version you read. In certain areas of Germany and Holland it was once the custom of children to say, whenever they picked these plants, 'Our Lady slept on this'. Sentimental, superstitious tosh, someone may say, but I believe that if those children thought about Mary the mother of Christ as a result of holding those plants, then it cannot have been a bad custom. And if we, in adulthood, are led by bedstraw, thyme or clematis *to meditate on the mysteries of faith,* rather than to seek clear irrefutable answers to questions we do not really need to ask, then the symbolism of plants and the legends surrounding them can only do us spiritual good. But of course, being human, we have to picture the things we don't know, as well as the ones we do. This is clearly demonstrated in the main legend surrounding the parents of Mary, and in its depiction in the work of Christian artists such as Giotto and Dürer. Briefly it goes as follows: Joachim (from Nazareth) and Anna (from Bethlehem) are a childless but otherwise happily married and wealthy couple, who lead a righteous and charitable life. On the occasion of Joachim taking a double gift to the temple he is told by the high priest that it is an unlawful offering because he and Anna have not produced an heir. Joachim abandons Anna and in despair goes to live with shepherds in the countryside. Here he fasts and prays for forty days and nights. Meanwhile Anna goes into mourning for the loss of her husband and because of her barrenness. She too prays, and she is visited by two angels. The first promises her that she will after all bear a child, who will be blessed throughout the whole world. The second angel tells

212

her that Joachim has received the same angelic promise and is on his way home. Anna goes out to meet him, they joyfully embrace at their reunion, and nine months later, the Blessed Virgin Mary is born.

The legend, which arose in the East and is therefore of early date, has definite echoes of the biblical account of Elizabeth, Zachariah and the conception and birth of St John the Baptist, and those who promulgated it clearly thought that Mary's origins *must* have been the occasion of even greater miracles which could not have involved the natural means of human conception. This version of events could have come about as a result of *pudeur*, the feeling being that it could not have been possible for the spotless virgin to be born in the usual way. Perhaps this in itself was because the doctrine of the Immaculate Conception of Mary had not been defined and, even if known, was imperfectly understood. For surely there is confusion here between Mary as immaculately conceived in the mind of God since before time began and her human birth in time. But I feel it is wrong to criticize the credulity of our ancestors from a standpoint of modern intellect and knowledge. We should be grateful to them because, despite the fantastic accretions they added to it, they still handed down to us the core of faith, without which we would still be walking in the darkness of total ignorance.

The post-conciliar Missal and Breviary stress that these are the *traditional* names given to the parents of the Blessed Virgin Mary. We are not asked, as an article of faith, to believe that they were so called. But the Church does not, now or at any other time, wish us to forget that the Virgin Mary did have parents and that they played an important role in her being and upbringing. If we dismiss them as people, because we can't accept the traditions surrounding them, then I believe we nod too far in the direction of fashionable scepticism and are in danger of missing both the point and a cause for gratitude and celebration. The marriage between the parents of Mary was most probably a happy one, but that is not my reason for choosing the Clematis 'Happy Marriage' today. I have chosen it because their union was indeed to turn out a very happy one for us, because Mary was born as a result of it. The Church would seem to take the same view since it is the burden of today's proper reading from *Oration 6: The Nativity of the Blessed Virgin Mary* by St John Damascene (*c.* 657–*c.* 749). It is entitled, 'By their fruits you shall know them'. In this case one might add, 'And all you need to know'!

St John says we are in the debt of Mary's parents for they presented to God and to us the noblest of human gifts, a spotless mother, who alone would be worthy to bear his Son. He of course willed it so, but, whoever

213

they were, they cherished Mary and nurtured her materially and spiritually. (It is clear from *The Magnificat* that she knew the scriptures.) Although her birth was natural, through grace her parents accomplished a thing beyond nature. We should, says St John Damascene, rejoice in them and be grateful to God for them because they produced a daughter of Adam and the mother of God: 'Break forth into joyful song and sing praises. Raise up your voice, raise it up, do not be afraid.'

Readings
Sirach 44:23b: He acknowledged him with his blessing, and gave him his inheritance.
Psalm 112:2: The generation of the upright will be blessed.
Isaiah 55:3: I will make a covenant with you.
Romans 9:4–5: Theirs are the patriarchs, and from them, in natural descent, sprang the Messiah.
Luke 12:42: A faithful and wise steward, whom the master will set over his household.
Luke 2:37, 36; 7:18: They worshipped the Lord day and night.

Intercessions
That we may approach the less verifiable traditions of faith with humility and in spiritual enquiry.
　For parents, particularly for our own.
　Thanksgiving for the parents of the Blessed Virgin Mary.
　Thanksgiving for the writings of St John Damascene.
For priests and people whose parishes and organizations are under the patronage of St Joachim and St Anne.

29 JULY
St Martha (first century)

ROSE 'MARTHA'
FLAX *Linum usitatissimum*
(see also Sage in *Thorn, Fire and Lily*, p. 58)

Cultivation, characteristics and lore
The rose 'Martha' is a Bourbon climber and was introduced in the 1920s. Its flowers are a delicate pink with a yellow base, and it climbs to 9 feet

and spreads for 6 feet. In the early nineteenth century, on the island of Bourbon (now Réunion) in the Indian Ocean, the 'Old Blush' China rose was crossed with a damask rose. Some of the resulting seed was sent back to France in 1817 from the island's botanical garden. As a result, not long afterwards, a recurrent-flowering shrub with luxuriant well-shaped blooms of fair fragrance became available. From this a strain with predominantly 'China' characteristics, almost thornless, was developed. The favourite 'Zéphrine Drouhin' (introduced 1919) is a Bourbon, and 'Martha' is a 'sport' from it. A 'sport' is defined as a climbing branch, thrown from the parent bush, which is then budded on. (The famous climbing 'Cécile Brunner' originated in this way.) The Bourbons, with their large in-turning flowers, became the template for many needlepoint designs, and it is this connection with domestic accomplishment that makes today's choice of rose doubly apt for the patron of housekeepers.

There are two types of flax, the taller with fewer branches and flowers, which yields fibre, and the shorter with more flowers and fruit, which produces linseed. *L. usitatissimum* is an annual and erect plant with narrow grey-green leaves. The sky-blue flowers are borne in summer and are followed by tiny, round seed cases containing the oval flat seeds. Flax thrives on well-drained dry to sandy soil in sun. Sow seed outdoors in spring and avoid transplantation. Cut mature plants for fibre and harvest seeds for immediate pressing for oil.

Flax has always been considered a female plant, and in northern European mythology Freya was the goddess of flax and the reins on her team of cats were adorned with its flowers. Everything to do with flax was considered to be under her protection, and she was frequently depicted as a woman spinning linen cloth. In later Christianization Freya was superseded by the Blessed Virgin Mary, and many customs and superstitions grew up around the plant. Flax was best sown on Maundy Thursday and Good Friday, and flax offerings and pilgrimages became common, with the purpose of imploring God to protect the crop. (Indeed flax became so important at one time that it was used as currency.) It was believed that the devil cannot fly over a field of flax and that all his demons fear it. Thread spun by a girl under seven years old was thought to be particularly powerful, and in some parts it was even placed under the altar cloth and had three Masses celebrated over it. Many of these semi-pagan beliefs and practices did not decline until the advent of cotton at the end of the nineteenth century. Flax has now been found to contain agents that are used in modern treatment of cancer. In the language of flowers flax, besides symbolizing domestic virtue, which clearly has its origins in Old Testament times and subsequent history, also sometimes signifies gratitude. I have many personal reasons for being grateful to St Martha, whose intercessions I am convinced have helped on occasions of domestic crisis.

St Martha and flax

Flax is found only as a cultivated plant and is one of the world's oldest crops, having been grown in Egypt since 3000 BC and in Mesopotamia a thousand years before that. In Old Testament times a good wife would work the flax 'with willing hands', put them to the spindle and the distaff, and then 'makes linen garments and sells them', her own clothing also being made of linen (Prov. 31:13–24). I am told that in the *Talmud* there are instructions for the harvesting, bleaching and preparation of linen cloth, and the priests were to wear breeches of fine linen, not of a wool/linen blend (Lev. 6:10; Deut. 22:11). It seems highly likely, then, that Martha would have been familiar with the plant and quite possibly knew how to make cloth, perhaps the linen for her brother Lazarus's grave clothes.

She appears in two important incidents in the Gospel, the first of which is responsible for her characterization ever since, as the busy housekeeper who offered hospitality to Christ but was in danger of overlooking 'the better part' chosen by her sister Mary (Luke 19:38b–42). (See 'The House at Bethany', by Rumer Godden, in Jane Mossendew's *Thorn, Fire and Lily*, p. 61). It is made clear before the raising of her brother Lazarus that she has already received teaching from Christ, saying to him of Lazurus, 'I know that he will rise again in the resurrection at the last day.' When Jesus then tells her: 'I am the resurrection and the life' and asks her if she believes this, she replies in a wholehearted affirmation of faith, 'Yes, Lord: I believe that you are the Christ, the Son of God, he who is coming into the world' (John 11:24–7). Outside scripture there is a legend that Martha went to Provence with her brother and sister, and in 1187 her supposed relics were found and enshrined at Tarascon, where she was alleged to have quelled a fierce dragon that was terrorizing the area. She sprinkled it with holy water and, wrapping her own sash around its neck, led it to Arles, where it was killed. In England, at Chichester Cathedral, she is represented in fine Romanesque sculptures of the raising of Lazarus.

Underlying the fictitious Provençal dragon legend is the power of faith she had expressed in John 11. But her proper Office reading, from St Augustine's *Sermon 103*, concentrates on the hospitality she offered to Christ. He characterizes her as one who received Christ as a pilgrim and as a servant receiving her Master. She had to feed him 'in the flesh' while at the same time she herself was fed spiritually by him. And of us, he says, lest we grieve because we are not born in an age when we can physically receive him into our material homes, that he has not taken the honour away, for we are able to receive him in our souls and bodies at Holy Communion. Further, we are asked to care for him in the guise of his poor and sick. St Augustine concludes that the rest from labour Martha was seeking will be totally irrelevant in the eternal life, where our pilgrimage will cease, and where there will be no dead to bury, no sick to tend, and none shall be hungry or thirsty anymore.

Readings
1 John 4:7–16: As long as we love one another God will live in us.
Psalm 34: Look towards him and be radiant.
Luke 10:38-42: Martha was busy about serving.
John 11:19–27: You are the Christ the Son of the living God.

Intercessions
For all involved in the growing of flax and in the linen industry.
For cancer sufferers.
Thanksgiving for the life, witness and intercession of St Martha.
That we may serve Christ through others and a life grounded in prayer.

For priests and people whose parishes and organizations are under the patronage of St Martha.

31 JULY
St Ignatius of Loyola, Founder (1491–1556)

SPANISH BAYONET *Yucca gloriosa*

Cultivation and history

This plant is a native of the warmer Americas, where many of the sons of St Ignatius have found themselves over the past four hundred years. John Gerard was given a yucca by the Exeter apothecary, Thomas Edwards. When Gerard's *Herbal* was published in 1597, it had still not bloomed. The first one to do so in England is believed to have grown in the Essex garden of William Coys (*c.*1560–1627) in 1604, half a century after its arrival. When the creamy white spike flowered, it caused such a sensation that it earned its name *gloriosa*, the specimen having reached 6 feet, according to some rumours. The name 'Spanish Bayonet' is perhaps an allusion to the history being played out in its homeland when it made its debut in Britain. The yucca is now often grown as a houseplant and, with its crown of sword-like leaves on top of a strong palm-like trunk, it is a splendid subject for a spacious hallway or room. It needs a deep, well-drained container, which can be taken out of doors in summer. In winter supply an unheated and well-lit spot indoors and keep the plant in sun whenever possible. Water generously from spring to autumn, less so in winter. Re-pot in spring every two years. As we have seen, the white bell-shaped flower may appear, if you are fortunate, after some years.

St Ignatius and the Spanish Bayonet

The plant is an obvious choice for St Ignatius, alluding as it does to his nationality and to the military symbolism of his Jesuits as 'soldiers of Christ' and their position at the forefront of the battle engaged by the Church in response to the Reformation. The yucca is not subtle; it is spiked and 'up front', as modern common parlance would have it. St Ignatius's movement is remembered as one of the more overtly practical and warlike prongs of the Counter-Reformation (although at the beginning the Society of Jesus was more concerned to convert the Muslims). I remind myself, however, that after his conversion he lived for ten months as a hermit at Manresa, near the monastery of Montserrat. It was during this intense period of prayer, study, meditation and penance, that he laid the firm foundation of his own spiritual life and also of his famous *Spiritual Exercises*, which enshrined his spiritual system and was to inform the Rules of countless religious Congregations founded in the centuries since his death. And today the *Exercises* are still popular as a basis for retreats made by both religious and laity. The prime aim of the *Exercises* is the salvation of the individual through first being made to choose Christ over the world. It is the Ignatian way to 'the conversion of life' of St Benedict and the *metanoia* of St Ephraem. However, one of the special characteristics of the Ignatian way is the emphasis on intense mental and spiritual visualization of the subject of any meditation. His *Spiritual Exercises* have thereby had immeasurable influence on the West's contribution to the visual arts as well as to its spirituality.

After leaving Manresa, Ignatius made a pilgrimage to Jerusalem, and on his return to Spain he learned Latin and studied theology. The disciples who gathered around him at the universities of Alcalá de Henares and Salamanca attracted the attention of the Church authorities and, although the *Exercises* were scrutinized and found to be orthodox, he was discouraged from forming a religious Order. He then spent periods in Paris, Spain and Rome and continued his own study, spent time in charitable works of mercy and began to train his followers in his spiritual system.

A profound spiritual confirmation from Christ himself convinced Ignatius that he was following the divine will, and by 1539 he and his followers had offered their services to the Church, in the person of Pope Paul III, and demonstrated their observance of Christ's second commandment by their charitable efforts during a Roman famine. The Society of Jesus received papal approval in 1540, and Ignatius had produced its formal Constitution by 1550. He died suddenly, and his body was placed in a shrine at the church of the Gesù in Rome.

His prayer 'to give and not to count the cost, to fight and not to heed the wound, to labour and not to ask for any reward, save that of knowing that I do thy will', was the first prayer I learned by heart (after the Lord's Prayer and Psalm 23), from an Anglican Sunday school teacher, and I can honestly remember being tremendously impressed, even at the age of eight, by its sentiments, which have indeed been informative during the rest of my life. One is reminded of that saying sometimes attributed to the Jesuits, that effectively claims: 'Give us a child in his formative years and he is ours for life.' Fr Martin D'Arcy is the only Jesuit I ever knew well, in an association that began when he gave me spiritual direction during my student years. But even at the age of twenty I appreciated and was privileged to benefit from his rigour and discernment. It now strikes me as odd that I was taught St Ignatius's prayer in 'the broad Church of England' during a period when divisions between Catholics and Anglicans were still intense, and even inimical. So I have to thank that certain Miss Green for her then unfashionable ecumenism and discernment.

'Discernment of Spirits' is the subject of the proper office reading for St Ignatius and is an extract from *The Acts of St Ignatius taken down by Luis Gonsález*. It describes the period of Ignatius's life when he was on the brink of conversion and tells how his reaction to his reading matter formed the 'starting point for teaching his followers the discernment of spirits'. The young and spiritually unformed Ignatius had discovered that if a piece of writing were intrinsically worthless, his initial enjoyment and pleasure in it would soon fade, and he would be left feeling dejected and empty. On the other hand, when he read the lives of the saints his enjoyment, and indeed joy, in what he read remained unabated, even when he stopped thinking about it. Thus it is with all spirits, whether in the form of the written word, or in the form of people.

I will not end today without reading some Gerard Manley Hopkins, and humbly close these thoughts on St Ignatius with the thought that, if the lasting delight, spiritual solace, and instruction in endurance found in this poet's work are anything to go by, then he was a good Jesuit but above all a 'good spirit'.

Readings
Psalm 91: The just shall flourish like the palm tree.
1 Peter 4: 8, 11: Whoever serves, serves with the strength God gives him.
1 Corinthians 10:31–11:1: Whatever you do, do it for the glory of God.
Luke 14:25–33: None of you can be my disciple unless he gives up all his possessions.

Intercessions
For the people of South America.
    For the entire people of God.
    Thanksgiving for the life of St Ignatius and for his immense contribution to Western spirituality and culture; that we may pray his famous prayer with a sincerity that will help to transform our lives.

For the Society of Jesus and the well-being of its individual members.
Thanksgiving for the life and work of Fr Martin D'Arcy SJ.
Thanksgiving for the poetry of Gerard Manley Hopkins SJ.

For all who follow the Ignatian way, either as members of religious
Orders or by making retreats based on *The Spiritual Exercises*, and for those
who conduct such retreats and give spiritual direction.

For priests and people who live and work in parishes and organizations
that have St Ignatius of Loyola as their patron.

1 AUGUST
St Alphonsus Mary de'Liguori, Bishop and Doctor
(1696–1787)

POMEGRANATE *Punica granatum*

Cultivation, history and uses

The pomegranate is a native shrub of the eastern Mediterranean and of
the Himalayas. It is evergreen in the subtropics and deciduous in
temperate regions. *Punica* is from the Latin *punicum malus*, that is
'Carthaginian apple', in turn derived from *Poenus*, 'Carthaginian', and
the Greek *Phoikes*, 'Phoenicians'. *Granatum* describes the crevices among
granite rocks where the pomegranate likes to grow. It was introduced to
Britain around the middle of the fourteenth century and produces large
brilliant red flowers with crumpled petals. If it is to fruit it will require a
long hot summer, which in Britain may now seem a thing of the past. In
the greenhouse, however, the fruits may ripen after flowering between
June and August. A minimum winter temperature of 45°F is necessary.
The pomegranate will grow to a maximum of 4 feet, and the dwarf 'Nana'
to 2 feet. Spread is between 3 feet and fifteen inches. The dwarf is slightly
hardier than the species and bears fruits about the size of a damson. It can
be grown in a container against a sunny outside wall but must be brought
indoors for the winter. Propagation may be from heeled, semi-hard
cuttings in July in a temperature of 64°F; seed can be sown in spring at
72°F; or root suckers can be taken from an established plant as they
appear and planted in autumn.
*Note: The use of pomegranate as a herbal medicine, particularly in the form of its
bark, is legally restricted in some countries.*

The pomegranate is mentioned in the *Ebers papyri* (*c.* 1500 BC) as a cure

221

for tapeworm, and it has been discovered to contain alkaloids that paralyse the parasites, so that they can be more easily expelled from the system. Pick the ripe fruits, remove the rind and dry for making decoctions and powders. On a more pleasant note, the seeds are surrounded by sacks of juice, and it is these that are eaten fresh or pressed to make grenadine. In 1897 André Gide (1869–1951) described the juice as tasting like unripe raspberries. If that sounds unpalatable, Henry IV of France took the pomegranate for his emblem, with the motto, 'Sour but sweet'.

In classical times the numerous seeds of pomegranate led to an obvious association with fertility and physical passion. However, its characteristics made it easy for the early Fathers to see the pomegranate as a type of the Church, and as illuminating Christ's suffering with its redness. And as the fruit hides its seed within a durable casing, so the Church guards the riches of the mystery of the hope of salvation, and as myriad pomegranate seeds are protected, so we who live in the Church are protected in her faith and love. In Christian art the pomegranate can be a symbol of hope and also of humility, since the fruit is not very attractive from the outside. Its roundness led to its Christianization as a symbol of the world as created by God.

St Alphonsus and the pomegranate

There is much in the Christianized lore of the pomegranate that justifies its choice for St Alphonsus. To begin with he was born in Naples and stayed in and around the city all his life. The pomegranate figures frequently in Neapolitan folklore, and it is quite possible that he would have known the legend of the sick young man who had a vision of the Virgin Mary holding a pomegranate, perhaps more so as his own middle name dedicated him to her. The fruit is thought of as something of a luxury, something for the idle rich who have nothing better to do than pick at the seeds with a pin – in 1352 five fruits cost ten shillings, an expensive purchase at the time! Alphonsus founded the Redemptorist Order to enrich the parched souls of the poor, and he spent twenty-six years of his life preaching the sweetness of the gospel in the villages and hamlets around Naples. Just as the pomegranate is difficult to grow, so Alphonsus experienced many difficulties in the course of the two major missions in his life.

The pomegranate is symbolic of hope, humility and unpretentiousness. Alphonsus was always against ostentation and aimed for simplicity in his explanation of the faith. But the final years of his life are a particular demonstration of his humility, hope and fortitude. Perhaps the most poignant and painful experience occurred when he was old, crippled from earlier rheumatic fever and partially blind. The Redemptorist Rule had already received the seal of papal approval, but because of the political situation it now had to be submitted to the civil authorities. Alphonsus was tricked, almost certainly as a result of his infirmities, into signing a false version of it. The pope refused the travesty he had mistakenly endorsed and would not acknowledge anyone who adhered to it as a Redemptorist. And so Alphonsus was excluded from his own Order until after his death, when Pope Pius VI, who had unwittingly been responsible for his plight, introduced the cause for his canonization, which eventually took place in 1839. Towards the end of his life, St Alphonsus had endured an appalling 'dark night of the soul', but it is recorded that before death he emerged from his ordeal, full of joy and hope.

In Christian allegory, the pomegranate often symbolized Christ in the lap or womb of Mary, as well as his own sacrifice of love. The proper Office reading for St Alphonsus is a meditation from his writings on that all-embracing, all-consuming love, and indeed it is a salient feature in his theology, the stature of which led to his being made a Doctor of the Church in 1871. In his *Moral Theology*, published in 1748, he had avoided both the rigorism of the Jansenists and the licence of the Quietists. Moreover, two years later, he had refuted the Jansenist opposition to Marian devotion in his *The Glories of Mary*. In our own time the Redemptorists are perhaps best known, at least in Britain, for their publications, notably of the weekly Mass leaflets to be found in many of our parish churches, not just Roman Catholic ones. And so they continue, with the help of modern technology, to disseminate the Word in the towns and villages of our land, just as their holy founder would have wished.

Readings
Sirach 49:3–4: In the day of sinners, he strengthened godliness.
Psalm 115: The Lord has been mindful of us; he will bless us.
Ephesians 4:1–7, 11–13: The work of service building up the body of Christ.
2 Timothy 4:1–5: Make the preaching of the Good News your life's work.
Luke 4:18: He has sent me to heal the contrite.
Mark 4:1–20: Imagine a sower going forth to sow.
John 3:9: A child of God does not sin because the divine seed remains in him.

Intercessions

For the peoples of the eastern Mediterranean, the Himalayas and Naples.

Thanksgiving for the Redemptorist Order, for God's blessing on its work and for the well-being of its individual members.

For the grace to adhere to the true faith and not to be led away by strange doctrines.

That we may each spread the gospel in our own small way.

For hope, fortitude, humility and a lack of pretension.

For priests and people who live and work under the patronage of St Alphonsus Mary Liguori.

ENVOI

This book has at its core the love God shows in his provision for us in nature and in that even greater love celebrated in June in the Person of the Son as 'The Sacred Heart of Jesus'. It therefore seems appropriate to conclude with the thoughts of today's saint, to whom God's love for us, and ours for him, was all in all. God created for us the earth with all its plenty so that we would, in gratitude for so many gifts, return him love for love. But St Alphonsus makes it clear, in his proper Office reading, that our mere gratitude is not the whole point, it is only the beginning:

> The soul's entire holiness and perfection lies in love for Jesus Christ, our God, our highest good, our Redeemer. Charity is the bond and safeguard of all the virtues that make us perfect.

PLANT INDEX